MANAGING SPORT FACILITIES AND MAJOR EVENTS

Sport events are inextricably linked to the places in which they are hosted. High-profile events require high-quality venues, and the proper management of facilities is crucial to their success. Now in a fully revised and updated new edition, *Managing Sport Facilities and Major Events* is still the only textbook to introduce the fundamentals of sport facility and event management in an international context.

With detailed real-world case studies and insights from professional practice, this book offers a systematic guide to the management issues and practical problems that sport managers must address to ensure financial, sporting, and ethical success. It covers all the key aspects of sport facility and major event management including the bidding process, facility development, risk analysis, budgeting, marketing, branding, and quality assurance, as well as completely new chapters on analytics, impact, and legacy.

Now supported by a companion website containing slides, test banks, a glossary, and sample syllabus, this is an invaluable resource for students and practitioners alike and is essential to any course on sport facilities, event management, or sport administration.

Eric C. Schwarz is a Senior Lecturer in Sport Management and Coordinator of the Postgraduate Courses in Sport Business and Integrity at Victoria University, Australia.

Hans Westerbeek is a Professor of International Sport Business, Pro Vice Chancellor – Sport, and Dean of the College of Sport and Exercise Science at Victoria University, Australia.

Dongfeng Liu is a Professor of Sport Management at Shanghai University of Sport, China.

Paul Emery is a retired sport management educator, as well as co-founder and honorary member of the European Association for Sport Management.

Paul Turner is a Senior Lecturer in Sport Management at Deakin University, Australia.

MANAGING SPORT FACILITIES AND MAJOR EVENTS

SECOND EDITION

ERIC C. SCHWARZ, HANS WESTERBEEK, DONGFENG LIU, PAUL EMERY, AND PAUL TURNER

Routledge
Taylor & Francis Group

LONDON AND NEW YORK

First published 2017
by Routledge
2 Park Square, Milton Park, Abingdon, Oxon OX14 4RN

and by Routledge
711 Third Avenue, New York, NY 10017

Routledge is an imprint of the Taylor & Francis Group, an informa business

British Library Cataloguing-in-Publication Data
A catalogue record for this book is available from the British Library

Library of Congress Cataloging in Publication Data
Names: Schwarz, Eric C., editor.
Title: Managing sport facilities and major events / Eric. C. Schwarz, Hans
    Westerbeek, Dongfeng Liu, Paul Emery and Paul Turner.
Description: Second Edition. | New York : Routledge, 2016. | Includes
    bibliographical references and index.
Identifiers: LCCN 2016021158| ISBN 9781138658608 (Hardback) |
    ISBN 9781138658615 (Paperback) | ISBN 9781315620695 (eBook)
Subjects: LCSH: Sports facilities—Management. | Sports administration. | Special
    events—Management.
Classification: LCC GV401 .M33 2016 | DDC 796.06/9—dc23
LC record available at https://lccn.loc.gov/2016021158

ISBN: 978-1-138-65860-8 (hbk)
ISBN: 978-1-138-65861-5 (pbk)
ISBN: 978-1-315-62069-5 (ebk)

Typeset in Melior
by Swales & Willis Ltd, Exeter, Devon, UK

Printed and bound by CPI Group (UK) Ltd, Croydon, CR0 4YY

Visit the companion website: www.routledge.com/cw/schwarz

DEDICATIONS

Eric C. Schwarz: This book is dedicated to my wife Loan for all her love and support throughout this project, and always. I would also like to recognise the work of Jonathan Robertson for his assistance and collaboration on this project. Finally, I would to acknowledge the support of my colleagues at the College of Sport and Exercise Science and ISEAL at Victoria University, and at Shanghai University of Sport.

Hans Westerbeek: To all hard-working professionals in sport facility and event management.

Dongfeng Liu: I would like to thank Lei, my dear wife, and two amazing little ones, Dayu and Youyang, for their understanding and support of my use of many family hours for work. I would like also to thank my long-time friend, colleague, and co-author Eric Schwarz, for his friendship, inspiration, and encouragement.

Paul Emery: Dedicated to our new grandson, Jack D'Arcy, who thankfully slept so peacefully whilst writing these chapters. One day may he fulfil his dreams at a sport facility or event of his choice.

Paul Turner: I would like to thank my family for their support in all of my scholarly endeavours.

CONTENTS

FIGURES

X
Figures

TABLES

CASE STUDIES

PREFACE

The title of this book, purposely combines the management of facilities and events. The sport or entertainment event is inextricably linked to the place and location in which it is being organised and hosted. High-profile events require high-profile facilities; high-quality events require high-quality facilities; big events require big facilities; community events require facilities that cater for the needs of community groups; and so on. The type of event brings with it an endless list of requirements, the fulfilment of which determines the eventual success or failure of the event. Transport to and from the event, overnight visitors' accommodation, a sizeable target market that is willing and able to attend the event, climatic conditions at the event location, specific athletes' or entertainers' requirements such as playing surface or acoustics – all are just a start to the list of matters that need consideration when matching the facility (location) with the event. In other words, a book on facility management is incomplete when the events that are to be hosted at the facility are not discussed. The same principle would apply to a book that dealt with event management without considering the event location. Although many of the examples used in the book will be related to professional sport, it needs to be understood that our facility and event definitions extend beyond the professional sport arena. That is, it is our intention to provide a context for the establishment and organisation of participative and spectator events, for community and elite events, and for profit and non-profit events. These events can be and are hosted in facilities ranging from state-of-the-art sporting 'temples' to local community halls. However, in the interests of providing a clear focus, we will look for our examples largely in the sport and recreation industry. An industry is a collection of suppliers to a marketplace who principally provide products that are substitutable. In this book, we will position 'sport facilities' and 'sport events' as sub-industries or sectors of the wider sport and recreation industry.

This book is also intended to provide you with an extensive insight into the different markets that are served by the events sector – to better understand how, when, and why to build new facilities, and to take a long-term perspective when managing either facilities or events. The latter is important in order to stay ahead of the developments in a sector that is long-term capital-intensive. In other words, if you incorrectly assess the needs of the target markets, leading to financing and building the wrong facilities, the (financial) consequences will also have a long-term impact. Rather than providing a purely 'technical' approach to how to plan and operate facilities and how to organise events, we have taken the perspective of the facility and event manager as our guide to writing this book. We will take you through the process of building a new facility, considering the research and preparation that goes into assessing the feasibility of setting up a new facility and event business. Having done this, we will guide you through the processes of building the facility and operating it by organising events in it, ultimately leading to intermediate performance monitoring and to determining the levels of success achieved.

In the first chapter, we provide a broad insight into the structure, size, and trends that typify the facility and events sectors. This 'big picture' information is used in Chapter 2 to briefly elaborate on the key drivers of success when planning, designing, building, and operating sport and entertainment venues, and when planning and organising events. Although there is a wide range of performance indicators that can – and need to – be considered when monitoring and measuring the successful management of facilities and events, we will limit our discussion in Chapter 2 to three key drivers of success. These are time, quality, and money. In Chapters 11 and 12, we will elaborate on measuring facility and event success by applying a scorecard approach to performance measurement (Chapter 11), and by looking at the impact of facilities and events from economic, social, and environmental points of view (Chapter 12).

Having considered the drivers of success, in Chapter 3 we show the steps through a process described as the feasibility analysis. Before committing to the major investment that comes with building large venues, a significant amount of research needs to be conducted in order to ensure its viability. In this chapter, we will analyse the stakeholders of both the newly planned facility and the events that might be hosted there. We will conduct a geographic analysis, an analysis of all potential customers, and, finally, a financial analysis in order to determine the overall feasibility of the new venue. Based on the outcome of research, in Chapter 4 we will consider design and building issues, ultimately leading to a comprehensive insight into facility and event logistics. This information can then be used in a building brief. Assuming that the facility has now been built, in Chapter 5 the facility management organisation is established – in other words, what needs to be done in order to operate successfully within the physical structures of the venue, which types of qualified personnel and how many of them we need, and what type of infrastructure is required. Having established a facility management organisation, we can start the process of organising our own events or, indeed, attracting events to our venue.

In Chapter 6 we will discuss the process of bidding for major events, how to structure the event management network, and how to start the process of event planning in the case of a successful bid. This process is continued in Chapter 7, where we start integrating our facility and event information. In other words, the venue now needs to be transformed to event mode, and an event project management structure needs to be merged with the existing facility management organisation. From both a facility and event perspective, this is also the time when risk management issues are considered.

In Chapter 8 we turn our attention to attracting the all-important customers (often better known as participants and spectators) to our venue and to our events. This can be done in a variety of ways, including the marketing of the venue itself, marketing the events, or positioning either the facility or the event based on specific strengths of the organisation (e.g. its ability to deliver exceptional service). In Chapter 9 we focus on the actual event, and on event operations from the perspectives of staffing, scheduling, crisis management, service delivery, risk management, financial management, and, of course, actual event management. Chapter 10 will expand on these event operations topics in terms of destination marketing, image, and branding. Then, as noted earlier, an in-depth discussion of performance measurement will be conducted in Chapters 11 and 12.

In the first part of Chapter 1, we overview briefly how events have always been an important part of human societies, leading to what we now call the facility and event management sector.

NOTES ON THE AUTHORS

Eric C. Schwarz from the United States started his career working in facility scheduling, special event management, and recreation programming for sport facilities. He has also worked at numerous major events including the NBA and NHL All-Star Weekends, the NFL Super Bowl, the Boston Marathon, and NASCAR auto racing events. He has been a sport management academician for the past 15 years at Daniel Webster College in New Hampshire, USA, and Saint Leo University in Florida, USA. Currently, he is a Senior Lecturer in Sport Management and Coordinator for the Postgraduate Courses in Sport Business and Integrity at Victoria University in Melbourne, Australia, as well as a visiting Professor at the Shanghai University of Sport in China. He has published two editions of *Advanced Theory and Practice in Sport Marketing* and two editions of *Sport Facility Operations Management: A Global Perspective* – the second edition of each with Routledge.

Hans Westerbeek is a Professor of International Sport Business. Currently serving as Pro Vice Chancellor – Sport and the Dean of the College of Sport and Exercise Science at Victoria University in Australia, he was the founding Director of the Institute of Sport, Exercise and Active Living (ISEAL). He has (co)authored more than 200 scientific, popular science, and opinion articles, 23 books, and 16 book chapters, and his books have been translated in to Dutch, Greek, Chinese, Russian, and Arabic. He is a past President (and founding Board member) of the Sport Management Association of Australia and New Zealand, and of the Netherlands Chamber of Commerce in Australia. He continues to serve as a Chair of Sport Management at the Free University of Brussels (Belgium) and as a visiting Professor at both the Read Madrid Graduate School in Spain, and the Central University of Finance and Economics in Beijing, China. He is a member of Club Melbourne and he was a foundation Board member of the Australian Football League (AFL) Europe, the AFL-endorsed governing body in Europe. Prior to migrating to Australia

in 1994, he worked as a marketing professional in the Netherlands. He co-founded the European Association for Sport Management and was a founding member of the European Union's European Network of Sport Science Institutes. He is also an active researcher, corporate facilitator, author, and consultant to more than 50 organisations and governments in a variety of countries including Australia, the USA, Malaysia, China, the United Arab Emirates, Belgium, the Netherlands, Brazil, India, Switzerland, New Zealand, India, and Japan. In addition to the first edition of this book, Hans has been involved with numerous projects with Routledge including *Sport Management: Principles and Practices*, *Global Sport Business: Community Impacts of Commercial Sport*, and *Australian Sport – Better by Design: The Evolution of Australian Sport Policy* among numerous other publications and experiences across the sport business management realm.

Dongfeng Liu is a Professor of Sport Management, and Co-Dean of the School of Economics and Management at Shanghai University of Sport in China. He is also International Professor at INSEEC Business School in Bordeaux, France. In addition, he holds visiting professor status at the University College in Dublin, Ireland; adjunct professor status at EM Lyon Business School in France; and was a post-doctoral research fellow at Sheffield Hallam University in England in the area of sport events and urban development. He is a member of China Sports Strategy Society, a think tank of China's Sports Ministry. A leading researcher and well-published author in the area of impacts and legacies of mega-sporting events, he is the co-author of a Routledge book – *The Global Economics of Sport*.

Paul Emery has more than 25 years of experience in sport management education. As an internationally renowned educator, facilitator, and manager, he has been awarded institutional and national awards for his innovative and engaging teaching. As a co-founder and honorary member of the European Association for Sport Management, Paul has taught on four continents, and supervised more than 60 research theses to successful completion. Paul has presented and published widely in the area of sport project and major event management, drawing considerably upon his theoretical studies as well as practitioner management experiences in both sport facility and sport event environments. He is one of the co-authors from the first edition.

Paul Turner is a Senior Lecturer in Sport Management at Deakin University in Australia. He has worked in Women's Soccer (National), State Soccer, and State Touch sporting associations in Australia. He also was the Competition Coordinator for Melbourne Football for the Sydney Olympic Broadcasting Organisation (SOBO) during the 2000 Olympic Games. He was also one of the co-authors of the first edition.

CHAPTER 1

INTRODUCTION TO SPORT FACILITY AND MAJOR EVENT MANAGEMENT

CHAPTER OBJECTIVES

In this chapter we will:

■ Discuss the key success factors and project drivers of managing sport facilities and events.
■ Provide an outline of the changing nature of the sport facility and event sectors.
■ Supply a broad survey of the structure, size and trends that typify the facility and events sectors.

1

- Identify a number of new markets for sporting events and discuss the implications for the construction of new facilities.
- Outline the added value of new facilities and events to user and non-user groups.
- Demonstrate the need for and application of managerial skills to facility and event operations.

INTRODUCTION

Throughout the last two decades, many managers of newly established sport and entertainment facilities were confronted with the inaccuracy of the well-known industry credo: if you build it, they will come. Times have changed quite rapidly. Modern day sport and entertainment venues are vastly different in their appearance and functionality compared with the previous generation of facilities. As we will discuss shortly, not only is the market for sport and entertainment events expanding and becoming more diversified but also the needs of old and new customers have changed, leading to the changing functionality of new venues.

THE CHANGING NATURE OF FACILITY AND EVENT MANAGEMENT

The current generation of stadia incorporate multipurpose facilities and have a sharper focus on catering for corporate hospitality, which in turn affects attendance (patterns) at events. With the corporate dollar becoming an increasingly important source of revenue for facility and event operators, more space in facilities is being devoted to corporate clients, necessitating a reassessment of facility and event positioning strategies. This leads logically to a reassessment of the facility's (and its tenants') target markets. Based on this shift from what were largely 'community' customers to a wider range of clients (including the much more cashed-up corporate clients), KPMG (2011) notes an increase in the commercial orientation toward stadium design in large European stadiums such as increasing the relative construction cost per seat to include more high-end amenities (e.g. corporate boxes, catering, and retail) and the increasing presence of facility naming rights sponsors.

As a result of the reluctance of sport fans and local community to fund developments with tax dollars (as opposed to the previous generation of stadia developed three decades ago, where funding often consisted of nearly 100 per cent tax money), facility and event organisations have turned their attention to identifying alternative funding strategies. Not only are sport and entertainment venues more likely to be privately funded and owned, but this situation has resulted in the 'unbundling' of commercial activities (concessions, pouring rights, merchandising rights, media rights)

2

that can operate within the facility. At the same time sport teams are relying less and less on match day revenue due to increasing revenue generation from, for example, media rights. Television coverage and live streaming of sport events further decreases the need for the average spectator to attend a given event, whilst increasing the expectations about an engaging viewing experience once at the event itself (i.e. it should be 'better' than watching at home). That is why a shift of focus to the business-to-business customers can be observed as corporations are prepared to pay top dollar for luxury boxes and club seating. KPMG (2011) found that the typical amenities provided in many European stadia included covered seats, in-house restaurants and bars, conference facilities, corporate boxes, high-end catering, merchandising outlets, at least 10 per cent premium seating, retail and leisure facilities, and (in the case of mega-stadia) an in-house museum. The new 2 million square foot, 71,000 seat, Mercedes-Benz Stadium built in Atlanta cost US$1.4 billion, received a mixture of public and private funding, contains 190 corporate suites, 7,500 club seats, 700 concession stands, 7 bars and restaurants, and an amazing 63,800 square feet of scoreboard wrapped around the playing surface and rising nearly 58 feet off the ground (Mercedes-Benz Stadium, n.d.).

With high-quality facilities such as the Mercedes-Benz stadium, which are fitted and resourced to service a demanding on-site (corporate) audience and a remote (television) audience, comes the need to continuously improve the levels of service quality. Not only do customers demand higher quality events on the field, and more of them, they also wish to be served in a way that matches the event and its facility surroundings. Well trained, friendly, immaculately dressed, and highly knowledgeable staff are required to serve better food to sophisticated, information- and spectacle-hungry audiences in more convenient, ergonomically outfitted physical surroundings. In summary, changing customer needs have driven a change in the type (and number) of events that are organised, in turn leading to facilities that are purpose built to cater to a wider variety of audiences and events. The higher quality of the new venues has led to higher customer expectations, which in turn has sparked a sharper focus on delivering high-quality service by facility and event owners.

THE EMERGENCE OF THE FACILITY AND EVENT MANAGEMENT SECTOR

As already noted, we refer to one sector (facilities and events) rather than two separate sectors, which we justify by the fact that events cannot exist without the facilities that host them. We also argue that excellent sport facility managers require substantial knowledge of how to organise world class events. Event managers, in turn, require a wide range of facility management skills in order to make their events top class. It goes without saying that the use of the term 'facilities' only refers to those facilities that are suited to host events. It makes little sense to also consider, for example, offices of a major bank or the retail facilities of a supermarket chain as part of our industry discussion.

Special events have always been part of human history. Anthropologists have traced human civilisation for tens of thousands of years, and at the heart of their observations are the 'special events' that typify and explain the tribal behaviour of that time and place. The supposed longest continuous human civilisation on the planet, that of the Aboriginal people of Australia, can be traced back 40,000 years, and many of their ancient rites and rituals survive into modern times. Rites and rituals represent 'special and important occasions' for members of the tribe or community that either mark significant changes in position and responsibility or are more general celebrations or commemorations of significant moments in time, such as the arrival of spring, or the passing of an elder tribesperson. Many of the sites of these rituals were secret and sacred, and remain so today. In other words, the special 'event' is closely tied to a special 'place'. One without the other loses its significance.

From more modern times, records have shown that special events did not diminish in importance in the context of different societies. The Scandinavian Vikings celebrated successful explorations and hosted large festivities to honour their gods, as did the Native Americans. The ancient Greeks conducted large athletic festivals to celebrate human excellence as a direct expression of honouring their gods (seventh century BC), and the Romans organised gladiatorial events at massive colosseums to entertain the crowds and also to facilitate a culture of preparation for combat (third century BC). Hundreds of years before the discovery of gunpowder in Europe, the Chinese would celebrate the arrival of the New Year with elaborate displays of fireworks, and throughout the European Middle Ages more localised events would lead to the development of many country-specific events that still exist today. Examples are the 'Oktoberfest' in Germany and the 'Elfstedentocht' (eleven-city tour speed skating event) in the Netherlands. Largely through European imperialism (leading to the 'export' of domestic events) and the industrial revolution, events became more international.

Better information flow and transport infrastructure allowed people to travel more widely and created opportunities for joint celebrations. Events such as the first modern Olympic Games in 1896 are precursors to a movement that saw the twentieth century become the first century of truly international events. After an initial facility 'boom' during the ancient Greek and Roman civilisations, when hugely impressive venues (you can still go and have a look!) were purpose-built to host major events, a second building frenzy took place during the latter stages of the nineteenth century. The development of internationally standardised football codes led to the building of many stadia in the USA, the UK, and mainland Europe, as well as Australia, that could host up to 100,000 spectators. Many of those facilities have now been recycled three or four times in order to cater to the quality standards of the third millennium. If in the 1890s the second facility building boom was

4

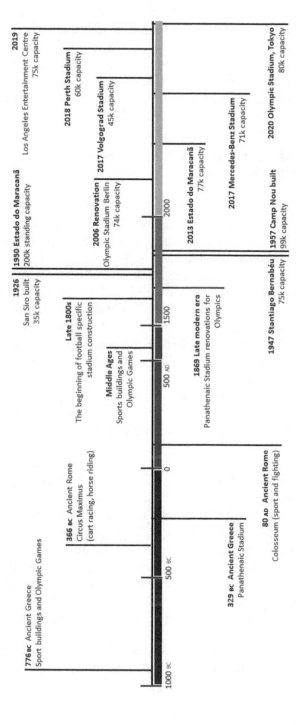

Figure 1.1 Timeline of stadium construction

Source: Adapted from KPMG (2013)

initiated, then societal changes in the 1990s led to the third global development period. Directly related to the 'continuous improvement' of facilities and events is the ongoing professionalisation of facility and event managers (Figure 1.1). In order to remain well prepared to deliver on ever increasing quality standards, managers need a continuous flow of cutting edge information and management systems, which is one of the main reasons for the publication of this book. We now discuss the global trends that have been and are still transforming the facility and events industry, leading to the construction boom of the 1990s and the growing number and variety of events that are being organised today.

TRENDS DRIVING THE GROWTH OF THE FACILITY AND EVENT MANAGEMENT SECTOR

Continuous improvement in the way fans and spectators consume the sport product, both within the venue or via a form of broadcast, is a driving force in the (re)development of global stadia. Editor of the Sports Facility Reports Paul Anderson (2009) observed that the 137 teams in the five major US professional sports leagues (MLB, NBA, NFL, NHL, MLS) are playing in 118 different facilities. During the 20 years to 2009, 88 new facilities were built, 15 renovated, and 15 remained unchanged. The cumulative cost of this facility construction was US$26.9 billion. Following the study, another five stadiums were built prior to 2016, with a further five scheduled to be completed by 2019. This means that by 2019 approximately 96 per cent of all major league teams will be playing in facilities that have been either renovated or newly constructed since 1989.

According to Pete Giorgio of Deloitte Consulting (2016, p. 5) the 'stadium of the future' is becoming the norm for teams and leagues as they are increasingly pressured to compete with the viewing experience available to sports fans in their homes:

> The home viewing experience has improved so dramatically in recent years that sports franchises must 'compete with the couch' in order to attract fans to stadiums and arenas on game day. From upgrading in-venue Wi-Fi to rolling out beacon-based location technology [to inform patrons of nearby services] and expanding mobile concession [food and drink] ordering and retail purchasing, teams must invest in the technological infrastructure of their current venues to heighten fan engagement. The challenge is creating an environment where unique and meaningful event experiences can influence fan behaviour over a long period of time and extend that experience beyond the game, beyond the venue, and beyond the season to create a true year-round relationship.

In the English Premier League, total attendance has historically been restricted by stadium capacity. The competition provides an interesting example of the importance of the variable 'stadium capacity' when interpreting overall attendance figures per club and per league. A SkySports (2015) study compared average league attendance for the 2014/15 season with ground capacity and found that, although all clubs in the Premier League averaged an occupancy rate of almost 95 per cent, the top eight clubs had occupancy rates of 98 per cent or higher. However, the reverse turned out to be the case for less successful teams (often first, second, and third division teams). Boosting stadium capacity in order to improve gate receipts may well have a negative effect on attendance, leading to the conclusion (Boon 1999, p. 15) that there is

> a clear need for some lower division clubs to temper their dream stadium plans with a degree of realism. It may be great to have a 20,000 capacity stadium, but an average attendance of only 4,000 creates a negative atmosphere. A 10,000 or 12,000 capacity stadium can provide a better atmosphere and – paradoxically – increased support.

The average occupancy rate of 94 per cent for Premier League teams drops away significantly in the lower leagues, with 36 out of the 92 professional football teams in the UK playing in front of half-empty stadia (i.e. crowds lower than 50 per cent stadium capacity). Boon's observation is particularly significant, in that having 'excess capacity' in stadia is not necessarily desirable for football clubs. Match day attendance can be positively stimulated by a limited supply of seats in the stadium. Therefore, it might be better to talk about optimum capacity, rather than maximum capacity.

The situation in Australia may serve as another example. Historically, the most popular domestic football competition, the Australian Football League (national governing body for the sport of Australian Rules football), was organised along the lines of most European soccer competitions. AFL clubs owned or leased their own football stadia and most home matches were played there. The Australian Rules football competition was predominantly based in the heartland of the code, the city of Melbourne, and in 'the old days' was a competition between different suburbs. In the 1980s, a sea change occurred in Australian football. For the code to remain financially healthy and competitive against 'new' booming sports such as basketball and soccer, the competition's operating systems needed dramatic rationalisation. League administrators, the AFL Commission, turned the League into a national competition, in the process setting up teams in different states, some of which were new teams and some teams relocated from Melbourne. A facility rationalisation strategy was adopted by the League as one of the drivers of success for the national competition. Clubs had to move from their small, outdated, and often unsafe suburban stadia to the few AFL designated playing facilities throughout the country. In Melbourne this led to multiple teams adopting either the Melbourne Cricket Ground (MCG) or Waverley Park, (later replaced by the Etihad Stadium), as their home ground. Both the MCG and the Etihad Stadium offer a range of facilities, from 'purchase at the gate' access to long-term corporate box leases. The moral of the story is the market in a domestic football competition such as the AFL is not able to sustain a wide range of low-capacity yet high-quality outfitted (corporate hospitality) stadia. Rather, costs need to be shared by a number of professional clubs playing at the same venue, in the process cross-subsidising the maintenance of high-quality entertainment opportunities at a limited number of venues. (Here it also needs to be stated that the playing surface required for Australian Rules football is about twice as big as a soccer pitch, leading to bigger and wider venues. Larger crowds are therefore needed to create a good game atmosphere; hence, consumption of football needs to be artificially concentrated by limiting the number of consumption outlets.)

OTHER REASONS TO BUILD NEW FACILITIES

Apart from these 'capacity specific' reasons to become involved in the construction of new facilities, Anderson (2000) provided five features that may explain the global 'facility boom'. First, he argues that it is more efficient to build new facilities than to renovate existing facilities in an effort to upgrade them to current standards and expectations. Second, new facilities are likely to become more than just an entertainment venue. Modern facilities are integrated into comprehensive community localities that include residential, office, and retail space. Third, new facilities are more likely, through the novelty factor and expanded services, to boost attendance. Fourth, when certain sporting teams or competitions as a whole come to play in new facilities, competitors will have to follow or suffer the consequences of becoming a less attractive entertainment option for the fans. Finally, the 'increasing cost theory' posits that only new facilities can generate the necessary revenue streams to return a profit to the operators of the facility. In an age of diminishing financial support from the State and increasing capital costs required to build or significantly renovate stadia, 'technological renovations' may provide a cost effective enhancement to the consumer experience. Technological renovations would necessarily focus on new technologies that add to the value proposition of live match day viewing at venues, including improved Wi-Fi access, screens and scoreboards, digitising purchases at concession stands, and making the ticket purchase and entry process seamless. We have already explained that corporate customers have become more important to the facility and event bottom line than the revenues generated from the 'average spectator'. A more recent move in the USA to revert to building 'single-purpose' facilities – that is, baseball- or football-only grounds – is directly linked to wanting to control all revenue streams generated through the sport facility rather than share them with co-tenants. It can also be seen from Table 1.1 that, when looking at the five major professional sporting leagues in the USA, the trend is away from paying for the construction of new sports arenas with public money; hence the need to create a 'return on private investment'.

8

Table 1.1 Proportion of single vs. multiuse facilities in the USA five major leagues in the 1980s and 2000s

% Single-use stadiums (single-use/no. of facilities in league)		
League	1980s	2000s
National Hockey League (NHL)	67% (14/21)	63% (19/30)
Major League Baseball (MLB)	52% (13/25)	93% (28/30)
National Football League (NFL)	57% (16/28)	84% (26/31)
National Basketball Association (NBA)	74% (20/27)	62% (18/29)
Major League Soccer (MLS)	N/A	80% (12/15)
Average across leagues	62% (63/101)	76% (103/135)

Source: Adapted from Long (2013, pp. 42–3)

As can be seen in Table 1.1, Major League Baseball is the only sport that has slightly increased the amount of public funding spent on building new stadia in the 1990s. This in itself does not come as a big surprise, given the fact that baseball, like no other sport in the USA, is the sport of the people. 'Funding' baseball from the public purse is least likely to meet with public backlash; hence it attracts the highest proportion of public funding of all major sports, and is the only sport that has increased its level of public funding throughout the 1990s. Ice hockey and soccer, in particular, seem to be perceived as sports that need to generate their own, private support. They are indeed niche market operators, compared with their all-American counterparts of football, baseball, and basketball. The averages across leagues show a clear trend towards privately funding the establishment of new sporting facilities.

In Australia, Etihad Stadium in Melbourne is 100 per cent privately funded. The stadium incorporates a retractable roof covering an oval shaped pitch capable of hosting cricket and Australian Rules matches, seats just over 56,000 spectators, and has become known for its strong focus on catering to the corporate dollar. The stadium was proposed to the market as an investment project and was completed with a range of major equity partners as venue shareholders. The growing requirement to 'return on investment' further explains the focus on catering for the more lucrative corporate customers. Although the stadium did not turn a profit during its first few years of operation, leading to shareholder buyouts, the facility continues to be privately owned.

Australia's premier sporting stadium, the Melbourne Cricket Ground, was redeveloped into 'a major entertainment destination', rather than just a place to host some sporting contests. A range of daytime cafés, bars, and restaurants combined with conferencing facilities encourage seven-day traffic at the venue. This is

9

Introduction

further boosted by the National Sport Museum (including the Gallery of Sport, the Olympic Museum, and the Sport Australia Hall of Fame) that is hosted in the facility. Approximately 70 per cent of the existing stadium has been redeveloped. The capacity of the venue was brought back to its original 100,000 seats for the 2006 Commonwealth Games. Funding for this near AUD$600 million project largely came from private sources. On the back of preparing for the 2006 Commonwealth Games, the federal government committed $A90 million, but a large proportion of the loan repayments – $A29 million per annum, to be precise – was generated by the 100,000+ members of the Melbourne Cricket Club (MCC). The MCC has had the long-term management of the MCG, on behalf of the state government and the MCG Trust, and has recently secured the rights to manage the facility until 2042, also extending the club's lease of the members' reserve until 2067. The loan is to be repaid in 20 years. Other funding comes from the Australian Football League, the most important tenant of the facility, at $A5 million per annum, and from renegotiated service supplier contracts such as catering, security, advertising, and ground sponsorships (Melbourne Cricket Club 2002). It needs no further explanation that with such levels of capital commitment, facilities such as the MCG need to host a continual supply of new events.

GROWTH IN THE NUMBER AND TYPE OF EVENTS

Globally, AT Kearny (2014) estimate that the sport industry (including events, sporting goods, apparel, equipment, and health and fitness spending) could generate as much as US$700 billion per year, or roughly 1 per cent of global GDP. Within the sport industry, the sport event market was worth US$80 billion in 2014 and with projected annual growth of the industry to be around 7 per cent, the global sport events market is expected to reach US$91 billion by 2017 (AT Kearny, 2014). In 2013 Europe, the Middle East, Africa (43 per cent), and North America (38 per cent) account for the major sport event geographic areas. Asia Pacific (13 per cent) and Latin America (6 per cent) combined were only half the size of the US sport events market (AT Kearny, 2014).

According to Goldblatt (2000), there are four factors that largely explain the growth in the number of events organised worldwide. The first relates to the demographic shift that is currently changing the makeup of most of the developed first world. The population of most Western nations is ageing rapidly, leading to more older people – lots more. Not only do older people have more time, they also have more money to spend during that time; and because they are growing older there are also more reasons to celebrate. The second factor relates to the exponential development of new technology, which in turn leads to a high-tech environment in which human contact (both face-to-face communication and physical contact) becomes increasingly rare. To balance their high-tech lives, people are looking for 'high-touch' opportunities to preserve their humanness. Events are excellent providers of 'high-touch' experiences. Booming economies around the world constitute the third reason for the growth of the event sector. In particular, tourism and leisure industries have benefited from the extra disposable income earned in many countries around the world. Moreover, the events we are referring to here are obviously not limited to sport. As a matter of fact, sport represents only a small part of the global events industry, which includes cultural festivals, food festivals, art fairs, and religious gatherings. However, sport is one area of events that is experiencing significant growth. The final factor leading to growth in the number of events relates to time. Time, particularly in Western nations, has become a precious commodity to be traded against other valuables. Work and leisure have merged to become almost a continuum in the West. People are opting for more, shorter breaks, which in turn should offer different experiences every time. Gone are the days of families travelling to the same holiday destination for 20 years in succession. More varied events, throughout the whole year, are needed to satisfy the requirements of increasingly diversified and demanding customers – customers who are prepared to pay for those events that allow them to 'economise' on the time they have available.

MUSIC FESTIVALS: A GROWING EVENTS AREA

Contrary to the focus on permanent facilities outlined throughout this text there is a rise in temporary facilities for annual events around the world. Nowhere is this more applicable than in the music festival sector and in particular Boom, Belgium. Boom has a population of a little below 20,000, yet since 2005 it has hosted the 'Tomorrowland' music festival featuring international acts from all over the world. The event brings more than 165,000 people to the small town and typifies the resurgence of the music festival as a major event over the past two decades. In 2015 the event attracted the best electronic dance performers including Avicii, David Guetta, and Armin Van Buuren. Apart from a great music line-up, Tomorrowland's central value proposition is escapism. The festival typifies the forthcoming Dream Society discussion as it applies to the music industry. At the festival, patrons are provided with fixtures in the form of castles and rainbows, concession stands in the form of small towns, digital promotions that take on the style of a fairy-tale, and aspirational communications to target global youth. Since its inception, the festival has now expanded the concept to Brazil and the United States. The continued success of this type of event demonstrates that substantial permanent infrastructure and the associated capital costs are not always required to satisfy today's consumer.

NEW MARKETS FOR SPORTING EVENTS AND IMPLICATIONS FOR FACILITIES

Westerbeek and Smith (2003) used the work of futurist Rolf Jensen (1999) to identify a number of marketplaces for sport products of the future. Jensen argued that wealthy, developed nations are about to enter what he called the 'Dream Society'. Humankind has moved from hunting and gathering to farming in an agricultural society. With the industrial revolution, the UK and other Western European nations, as well as the USA, entered the industrial society. Growing wealth as a result of dramatic technological advances resulted in people moving from the country to urban centres; cities were constructed, which in turn facilitated the establishment of transport infrastructure. People and organisations also became involved in what we now define as 'planning'. Increasingly, people allowed themselves the luxury of forgoing short-term results for longer-term prosperity. About three decades ago, the leading industrial nations moved into the so-called information society. Because production jobs were largely automated, knowledge became more important than capital. Intellectual capital is now valued more highly than physical capital. In the information society, however, success is still predominantly measured in tangible, materialistic wealth. According to Jensen (1999), the Dream Society will drive people towards achieving the emotional wealth that typified the very early human societies. The Dream Society is the ultimate societal type, because it combines material wealth (we no longer struggle to survive) with emotional wealth and fulfilment. The Dream Society perspective neatly fits in with the trends explaining the growth of the events industry, as observed by Goldblatt (2000). New events need new facilities (and also more of them). This is why it is prudent for sport facility and event managers to take stock and imagine what types of products are likely to be delivered through their facilities and with their event management structures. Westerbeek and Smith (2003) formalised the relationship and influence of the Dream Society in terms of the sport facility and event management industry under the umbrella term 'DreamSport Society'. They proposed six new markets for sport products in this 'DreamSport Society' that would have a significant influence on the future of sport facility and event management. These markets include sport entertainment, sport fantasy, sport quality, sport identity, sport tradition, and sport conscience.

NEW MARKETS FOR SPORT PRODUCTS

Sport entertainment[1]

People have an increasing emotional need for adventure, as evidenced by the escalation of such activities as bungee jumping and extreme sports. The sport theatregoer, who attends sporting contests with the express desire for entertainment and spectacle, exemplifies this need for adventure. Theatregoers of the future, how-ever, are more about being entertained by satisfying their need for adventure than merely sitting on the sidelines and passively watching a sporting contest. This is not to say that theatregoers necessarily want to be in the game, but in order to real-ise their emotional peak they must have some influence on the game. As this is impossible in a practical sense, they instead require an interactive presence to best fill their emotional needs. What does this mean for facility and event managers? Well, if interactivity is the key, then technology that facilitates spectators' emo-tional connection to the sport product by engaging them in ways they have never experienced before will triumph, and will ultimately revolutionise sport delivery. This will have vast consequences for facility design and construction. It also needs to be noted that, although we are looking forward to future consumption behaviour, those facility and event managers that want to remain ahead of the game will need to incorporate the opportunities to deliver those products in their design and construction plans today!

Sport fantasy

Achieving the emotional need that can be described as togetherness revolves around products that can bring consumers together. Naturally, most sport teams and some events capitalise on this emotional bond that sport can provide better than any other products, including beer, fast cars, and film. At the heart of this emotional requirement is the desire for comradeship and direction. In other words, the interest in sport – whether conscious or not – is more about the other fans that sport attracts than about the game itself. This can be seen in participation-based events like University Games, the Gay Games, and the Masters Games. However, only a comparative minority of people seeking to fulfil this need for togetherness do so directly through involvement in sport. Most attempt to meet this need through 'champ-following', particularly of team sports. The champ follower of the future is different in that he or she selects winning teams to support because these provide a convenient opportunity to experience the pleasure of togetherness that only success can deliver.

Champ followers are principally motivated to watch sport because they have an interest in a specific team or club that is winning. They are reluctant to watch sport by themselves. The new champ followers will increasingly look for opportunities to share the emotional experience of sport consumption with other like-minded indi-viduals and groups, to share around their winning affiliation and reinforce to them that the world is viewing them as a winner. For facility and event managers this has some implications. First of all, champ followers do not necessarily meet in the traditional stadium. Increasingly they are using the Internet to chat with kindred spirits all around the world. Merely sitting in a stadium with other sports fans is not enough. Champ followers must derive a sense of importance from belonging to the group; the others in the group must care about their presence and recognise them as winners, just like the team they are supporting. Channelling sport exclusively through pay television is therefore a certain way to ensure that the new champ followers will find it more difficult to access the groups they need in order to reach satisfaction. Facility and event managers need to offer a range of opportunities to share that 'winning feeling' with other 'winners'.

It is important to note that Westerbeek and Smith (2003) see the boundaries between the different markets as not necessarily concrete. The need for togetherness can be found in other fan types, and the new champ follower is not exclusively interested in meeting an emotional need for togetherness.

SPORT FANTASY

Over the past decade, two factors of online sport fantasy participation and handheld technological devices have contributed to an explosion of sport fantasy gaming. The champ follower is particularly predisposed to engaging in online sport fantasy gaming due to the satisfaction and sense of importance the individual derives from demonstrating their sports knowledge within a given sport fantasy community and 'winning' against a given opponent (see fantasy. nfl.com for an example). Nearly all major leagues around the world have multiple variants of online fantasy leagues and several have made the extension into associating real-world monetary rewards for success on the digital platforms. In 2011, the explosion in fantasy sport led to the NFL directing all 32 clubs to display fantasy points live on the big screen at venues during games – a move that has been followed by several leagues around the world both in-game and during broadcasts on television. Furthermore, whilst the ubiquity of 'smartphones' is not new, the data management and Wi-Fi access requirements for large stadia are leading to an array of technical redevelopments in venue design to boost the fan experience and avenues for engagement. The need for fans to remain connected has led to design innovation; for example, in the US Bank Stadium, the new home of the Minnesota Vikings, Wi-Fi hotspots have been installed within the handrails around the stadium to boost the Wi-Fi speed and capacity for spectators.

Sport quality

The sport quality segment of the DreamSport Society is a combination of the expression of care and the intrinsic enjoyment of the sport product being consumed. Sport organisations are full of opportunities for members and fans to demonstrate that they care.

Volunteers are the backbone of club-based sport systems like those in Europe and Australasia. The composition of the sport quality segment reflects a slightly new role for the sporting aficionado who has traditionally been interested in sport because it possesses the intrinsic aesthetics that they find alluring, or even addictive. In the DreamSport Society, the new aficionado is no longer satisfied with the position of semi-detached sports lover. The visual pleasure of watching a good game is not enough as other competing products offer more than quality skills on show, seeking to reach consumers on an emotional level. New aficionados want the quality sport experience to reach a deeper level – one that allows them to fulfil their need to show they care intensely about their sport and the level at which it is played. For athletes to appeal to this segment, they need to care as well – care about the people and communities that allow them to reap the benefits of their superior athletic performances. As athletes are increasingly viewed and positioned as 'good corporate citizens', the interest to celebrity marketers has also increased. Sport performers will continue to earn their sometimes outrageous salaries only if they show their fans they care about them. Sometimes this comes naturally to athletes, for example to Swiss tennis ace Roger Federer, who has set up his own charity, the Roger Federer Foundation. Other athletes may need the assistance of their agents to select appropriate charities to support and donate parts of their earnings to, in order to convince the public that they do care about the communities that they benefit so much from. From the event management point of view in particular, those events that offer a 'care' factor are most likely to attract the sport quality niche of the events marketplace.

From the sport quality perspective, the influence of money and finances can be significant. Trends and pressures that affect the intrinsic quality of the sport itself will determine the commitment of the sport quality aficionado. For example, where economic imperatives drive the amount of money associated with sport and force the evolution of new 'elite of elite' leagues, and foster the development of super-athletes to perform in these competitions, the sport quality segment will happily consume sport. However, where these pressures erode the quality of the game, or manipulate it to an extent that the 'pure' element of the game is lost, then the segment will react unfavourably. This segment will make assessments about the value of the sport's quality, and this value assessment will be mediated by the actual ability of segment members to show that they care about quality.

Sport identity

Sport fans have a history of eliciting a sense of identity and meaning from their association with sport teams and clubs. The sport identity segment of the DreamSport Society combines the emotional need for identity. Jensen (1999) refers to this as the 'who-am-I' need, with the strength of conviction held by the passionate partisan. The sport identity segment will seek the emotional satisfaction of a strong sense of belonging and identity, married with the unwavering loyalty of the passionate fan. At the superficial level, the sport identity segment comprises focused sport watchers, keenly observant about the state of the game and their team, and compelled by the most trivial team-related information. However, at the deeper level, this segment is looking for self-definition. At this deeper level, that search is realised by a close affiliation with a team or club, where a personal identity can be moulded indistinguishably with a club or a supporter group. As a result, the sport identity group define themselves in a way that is consistent with their association with a team of choice. For facility designers, this means that the 'space' allocated to these passionate fans needs to reflect their passion for the team they follow, and to offer opportunities to claim that space as if it were theirs. From the event point of view, it is important to note that these passionate fans are willing to spend significant sums of money in pursuit of ongoing self-identification through the purchase of sport spectating services including tickets and pay television subscriptions; endorsed products such as club credit cards or home loans, and product extensions offered through concessions (food and beverages, merchandise, and memorabilia. But they can also be easily alienated. As with any of the segments, forces that interfere with the identification process are harmful to this consumer. For example, when fans are locked out of venues in favour of corporate ticket holders and hospitality services, there will be a distancing of the fans from their beloved club and a consequent weakening of their identity.

THE NEXT FRONTIER: VIRTUAL REALITY

In line with the rise of technology the use of virtual reality and 'in-game' experiences may be an option for facility managers to consider for enhancing the sport identity consumer segment. Sport identity consumers derive part of their identity from a team or player, virtual reality facilitates such a transfer by taking the viewer from the couch 'into' the game. Virtual reality has been activated at events like the US Open tournament tee-box, to wearable cameras in player's helmets in the NFL and cricket and in the vehicles of most motor sports. Wearable technology such as this enhances the viewer's sensation and identification with athlete and event of being one of 'them' and being 'there', of 'me' or 'us' versus 'them'. In doing so, these tools strengthen the emotional association with club and athletes and as such may improve the perception of affiliated brands.

Sport tradition

The sport tradition segment is a particularly interesting one from a facility management point of view. The emotional need to be met relates to the 'peace of mind' that comes through reminiscing about better times in the past. Of course, history is important to sports fans, but none so much as the sport tradition segment. Sport traditionalists are born of a combination of the 'peace of mind' element, which focuses on the good feelings and 'old-time' values that the consumption of some products can elicit, and the reclusive partisan sport fans, who will come back to fandom from the bench when the right set of circumstances seizes their interests. The sport tradition fans are therefore sophisticated in the way they assess the value of sport watching. Their emotional interest is engaged when sport can offer them a chance to reignite past values, to bask in a new winning streak that reminds them of the glory days, or to inspire them with confidence and trust. This is why corporatisation can disenfranchise the fan and take sport away from that special traditional base that is so important. On the other hand, corporatisation in the form of corporate hospitality, for example, can offer some of the special treatment that the sport tradition segment needs to satisfy its sense of personal service and value. Technology and innovation can also deprive this segment of the personal touches that sport can provide, such as the suburban stadium that is replaced by a heartless but architecturally stunning multi-purpose venue, or the old memorabilia-filled pub or bar that was sold to make way for yuppie apartments. Major League Baseball in the USA has continually managed to attract reclusive partisans to the game in the normal cycles in which they take an intermittent interest. Many of the MLB clubs are, or have been, involved in stadium renovation or rebuilding in the style that was prominent at the height of baseball's community success during the early 1900s. To cater for the sport traditionalist, KPMG (2011) identified that almost every modern stadium in Europe above 60,000 seats included a museum within it, whereas smaller stadiums often did not contain museums as an amenity. This could be in part to maintain a legacy story needed to legitimise new stadium (re)developments in the eyes of the sport traditionalist, whilst meeting the increasing experiential needs of other consumer types in terms of design and technology.

Sport conscience

The final segment we are using to help sport facility and event managers focus on the future has been named sport conscience. The name is a reflection of the emotional requirements of consumers more interested in the broader picture than they are necessarily with sports or clubs themselves. The important element is a sincere desire that something worthwhile is accomplished that affects people at a greater level than the mere enjoyment of sport participation or spectatorship. There is a moral conviction at work. Allied to this is a sense of community. The main consumers in this segment are the community partisans, who are concerned with the needs of others in their association with sport. In particular, this fan type attends sport to please others and to contribute to the community interest. These are the mothers and fathers who bring the halftime tea or oranges, provide the taxis, and coach the team. These are also the individuals who turn up to the local game because the team 'needs the support', or because they view it as a manifestation of their community pride.

A combination of the community partisan and the need for some conviction to be realised can be seen in the sport conscience segment. Their principal emotional necessities revolve around feelings of moral righteousness, usually achieved through benefits to the community or at least to people other than themselves. These people use sport, like some people use charity, to alleviate guilt and to sustain a sense of personal rectitude. They will buy only the shoes that were manufactured in 'appropriate' circumstances, consume healthy, organically grown foods, and attend sporting contests and events that show them to be worthy community contributors. These are the consumers that need to be targeted by the organisers of community festivals or mass participation events such as the Gay Games and the Masters Games, and of sports (events) with definitive moral philosophies about such issues as racism and gender inequality.

Table 1.2 provides an overview of sport product examples in all DreamSport Society marketplaces. It can be seen that the days of the simple football match as the only 'sport product' hosted in a sport arena or community sport facility are gone. For (recreational) sport entertainment people visit theme parks or jump off cliffs; for sport fantasy they interact with other fans online or at events; for sport quality they volunteer at events in a meaningful manner; for sport identity they publicly support teams that offer them opportunities to be 'part of the family'; for sport tradition facilities and service providers replicate the 'good old days'; and for sport conscience people will support those events and athletes that contribute to society as a whole.

Table 1.2 DreamSport products and implications for facility and event managers

DreamSport Society marketplaces	Example products	Implications for facility and event managers
Sport entertainment	■ Sport-themed consumption (theme park, museum, facility tours) ■ Sport tourism products (sport adventure packages to Queenstown, New Zealand including rafting, bungee jumping, etc.)	■ Customer in the game ■ Customer part of the action ■ Active manipulation or influence on outcome ■ Facility features to allow for integration of the 'spectating' and 'participating' roles

DreamSport Society marketplaces	Example products	Implications for facility and event managers
Sport fantasy	■ Team-based spectatorship (Newcastle United, Los Angeles Lakers, Collingwood Football Club) ■ International, event-based (based on nationality or alma mater) spectatorship (at the Olympic Games or at the World University Games)	■ Integration of online and onsite togetherness ■ Vastly expanding marketplaces through online supporter communities ■ In-stadium interactive and 'between fans' communication features
Sport quality	■ Team-based volunteerism (domestic teams, ethnically based teams, local clubs) ■ International event-based volunteerism (e.g. the Rio 2016 Olympic Games)	■ Culturally sensitive event communication (understand us and care about us) ■ Events that give back or contribute to the community ■ Events that incorporate opportunities to help others ■ Athletes who care about fans ■ 'Pure' sport (drug-free, traditional rules)
Sport identity	■ Sport participation products (Auskick, as a national participation program marketed by the Australian Football League) ■ Sport spectatorship products (FIFA World Cup and fanatic country/team support) ■ Packaged athlete and team products (LeBron James, Manchester United, the Brazilian soccer team)	■ Separate 'space' allocated within the facility to passionate partisans ■ Opportunities during events to publicly express the passion people feel for a team or athlete ■ Fit between the object of passionate following and tangible products offered for sales to commodify that relationship
Sport tradition	■ Sport-themed consumption (theme park, museum, facility tours) ■ Hallmark sporting events (Wimbledon) ■ Broadcast- and film-produced sporting entertainment (the FA Cup final) ■ Sport tourism (the British Lions Rugby Union tour)	■ Traditional architecture ■ Traditional or recycled building materials ■ Recreation of 'old' experiences ■ Marketing programs that have a high 'hero and ritual' content

DreamSport Society marketplaces	Example products	Implications for facility and event managers
Sport conscience	■ Culturally specific sport sponsorship based on convictions (e.g. sun protection products and surf lifesaving in Australia) ■ Culturally global sport sponsorship based on convictions (Coca-Cola and the Olympic Games)	■ 'Green' buildings ■ 'Green' events ■ Corporate sport citizenship ■ Sport, facilities, and events as tools to 'make things better'

In this table's overview of the type of products that will be delivered to the DreamSport Society marketplaces, also outlined are the implications for facility and event managers when they consider the delivery of these products. It has now also become clear that few facilities can cater to the needs of all sport consumers. In the remainder of this book we will therefore consider the following types of sport event facilities:

■ natural facilities (e.g. speed skating contests on natural ice such as lakes or canals);
■ spectator facilities (e.g. football stadia);
■ participative facilities (e.g. gymnasia or community swimming pools);
■ multi-use facilities (e.g. facilities that include retractable or removable seating systems, allowing them to be used for community and elite purposes).

THE ADDED VALUE OF FACILITIES AND EVENTS TO USER AND NON-USER GROUPS

As noted earlier, we will comment on the drivers of facility and event success more elaborately in Chapter 2, and will consider performance management issues in Chapter 11 and 12. This chapter concludes with a closer look at how the construction of facilities and the hosting of events are justified by the organisers and governments that determine how (community) resources are invested. There are four areas that are most often used to show to investors or to the local community why a new facility or major event will add value to all stakeholders involved. These areas are community development, economic development, destination development, and social and cultural development.

Community development

As has been shown, communities of local, regional, or national citizens have significantly contributed to the establishment of new facilities and to the attraction of hallmark sporting events to their cities and regions. However, only recently have governments realised that they are to be publicly accountable for the community resources they invest in venues and sporting events. Not only are they accountable economically – that is, to show professional financial management skills – but they also need to outline how community resources are used to provide a return for the community. This is when the establishment of facilities and the attraction and organisation of events are considered in light of added value. For example, will the new facility offer more opportunities for local community members to come together, to get to know each other better, to organise or become involved in community events, to allow minority communities to congregate and integrate with other community members? A multi-purpose facility such as the Coomera Sports Centre on the Gold Coast, Australia, is an example of this. The venue is been redeveloped for the Commonwealth Games to be hosted on the Gold Coast in 2018. The AUD$40 million indoor sports centre offers facilities for elite and community sport in basketball, netball, gymnastics, and soccer, and, it further accommodates a number of function rooms to service local community events. In short, the facility brings people from different (sporting) backgrounds together. With regard to events, do they provide community members with the opportunity to experience new cultures? Do the events, indeed, bring people together? Events can be used to showcase the uniqueness of local communities to the rest of the world, or at a more local level to invite people from various communities to come along and meet their neighbours. However, where community development remains a quite 'intangible' way of justifying the new facilities and events, calculating the economic effect of facilities and events on communities clearly focuses on measurable (quantifiable) contributions to the host society.

Economic development

Economic impact studies are attempts to demonstrate how expenditure related to the sporting event circulates through the economy. A positive economic impact (leading to economic benefits) can result from spending by visitors (locals, non-business, and business 'tourists') on food, accommodation, and transport. Added to this is the expenditure of government authorities and private investors when a new event related infrastructure is developed. In addition to this direct impact, there is the contribution of indirect spending when businesses produce goods and services (e.g. building materials) for organisations that spend money directly related to the event. Finally, there is a component called induced impact, when extra income gained by employees of firms that create direct and indirect impact is spent in the economy. The most common economic benefits that are the result of positive economic impact are the generation of new jobs, an increase in tourism in the region, the attraction of new business to the region, the growth of existing businesses, and a legacy of new or upgraded capital works (including sport facilities) for the region. It should be noted that the economic impact of major sporting events such as the Olympic Games and World Cups are continually over-estimated by potential hosts and communities. In contrast, Matheson (2009) and many academics suggest that the actual economic impact of hosting such events may be inflated due to inappropriate measures of economic assessment such as the number of times money invested in the Olympic Games circulates around the host community and nation (i.e. the multiplier effect). The deteriorating confidence in the economic impact of the Olympic Games was highlighted in the bidding process of the 2022 Winter Games in which several countries pulled out of the bidding process due to concerns regarding the economic viability of the event and the corrupted bidding process to attract the Games.

Destination development

The information age has resulted in an increased conceptual proximity of nations, cities, and people. Lightning-fast, long-distance exchange of information is leading to the redevelopment of urban regions from monocentric to polycentric cities. New economy cities are typified by the concentration of knowledge-based services and activities, not by building around a church or city hall. In other words, commercial activities are becoming the new centres of agglomeration and these centres both compete and cooperate with each other. Berg, Braun, and Otgaar (2000), at the European Institute for Comparative Urban Research (EURICUR) in Rotterdam (the Netherlands), argue that the potentially successful polycentric city will be formed around knowledge-generating institutions like multinationals, universities, and research organisations.

From that perspective, it is no longer sufficient to be (or become) a city that is built in an attractive location. Potential (and current) citizens, business organisations, investors, and visitors determine whether a city is attractive enough to be considered as a destination. Access to information, new knowledge, cultural services, and a healthy environment are becoming the competitive drivers of success for cities to attract 'clients'. In other words, how can cities be marketed as an attractive alternative for all identified client groups? Increasingly, sport is being used as one of the drivers of city marketing strategies. This is because sport events allow targeting of all (domestic and international) client groups through one powerful medium. London used the 2012 Olympic Games as an opportunity to regenerate East London (areas such as Stratford were previously run-down, polluted industrial areas full of factories). The regeneration of East London, just

11 kilometres from the centre of London, was a central pillar in the legacy of the 2012 Olympic Games. The Olympic Park was built in East London, rejuvenating the local environment alongside driving the building of key infrastructure such as new train stations and connections, and local commercial infrastructure such as new retail and residential zones.

Social and cultural development

There are a multitude of social benefits that can be identified, and it is common for governments and event organisers to highlight those benefits that are most likely to fit current policy and generate positive attitudes towards the event. From a sport specific development point of view, the event will contribute to the exposure of the sport, the development and preparation of officials and volunteers, and the generation of event-specific knowledge. The net benefits to the sport include new knowledge, experienced people, and marketing benefits. It is also important to acknowledge that the contribution of the event to national identity and citizenship should not be underestimated – in other words, the development of 'esprit de corps' of a nation or city. Furthermore, the event can contribute to programmes that focus on youth development, gender equity, multiculturalism, and health and fitness. One category of social benefits that is increasingly identified as a priority is the area of environmental legacy. Benefits that the event needs to deliver to its host society include the development of new environmental policies, the contribution to human health, the active pursuit of resource conservation, and pollution prevention and environmental protection. Stated differently, it is not sufficient for the event to merely ensure that the natural environment is not damaged: rather, the event will be used as the instigator for enriching the living environment and, hence, will leave an environmental legacy. The Sydney 2000 Olympic Games were tagged as the first 'green games', largely because the principal site of competition at Homebush had been a toxic waste dump for years before it was singled out as the future venue of the Games (a strategy that was repeated in London 2012 in East London). Sixteen years later, the Rio 2016 Olympic Games had one of the most comprehensive sustainability management plans in Olympic history including meeting international standards on environmental and social impacts. The sustainability approach has two main foci: environmental and social inclusion. The main environmental goal was to reduce the environmental footprint as much as possible, considering transport and logistics, sustainable construction and urban improvements, environmental conservation and clean-up, and waste management. The social aspect titled 'games for everybody' considered the involvement and raising awareness of diversity stakeholder groups, universal accessibility, and diversity and inclusion strategies (Rio 2016, 2013).

Cultural benefits may relate to the level of inclusiveness of linguistic and cultural aspects of the event. How accessible is the event to cultural minorities? And is the event actively used and promoted to offer minority groups opportunities to participate? The alternative is obviously that governments need to spend taxes on developing cultural inclusiveness programmes of their own (hence the need to conduct a cost–benefit analysis). The IOC has enforced the inclusion of a cultural programme directly linked to the hosting of the Olympic Games, to offer the host city opportunities to produce cultural benefits. Not only does it allow the host nation to expose its particular culture and its values to the rest of the world (media benefits), but the inclusion of arts and heritage groups and activities in the event's programme will deliver 'inclusiveness' benefits to a large cross-section of the host society.

SUMMARY

In this chapter, we have provided an outline of the changing nature of the sport facility and event sector. Because of its changing nature, the sector, more than ever, needs managers who are skilled in the areas of managing facilities and events. Throughout the rest of this book, you will be taken through the processes that range from establishing the facility and event infrastructure, to the actual running and performance evaluation of facilities and events. These processes will be outlined on the back of knowledge about the structure, size, and trends that typify the facility and events sectors. The latter information is of critical importance because it largely determines which markets the facility and its events need to cater for. This is why we have identified a number of new markets for sporting events and discussed the implications for the construction of new facilities. In this age of economic rationalisation and increasing social awareness, the business plan for constructing new facilities and attracting expensive events needs to be broader than a mere outline of the economic benefits. Our brief overview of the added value of new facilities and events to user and non-user groups presages a more detailed discussion of these issues in chapters to come.

CASE STUDY

The Coomera Sports Centre: customer needs and relationship management

This chapter's discussion of six different DreamSport Society marketplaces centred on the future needs of facility and event customers. Meeting customer needs is essential to the success of any facility or event, but customer needs are many and varied and continue to evolve.

One facility that meets the needs of many different customer groups and continues to adapt to changing customer needs is the Coomera Indoor Sports Centre (CISC). Located at the edge of attractive parkland and next to 'Dreamworld', one of Australia's largest theme parks, this impressive multi-purpose centre caters to a diversity of sport and leisure participants, spectators, and organisations. The facility is one of several new construction projects and redevelopments in the area in the lead up to the 2018 Commonwealth Games to be held on the Gold Coast, Queensland, Australia. The facility comprises a 7,600 seat show court that will reduce down to 350 permanent seats after the games, and will host the gymnastics and the netball final at the games. Additionally, the AUD$40 million facility will comprise eight mixed-use sports courts, a gymnastics arena, a kiosk, meeting and function rooms, and approximately 200 car parking spaces.

However, it is not only its multi-purpose nature that enables CISC to meet so many customer needs. The centre is one of several developments that the State government is undertaking in the lead up to the games in an effort to meet the needs of a rapidly growing and geographically spread population. The organising committee and local and state government are heavily focused on 'embracing the games legacy' in three main areas: economy, lifestyle, and community. In partnership with the organising committee and local government the State government has funded more than AUD$320 million ($237.3 million USD) in new stadia construction and facility upgrades including three new facilities and upgrades to seven further facilities. This investment is likely to generate more than 1,000 full-time equivalent positions and substantially improve the access and quality of sport and recreation services in the region.

To complement the investment in infrastructure, part of the legacy for the region is to incorporate programmes to curb health problems that have been increasing caused by a sedentary lifestyle in an ageing population. To do this, the organising committee in combination with the local government have introduced an 'Active and Healthy' programme in the lead up to the games that aims to 'create a city which embraces an active and healthy lifestyle' (Commonwealth Games Legacy, n.d.). The programme involves educating and supporting the local community in the incorporation of physical activity and healthy eating into their lives using the local infrastructure that is been built for the games and the local sport networks (clubs, schools, and businesses) that prosper from the new facilities. Furthermore, the local government is providing over 150 free or low-cost community physical activity programmes in the lead up to the games to try to achieve this goal.

The facility and event management landscape is changing globally. The citizens in several nations no longer accept the business case of significant investment of taxpayer funded money for only the two-week period of an event. For example, several of these nations quickly dropped out of the running for the 2022 Winter Olympics. Instead, approaches like that of the Gold Coast 2018 Commonwealth Games organising committee are becoming more common. This book is a resource for facility and event managers as well as students aspiring to work in the field. While not necessarily taught in sport management education programmes, central to anyone's success in this field is the ability to seek out, nurture, and maintain relationships with key stakeholders and provide value to the local community. In addition to the key success factors discussed in Chapter 2, successful relationship management is essential to the effective operation of any facility or event.

Questions

1   Identify at least 10 of the CISC's business customers.
2   Select two of these business customers and describe the interdependent nature of their relationship with the CISC.
3   Adopting the role of the local government manager for sport and recreation on the Gold Coast, what strategies could you use to leverage the new sport facilities in your area to provide long-term health impacts to your local community? What programmes would you offer? What deals could you provide (e.g. memberships, discounts, affiliations)? How would you measure the effectiveness of these programmes?
4   Physical activity and sport are increasingly being used as justifications for public spending and major events on the basis that they address public health problems linked to a sedentary lifestyle and poor diets such as diabetes and heart disease. Put yourself in the place of an international organising committee (e.g. FIFA, IOC), what stipulations would you put in the bidding documents to ensure that major events had a positive health impact on the local community?

NOTE

1 Parts of this section have been published earlier in Westerbeek, H., & Smith, A. (2003). Sport Business in the Global Marketplace. Palgrave, London. Permission to reuse this material was kindly granted by the authors.

REFERENCES

Anderson, P. (2000). *Sport facilities reports*. Milwaukee, WI: National Sports Law Institute of Marquette University Law School.
Anderson, P. (2009). An analysis of sports facility costs and development from 1989–2009. *Sport Facility Reports, Marquette University Law School, 10*(Summer), 1–16.

26

AT Kearney (2014). *Winning in the business of sports.* Chicago, IL: AT Kearney.

Berg, L. van den, Braun, E., & Otgaar, A. (2000). *Sport and city marketing in European cities.* Rotterdam, Netherlands: Erasmus University.

Boon, G. (1999). *Deloitte & Touche annual review of football finance (1997–1998).* Manchester, United Kingdom: Deloitte & Touche.

Chard, H. (2016). *Your ground's too big for you! Which stadiums were closest to capacity in England last season?* Retrieved from http://www.skysports.com/football/news/11095/ 9915096

Delloite Consulting (2016). *Deloitte sports' starting lineup: Sports trends that will disrupt and dominate 2016.* New York: Author.

DTESB (n.d.). *Our legacy stories: active and healthy program.* Retrieved from http://www.embracing2018.com/page/Our_Legacy_Stories/Active_and_Healthy_program

Goldblatt, J. (2000). *A future for event management: the analysis of major trends impacting the emerging profession.* Paper presented at the proceedings of conference on event evaluation, research and education, Australian Centre for Event Management, School of Leisure, Sport and Tourism, University of Technology Sydney.

Jensen, R. (1999). *The dream society.* New York: McGraw-Hill.

KPMG (2011). *European stadium insight 2011.* Budapest: Author.

KPMG (2013). *A blueprint for successful stadium development.* Budapest: Author.

Long, J.G. (2013). *Public-private partnerships for major league sports facilities.* New York: Routledge.

Matheson, V.A. (2009). Economic multipliers and mega-event analysis. *International Journal of Sport Finance, 4*(1), 63–70.

Melbourne Cricket Club (2002). *Press release: MCC commits $580 million to MCG redevelopment.* Melbourne: Author.

Mercedes-Benz Stadium (n.d.). *Fast facts – Mercedes-Benz Stadium by the numbers.* Retrieved from http://mercedesbenzstadium.com/stadium-info/fast-facts

ROCOG (2013). Sustainability management plan. Rio de Janeiro: Author.

Westerbeek, H., & Smith, A. (2003). *Sport business in the global marketplace.* London: Palgrave Macmillan.

CHAPTER 2

KEY SUCCESS FACTORS OF OPERATING SPORT FACILITIES AND RUNNING SPORT EVENTS

CHAPTER FOCUS

1 Introduction to sport facility and major event management
2 **Key success factors of operating sport facilities and running sport events**
3 Feasibility analysis and market research for planning new sport facilities and events
4 New sport facility development: planning, design, and construction
5 New sport facility development: preparing the facility management infrastructure
6 New sport facility operations: attracting events
7 New sport facility operations: planning the event management infrastructure
8 Attracting customers: marketing sport facilities and events
9 Running the sport event: event operations
10 Destination marketing, image, and branding through major sport events
11 Performance management: evaluating operations
12 Performance management: legacy and measuring impact

CHAPTER OBJECTIVES

In this chapter we will:

■ Demonstrate the complexities of real-life sport management through the introduction and analysis of an international sports event.

28

- Provide an applied overview of the management lifecycle phases of a sport event and facility from the perspective of the local organising committee.
- Introduce the basics of performance management by adopting a systems approach to organisational analysis.
- Discuss the key success factors and project drivers of managing sport facilities and events.

INTRODUCTION

Whereas Chapter 1 sets the scene and provides an essential overview of the current and future sport facility and event industry, this chapter will primarily establish the framework for the successful planning, design, building, operation, and evaluation of sport facilities and events. As in any business setting, continuously exceeding performance expectations presupposes a comprehensive understanding of the relevant concepts, principles, and processes of management. For this reason, we introduce the boundaries and constraints of effective facility and event management, providing a holistic context for applying the analytical processes and tools that will be introduced in subsequent chapters.

To ensure practical relevance and meaning, we begin with a management case study of the Olympic and Paralympic Games. With its global recognition and hallmark status, there is arguably no better example to study, since it exemplifies the complexity of multi-project management across industry sectors (Silvers & Nelson, 2009). Analysis of international and local impacts of this multi-sport event includes forming an understanding of facility build and development, a conceptual framework is presented from which all event and facility managers can operate. Drawing from event and project management bodies of knowledge, project management principles, systems theory, and the micro-management drivers of quality, time, and cost are discussed. Adopting this approach will demonstrate the complexity of real-life sport management across the breadth of an event or facility lifecycle, as well as highlight the importance of clarifying organisational and individual relationships that determine performance measurement. Understanding the often diverse and sometimes conflicting inter- and intra-organisational requirements of contemporary sport will help more informed managers to reliably analyse and predict human behaviour, and thereby meet the ultimate goal of optimising sustainable organisational performance.

THE OLYMPIC AND PARALYMPIC GAMES: LOCAL ORGANISING COMMITTEE PERSPECTIVE

The Olympic and Paralympic Games (the Games) are the 'biggest sporting event on the planet' (Rio 2016, 2016), providing a unique catalyst for cities and countries to invest in their future (IOC, 2015). This global, multi-sport, elite-athlete mega-event is owned by the International Olympic Committee (IOC), an international, private, non-profit organisation responsible for the Olympic Movement. Operating through a constitution, protocols, regulations, and codes of conduct, the IOC awards the hosting of the event to a city every four years (an Olympiad). As the owner and guardian of the Games, the IOC selects the host seven years in advance of the event implementation, requiring the National Olympic Committee (NOC) of the host country and the host city to sign a Host City Contract, specifying the IOC operational requirements for effective Games delivery.

Within five months of selection, the hosting country and city establish an Organizing Committee for the Olympic Games (OCOG), which acts as the lead body and legal entity to exclusively plan and organise the Games. Given that mega-events are characterised by numerous interrelated subprojects that meet a mandatory delivery deadline (Locatelli & Mancini, 2014), the OCOG needs to fully engage with all stakeholders affecting the successful Games delivery, particularly the government and city authorities of the host destination. This is typically achieved by establishing an Olympic Public Authority (OPA) that coordinates the Government's infrastructure of the Games. Engaging with other important stakeholders such as the International Sport Federations (IFs), the International Paralympic Committee (IPC), The Olympic Program (TOP) (sponsors), broadcast partners, United Nations agencies, and Federal, State, and Municipal Governments, to name but a few, managing the Games under the intense scrutiny of worldwide media is no easy task.

To demonstrate many of the practical yet complex logistics involved in managing the Games and its venues, let us refer to the local organising committee perspective of Rio de Janeiro (the 2016 host city and local organiser of the XXXI Olympiad and XV Paralympic Games) as illustrated in Table 2.1.

Table 2.1 Summary details of the Rio 2016 Olympic and Paralympic Games

Event aspect	Rio 2016 details
What	▪ **Olympic Games** – 17-day world-class competitive event involving 10,500 athletes from 206 countries, competing in 42 sports ▪ **Paralympic Games** – 12-day world-class competitive event involving 4,350 athletes from 160 countries, competing in 22 sports
When	▪ National candidate city chosen by Brazil Olympic Committee (BOC) – 1st September, 2006 ▪ International host chosen by International Olympic Committee (IOC) – 2nd October, 2009 ▪ 2016 Olympic Games – 5th–21st August, 2016; Paralympic Games – 7th–18th September, 2016
Who	▪ 23,000 athletes/team officials ▪ 163,000 Organizing Committee Workforce (70,000 volunteers; 85,000 contractors; 8,000 employees)

Event aspect	Rio 2016 details

- 27,500 media and broadcasters
- 3.7 billion television audience (more than 100,000 hours of Olympic broadcaster Games coverage)
- 7.5 million Olympic tickets and approximately 500,000 visitors to Rio

How   **Event organisational basic structure**

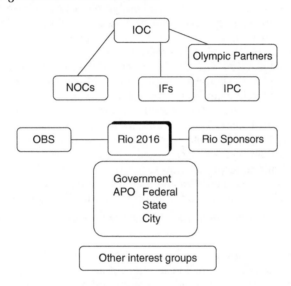

Key:

- **IOC** – International Olympic Committee (selects the city to host the Games)
- **Worldwide Olympic Partners** (e.g. Coca Cola, Visa)
- **NOCs** – National Olympic Committees (organise national involvement and participation)
- **IFs** – International Sport Federations (eg. IAAF; FINA)
- **IPC** – International Paralympic Committee (leads the Paralympic movement)
- **OBS** – Olympic Broadcasting Services (the host broadcaster of the Games)
- **Rio 2016** – Local organising committee (private and non-profit association that plans, organises, and delivers the Games; mediates the relationship between the IOC, IPC, and federal, state, and city governments)
- **Rio 2016 Sponsors**, including supporters and suppliers
- **OPA** – Olympic Public Authority (coordinates the host city venues, infrastructure and legacy)
- **Other interest groups** – e.g. tourism agencies, emergency services

Details:

- **Budget** – Local organising committee operational budget – R$7.4 billion ($2 billion USD)
- **Facilities** – 32 competition venues primarily spread across four zones of one city – Rio de Janeiro (47% of competition venues already existed, 25% temporary; 28% required building)

31

Event aspect	Rio 2016 details
	■ The exception to this is the 58 Olympic football matches that used many of the 2014 FIFA World Cup football stadiums (7 venues across 6 cities) ■ **Logistics** – The Rio 2016 logistics team must, for example, plan and accommodate 800 boats and 315 horses for the sailing and equestrian events
Other	■ 44 test events (34 Olympic; 6 Paralympic; 4 Olympic and Paralympic sport disciplines), involving 7,800 athletes and 16,000 volunteers, were hosted in the final 18 months before the Games commenced. ■ Rio's 2016 Olympic torch relay started in the Greek city of Olympia and visited 83 cities. On the 95-day tour of Brazil, it reached an estimated 90 per cent of the country's population, and was carried by approximately 12,000 torchbearers. Its journey was concluded on 5th August when the last torchbearer lit the Olympic cauldron to officially open the 2016 Games. ■ Rio 2016 Truce (a United Nations supported series of international sport activities that promote peace, solidarity, and protection of children) was hosted during the Games period. This is a resurrected ancient Olympic symbolic concept that aims to use sport to establish contacts between communities in conflict and offer humanitarian support in countries at war, as well as create a window of opportunities for dialogue and reconciliation.
Example of hosting of Games outputs/ outcomes	**A post-evaluation report (DCMS, 2013) of hosting London 2012 revealed the Games:** ■ Were the catalyst for improved elite sporting performance in the UK, ■ Created a substantial boost to the UK economy, ■ Accelerated the physical transformation of East London, ■ Set new standards for sustainability, ■ Inspired a generation of children and young people, ■ Improved attitudes to wards disability and provided new opportunities for disabled people to participate in society, ■ Increased enthusiasm for volunteering, ■ Increased active participation in sport. **A BBC (2013) ComRes poll revealed;** ■ More than two-thirds of the UK public believes the £8.77bn cost of the London 2012 Olympics was worth the money. ■ 74% would welcome the Games back to the UK.

Sources: BBC (2013), DCMS (2013), IOC (2013), IOC (2015), IOC (2016), Rio 2016 (2016)

As a concise analogy, Rio 2016 (2013, p. 8) summarises the relationship and role of some of these key organisations:

> if the Games were a stage play, Rio 2016 would be responsible for the production and staging of the play, and the governments and the OPA would be responsible for building the theatre, while the IOC and IPC would be the authors of the screenplay.

32

In essence, while the local organising committee (Rio 2016) is the primary planner and deliverer of the Games, it is not responsible for the building works. Instead, the planning and costs of building works for the Games venues and infrastructure are managed by the three levels of host country government (Rio 2016, 2016).

The Games' operational locations are also numerous. Whereas sport competition venues are perhaps the most obvious facilities, since they are the showcase of the entertainment experience, there are many other sites that require attention and effective management. For example, non-competition venues include the international and local transportation hubs, the Olympic Village, the 'Live' sites, the Main Press and International Broadcast Centre, pre-games training venues, the IOC hotel(s), warehouses, and support depots. Since no Games site operates in isolation, integrated planning and fully tested systems are essential components for successful delivery (London 2012, 2011).

The Games competition venues are always likely to involve the use of:

- existing venues with normal event infrastructure,
- new venues,
- existing venues with some, little, or no event infrastructure,
- temporary venues.

In the case of London 2012, Wembley Stadium was an example of an existing venue with a normal event infrastructure. However, even this well-established event venue would require some physical dressing and operational adjustments to accommodate the integrated system requirements of the Games. By comparison, the ExCeL London exhibition and international convention centre was a multi-use existing venue whose indoor halls could be reconfigured to designated sport requirements. For the Games, the fields of play, the stands, and all client and functional spaces were built to meet stakeholders' needs and specifications. New cutting-edge and by definition very expensive venues, such as the Olympic Stadium and Aquatics Centre of London 2012, are often built for Games use, with post-event legacy an important justification for their cost. Temporary venues, such as the Greenwich Park equestrian venue at London, are by contrast designed and built for the Games, and then removed immediately afterwards.

Regardless of competition venue nature, venues or portions of their facilities are handed over for the OCOG's exclusive use anywhere from several months to a few weeks before the Games commence. A Games Overlay (physical and operational adjustment) is then applied to all venues, to ensure consistency in implementation of policies, procedures, and levels of service during the Games time period (often in the region of seventy days).

Early establishment of the perimeters and boundaries of these competition venues is important to define the Games management systems and interdependency of network operations. For example, precinct venues (a group of venues within a common security perimeter, e.g. Olympic Park and ExCeL) require significant coordination of event schedules to coordinate pedestrian flows and replenishing activities to optimise shared resources. While the relative proximity of clustered venues (geographically close venues with separate perimeters, e.g. London's Outside Races – road events) requires interdependent planning, they may not have any significant operational sharing of resources to create management efficiencies. Stand-alone venues (e.g. Weymouth – hosted the Olympic sailing events), by their very nature are less complicated to manage. They operate as part of the Games network, but possess relatively low impact on the overall Games systems.

Defining clear boundaries for the competition venues helps to address fundamental security needs, ensuring a safe, friendly, attractive environment for each of the Games' client groups. Indeed, London 2012 explicitly defined and justified their IOC initiated client group focus in their Concept of Operations documentation (London 2012, 2011, p. 4–5):

> Given the interdependencies and interfaces between operational partners, it is strategically and operationally important to adopt consistent terminology and approach to client group segmentation in order to design and deliver seamless end-to-end experience for each client group. The following are our Client Groups and their definitions:

- The Athletes Client Group is comprised of athletes and their supporting Team Officials participating in the Games as accredited members of an NOC or NPC delegation.
- The Technical Officials Client Group is the team that oversees and manages the field of play and athlete areas (including Technical Delegates, International Technical Officials, National Technical Officials, and International Federation staff).
- The Press Client Group comprises representatives of photographic and written press from the UK and overseas, as well as a limited number of broadcasters that are not part of rights holding organisations.
- The Broadcast Client Group includes the Olympic Broadcast Service (OBS) and all the rights holding broadcasting organisations.
- The Olympic and Paralympic Family Client Group is defined as the IOC and IPC organisations (and their constituents), Chairmen and CEOs (or equivalent) of sponsors and broadcasters, international and domestic dignitaries, Presidents & Secretaries General of the NOC/NPC, IFs/IPSFs, future OCOGs, candidate cities, WADA, CAS & other eligible guests.
- The Marketing Partners Client Group includes The Olympic Program (TOP) partners and domestic Tier 1, Tier 2, and Tier 3 partners.
- The Workforce Client Group is defined as all persons who are paid employees, volunteering or contracted by LOCOG to directly deliver the Games.
- The Spectators Client Group includes those who have purchased tickets, and those who will attend a non-ticketed road event.
- The General Public includes members of the public from London, the UK and overseas. Ticket holders are not included (part of the Spectator Client Group). Members of other client groups can transition to or from the General Public Client Group at any time.

Adopting this focused client experience approach towards competition venues helps managers to determine very specific service and operational needs, and hence plan the detailed requirements of hosting the Games. In practice this means identifying what is needed to be done, by whom and when, and then implementing the plan of action for each stakeholder group to achieve the short- and long-term performance targets of the Games.

Having determined to host the Games in established, temporary, and new specialist sport facilities, Rio 2016 (just like London 2012) agreed to effectively design, build, operate, and manage these venues by adopting sustainable management principles. Adhering to the Rio 2016 mission, 'to deliver excellent Games, with memorable celebrations, that will enhance the global image of Brazil and promote sustainable social and urban transformations through sport, contributing to the growth of the Olympic and Paralympic Movements' (Rio 2016, 2013, p. 6) meant demonstrating sporting, educational, and social legacy plans. As illustrated by two examples of Rio's world-class venue clusters (Table 2.2), this was a daunting venture of considerable magnitude and long-term commitment.

Table 2.2 Examples of world-class sporting facilities built for the Rio 2016 Olympic and Paralympic Games

Facility	Facility features, funding, and use after the Games
Barra Olympic Park	**Facility features** ■ 44-acre park and focal point of the Olympic and Paralympic Games. Hosted 16 Olympic and nine Paralympic sports, the athletes' village, the main press centre, and the international broadcast centre. ■ Entailed the construction of new sports competition and training venues, improvements in transport infrastructure (city metro, bus, and road improvements) and new residential, shopping, and entertainment areas. **Funding** ■ Olympic park and public transport costs – R$29.6 billion (public R$15.16 billion/$4 billion USD; private R$14.48 billion/$3.85 billion USD). **Use after the Games** ■ Of the nine competition venues, seven remained and two were removed having their parts reused for new projects. The materials used to create the Future Arena (hosting of Olympic handball and Paralympic goalball), were used to construct four public schools, each with a capacity of 500 students. ■ The Olympic Aquatics Stadium used its parts to construct two aquatics centers, both with 50m Olympic swimming pools – one with a grandstand of 6,000 seats, the other with seating for 3,000 spectators. ■ Carioca Arena 3 (hosting Olympic fencing, taekwondo, and Paralympic judo) was planned to become an Olympic Experimental School, combining academic teaching with top-level sports training for 850 full-time students.

Facility	Facility features, funding, and use after the Games
Deodoro Park	**Facility features** ■ A multi-venue hub that played a prominent role in the 2007 Pan-American Games, consisted of three existing venues, three new, and one temporary required for the Games. ■ Provided the competition venues for the aquatics, basketball, BMX, canoe, equestrian, hockey, modern pentathlon, mountain bike, rugby, and wheelchair fencing competitions. ■ The Olympic Park project dealt with the issues of a suburban context comprising a military neighbourhood, a densely populated favela, a rough industrial area, and a vast wild landscape. **Use after the games** ■ As well as continuing to offer facilities for high-performance sport, Deodoro was planned to become home to Rio's second largest public leisure area (500,000m2), the X-Park, serving about 1.5 million people. ■ While the post-Games plans for the canoe slalom venue was to become a large recreational lake, the Olympic BMX track was to be maintained, with additional multi-sports courts, a mini mountain bike track, a beginners BMX track, nature trails, bike paths, a skating rink, outdoor fitness equipment, gardens, and barbecue areas to be installed.

Sources: Rio 2016 (2015); Rio 2016 (2016)

This case study has provided a broad context and array of practical issues in which to comprehend sport event and facility management from. To better appreciate the requirements of successfully managing elements of the Games, let us now draw from event and project management theory to inform best practice.

THEORETICAL UNDERPINNING

The international event management body of knowledge (EMBOK) model illustrated in Table 2.3 provides a useful overview and framework in which to study events. Customised to meet the needs of various cultures, organisations, and event offerings, this model proposes four interdependent components of event management, namely phases, processes, core values, and knowledge domains (Silvers & Nelson, 2009). Whereas the phases provide the structure and cyclical sequencing of an event, the processes provide guidance on how activities are administered. Values, on the other hand, refer to the personal and business skills needed to orchestrate the event, and domains, the functional activities constituting event management responsibilities (Robson, 2008). With each component possessing a further five elements of description, a logical conceptual event framework is presented for analysis, design, and application (Silvers & Nelson, 2009).

Key success factors

Table 2.3 Overview of the international event body of knowledge model

Component	Elements	
Phases	Initiation, planning, implementation, event, closure	
Processes	Assess, select, monitor, document, communicate	
Core values	Creativity, strategic, continuous improvement, ethics, integration	
Knowledge domains	Administration	Financial management, human resource management, information management, procurement management, stakeholder management, systems management, time management.
	Design	Catering design, content design, entertainment design, environment design, production design, programme design, theme design.
	Marketing	Marketing plan management, materials management, merchandise management, promotion management, public relations, sales management, sponsorship management.
	Operations	Attendee management, communications management, infrastructure management, logistics management, participant management, site management, technical management.
	Risk	Compliance management, decision management, emergency management, health and safety management, insurance management, legal management, security management.

Source: Adapted from Silvers and Nelson (2009)

This model draws heavily from the more established project management literature and in particular the Project Management Institute's project management body of knowledge guide (PMBOK). For example, EMBOK's phases of initiation, planning, implementation, event, and closure are nearly identical to PMBOK's process groups of initiating, planning, executing, controlling, and closing. One reason for this is that events and facilities are often considered as projects, defined by the Project Management Institute (2013, p. 3) as 'a temporary endeavor undertaken to create a unique product, service or result'. While the event or facility is the deliverable, project management is the overlay integrating all tasks of the deliverable.

Indeed, one of the earliest descriptions classifies project management as 'the use of tools and techniques applied to diverse resources in order to accomplish a unique, complex, one-time task within time, cost and quality constraints' (Drury-Grogan, 2014, p. 507). Clearly, the management of an event such as the Games fulfils this definition where each project – building a facility, planning the torch relay, managing the closing ceremony, coordinating the media coverage of the Paralympic Games – can be considered a collection of integrated projects.

PROJECT MANAGEMENT ENVIRONMENT AND KEY DRIVERS TO SUCCESS

In the complex, uncertain, and accountable environment of hosting the portfolio of projects that constitute the Games, each project manager needs to understand their operational environment (see Figure 2.1).

The outer ring in Figure 2.1 represents the key environmental and stakeholder influences on the project manager decision-making process; the inner ring identifies the golden triangle or project drivers for successful management – namely, the essential and critical performance measures of quality, cost, and time (Drury-Grogan, 2014).

Elaborating in more detail on both rings, regardless of the nature of involvement in sport facilities or events, each organisation possesses its own unique purpose and attempts to measure its success by the achievement of goals. These are achieved through an ongoing interaction with the organisation's general and specific macro-environment. As illustrated in Figure 2.2, effective sport management can be explained by each organisation (the grey area) obtaining and using inputs from its environment, and implementing systems (referred to as conversion processes or throughputs) to produce and discharge outputs (services and short-term objectives) and outcomes (impacts and long-term aims) into the environment. This is known as systems theory, and is increasingly being used to understand the means of sport facility and event management performance.

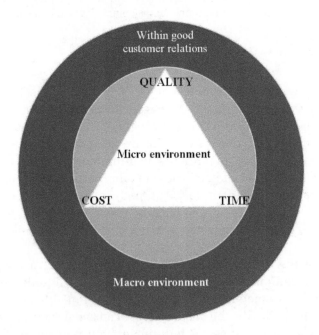

Figure 2.1 The project management environment

Source: Adapted from Kerzner (2013, p. 6)

Understanding this systems model places in context the interlinked core management processes of hosting the Games, namely planning, organising, leading, and evaluating. From Figure 2.2, it can be seen that each sport organisation operates in an open systems environment, with each external and internal subsystem dynamically influencing one another. In effectively delivering the Olympic and Paralympic Games, the whole system – involving core and peripheral organisations across many different layers – has to be managed to achieve the high-risk yet publicly scrutinised short and long term performance indicators. From a local organising committee perspective, successful management implies establishing a closely knit or loose coalition of multi-organisational partnerships to achieve collective and individual organisational goals.

Applying a systems theory approach to project management success, Kendra and Taplin (2004) place great emphasis on the operational environment of project management, and this includes carefully managing the fundamental drivers or key success factors of the project, namely quality, cost, and time. Dependent on the unique demands of the project, the individual stakeholder perspective and the lifecycle development phase, one of the project drivers is likely to dominate management actions and become the primary limiting factor for success. Table 2.4 and the subsequent commentary illustrates a diversity of general sport project scenarios and highlights the management implications and typical trade-offs encountered between one or more project driver.

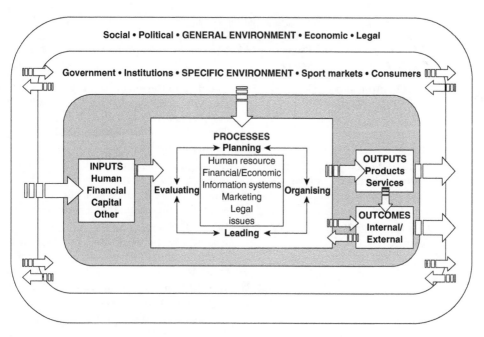

Figure 2.2 Organisation systems and relationships

Source: Adapted from Soucie and Doherty (1994)

The case study and Scenario 1 referenced in Table 2.4 below is driven by the notion of time, given that the Games, once awarded to the host city, progresses to an immovable date. If the project is behind schedule, the only options available to management are to reduce the quality of the event or facility (e.g. shorter Opening Ceremony or cheaper facility signage) or incur greater costs (e.g. employ more people and equipment, or pay overtime) to meet important milestones and deadlines. Scenario 2, a non-case study oriented scenario, on the other hand, is heavily influenced by financial resource constraints that directly affect the facility quality and timing. If the project costs escalate from the original estimates, the project manager could decide to reduce the quality of the synthetic pitch/surrounding area or postpone the project finish date until such time as the additional finance became available.

Scenario 3 is particularly important for managers to comprehend because external threshold performance standards must be achieved before the project can be implemented. For example, it is not uncommon for music concerts that include temporary structures to be issued a safety certificate just one hour before the doors open, due to additional work being completed to fully comply with the safety panel's conditions. The alternative option to this potentially higher cost could mean postponement or cancellation of the event, which equally would create additional management problems, bad publicity, and further costs. Finally, Scenario 4 presents an example where managers have more freedom in which to make decisions. Here,

Table 2.4 Sport project diversity and management implications

Scenario	Brief project description	Project driver	Management implications
1	The Olympic and Paralympic Games	Time	■ The date of the event cannot be changed, since it impacts global media and other event schedules. ■ The only variables that can be altered are quality and cost.
2	Synthetic pitch of a local voluntary hockey club	Financial cost	■ Maximum expenditure is likely to limit management options. ■ Time and quality decisions are dependent on availability of financial resources.
3	City Half-Marathon Road Race	Quality	■ Without adherence to the appropriate legal safety standards and sport technical requirements, the event simply will not take place. ■ Cost and time can be altered to achieve the required quality criteria.
4	The opening of a new private health and fitness club	Hybrid	■ No key driver of the project from the outset. ■ Time, cost, and quality can be played off against each other.

the private health and fitness club project could be phased over time, with building developments or membership packages, or conversely includes a new opening date if the image and quality of the establishment were paramount to its success.

Clearly, the components of this triangle (project drivers) are seen to be interdependent, where a change in one is likely to influence another to restore the project equilibrium. The intention of management is therefore to establish an appropriate balance between the elements of quality, cost, and time at any particular stage. This may vary throughout the project lifecycle as the key driver reaches its ultimate limit.

The very nature of many sport event management environments – namely, a finite activity with just one opportunity to get it right – often means that the component of time should receive considerable attention. Quality, in the form of technical facility specification, is usually controlled by international governing federation and building legislative standards, and finance by the commonly used techniques of budgeting and cash flow forecasts. To date, the use of time management techniques in managing even small events is quite rare. This is somewhat surprising given that:

> The event, unlike the normal ongoing program, is speeded up and delivered within a short space of time; this concentrates all the advanced planning and actions into specific hours and moments. Problems can thus be dramatic and could prove devastating.
>
> (Torkildsen, 2005, p. 474)

Stages	1. Pre-event			2. Event	3. Post-event	
Sub-stages	(a) Idea and feasibility	(b) Bidding process (if required)	(c) Detailed planning and preparation	(a) Implementation	(a) Clear away	(b) Feedback
Core management processes	← PLANNING → -------------------→					
	← ORGANISING → -------------------→					
	← LEADING →					
	← (Formative) EVALUATION (Summative) →					
Timeline	⟶					

Key:
← Start of Management Activity   → End of Management Activity   – – – – Management Application

Figure 2.3 Lifecycle stages and core management processes of managing major sport events

Source: Adapted from Emery (2003)

THE EVENT AND FACILITY LIFECYCLE

Given the importance of time in project management scenarios, let us now apply the life-cycle concept to both the sport event and facility management scenarios. Lifecycle models are an attempt to simplify the chronological and developmental process of managing projects. From a project management perspective, they integrate both general and specific planning requirements across a time-driven management context, so that each successive activity can be better prepared for, and cost-effectively managed within, the project.

As a useful starting point, the event lifecycle model in Figure 2.3 can be applied to the major and mega-sporting event environment. This model emphasises that there are three discrete stages – pre-event, event implementation, and post-event – each constituting a self-evident boundary of time and involving further EMBOK phases. Such a model, which includes the dynamic generic management processes of planning, organising, leading, and evaluating, can equally be applied and adapted to any type of sports event.

Pre-event management stage

The first and longest stage of the lifecycle, often involving up to 90 per cent of the total event duration, normally requires the majority of the resource investment spend. This pre-event stage can be subdivided further into the three phases of initiation, planning, and implementation (Figure 2.3).

Initiation phase

Historically, the decision of whether to host a sport event or not was often based on a personal and political whim rather than any careful appraisal of the project merits (Emery, 2003). However, with the escalating costs involved in hosting events and the greater levels of accountability experienced in all sectors of the sport industry, clarification and justification of any resource investment should now be regarded as the norm. Any organisation wishing to host a sport event, whether from an internally or externally generated idea, should be able to justify it on the basis of the strategic fit between present and future organisational competence as well as environmental need.

In the early phase of initiation, potential hosts need to clarify what it means to enter each stage of the event by means of concept definition and verification. By reducing uncertainty to acceptable levels, candidate cities can determine project viability and their commitment (or not) to the event as the proposal progresses through different phases of the internal and external selection and sanctioning processes. As will be explained in more detail in Chapter 3, this means that the feasibility of the idea should be objectively appraised via analytical techniques, and via comparison with both organisational selection and sanctioning criteria, as well as competitor offerings.

Bidding is not an inevitable event process, although it is required when seeking to host the Games or other internationally recognised sporting championships.

42

Where bidding is required, the local organiser is likely to experience increased resource commitment and greater levels of bureaucracy and uncertainty at each stage of the organisational, national, and international approval process. Ironically, it could be considered to be a business venture where many organisations may start the race but where realistically there is only one winner, since there are rarely any benefits for second place.

Sport events involving a bidding process place the winning host in the role of a 'time-bound' franchisee, unlike many other cases, where the sport event is created by an individual or organisation and is hosted at the same venue each year. This latter type of annual sport event, which still requires the respective national governing federation's permission to host the event, includes the Wimbledon Tennis Championships, local athletic road races, and invitational rugby tournaments. Regardless of the nature of the sport event, successful delivery is possible only through the event organiser's meticulous attention to detailed planning and preparation.

Planning phase

Once such permissions have been granted (or candidature confirmed) and a full commitment made to stage the event, the in-depth planning and preparation of requirements and tactics development can begin. Planning, establishing the terms of reference (future ends) and the systems/means of achieving them, should begin the moment the event is initiated. This, as highlighted in Figure 2.3, has a tendency to pervade all elements of the lifecycle. As more projects fail through bad planning than for all other reasons combined, it is likely that the planning phase will consume the lion's share of the allocated event resources. As Watt (1998, p. 25) explains:

> It is always a little dangerous to select one management function as more important than another, but in terms of event organisation, it would be quite legitimate to select planning as the prime factor of success ... planning is so valuable because it reduces uncertainty, focuses attention on goals, produces unity of purpose, makes for efficient operation and ensures appropriate control systems are established.

In essence, the core management process of event planning attempts to maximise positive impacts and to counter potential negative impacts through astute awareness and practical intervention activities (Bowdin, Allen, Harris, McDonnell, & O'Toole, 2012). It is considered to be so fundamental to the nature of any type of sport event and facility management success that it will be discussed in considerable depth throughout the book.

Organising

The second core management process initiated in the pre-event stage of event management is that of organising. According to Watt (1998, p. 35), this entails determining;

the special activities to be accomplished towards the end objectives; the gathering together of these activities into relevant structures, and the allocation of the achievement of objectives, through these activities, to the appropriate groups or individuals ... the framework within which individuals can cooperate together to achieve what they could not achieve on their own.

Inextricably linked to planning, organising can be seen to be about creating synergy, and hence optimising the effectiveness and efficiency of goal achievement while minimising coordination costs. The difficulty of managing this process in the mega-event management environment lies in the finite nature of the event; the complexity of the multi-stakeholder involvement; as well as the human resource demands that peak at the event delivery phase. In the Games context, the IOC (2015, p. 14) explains;

> Within the space of seven years, Olympic Games hosts will build an organisation from a few employees to an entity the equivalent of a Fortune 500 company, and then integrate that with a broad range of existing public authorities and institutions.

With a clear dissolution strategy in place, it is also not uncommon that the host organisation is then completely dissolved within eight months of the Games being delivered, as was the case with London 2012. As a temporary, flexible host organisation, the organising committee operates in a very dynamic and unknown environment, and, with new multi-agency partnerships, potentially creates all the ingredients for a coordination disaster. Furthermore, organisation theory would suggest that such an environment demands an organisational structure of low centralisation, job specification (horizontal and vertical), and formalisation. Paradoxically, local authority organisations are usually the drivers of major sports event local organising committees, yet they are historically characterised by functional bureaucratic cultures, the very opposite of what the event environment demands in theory.

For successful event management, this dichotomy obviously needs to be resolved, to create the many features cited for effective event organisation. Torkildsen (2005), for example, suggests that these should include:

- Clear objectives to which all parties are committed,
- A highly respected coordinator of calibre and authority,
- A synergistic organisational structure, with discrete units for specific tasks,
- Team effort, positive attitudes and enthusiasm,
- Efficient formal and informal lines of communication,
- Coordinated effort, with no overlap or wasted time and resources.

Leading

From such a list, it is apparent that one of the keys to successful event management is effective leadership, which must facilitate all stages of the event lifecycle.

This constitutes the third component of the core management processes, and entails balancing the performance needs of the task, team, and individual according to the event demands encountered. Achieving the task obviously dominates the desired behaviour of business activity, although human relations theorists draw attention to the importance of the team and comprehension of personal needs, particularly in light of the sport event scenario involving such a high percentage of their workforce as volunteers.

Given the previously established complexity of the event environment, it probably comes as no surprise that the role of the event leader is incredibly onerous, being multidisciplinary as well as multidirectional. For example, Rio 2016 leadership required looking upwards and downwards (e.g. leading IOC involvement and staff expectations), forwards and backwards (e.g. establishing performance targets and monitoring milestone deliverables), as well as inwards and outwards (e.g. managing personal goals and the event suppliers/contractors).

This additionally highlights the potential accountabilities of leaders, at both organisational and individual levels, and can be linked directly to Meyer's (2002) 'purposes of performance measurement' model as presented in Figure 2.4.

As Chapters 11 and 12 will further develop the concept of performance measurement, only a concise synopsis of the model is presented here. In briefly explaining this model, Meyer (2002, pp. 30–31) elaborates:

> the look ahead, look back, motivate, and compensate purposes of performance measures are placed outside the organisational pyramid because they are common from the smallest and least formal to the largest and most organised firms. By contrast, the roll-up, cascade-down and compare purposes, which become

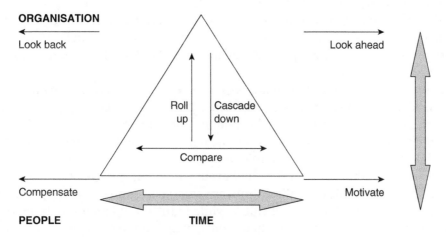

Figure 2.4 The seven purposes of performance measurement

Source: Adapted from Meyer (2002, p. 31)

significant as firms grow in size and complexity, are placed within the pyramid because they are the artifacts of organisation ... look ahead and look back are placed at the peak of the pyramid because measures having these purposes gauge the economic performance and past accomplishments of the firm as a whole, whereas motivate and compensate are at the bottom of the pyramid because measures having these purposes motivate and drive the compensation of individual people.

Clearly, event leaders at all levels of the operation must have the ability to establish the leadership style(s) of 'best fit' determined by the event phase, the leader, the subordinates, the task, and the specific goals of the organisation.

Implementation phase

Implementation involves coordination and contracting, verification and control. Bowdin et al. (2012) more explicitly suggest that it involves applying plans, monitoring, and controlling their implementation, making decisions based on differences between plans and reality, active risk management, and reporting on work-in-progress to key stakeholders. This usually means high activity as well as constant communication between involved parties.

Whereas rehearsal, execution, and evaluation are relatively easy to achieve in most sport operational management contexts, this is more difficult to practise in the unique environment of managing one-off mega-sporting events. This is not to say that it is impossible to achieve. For example, Aquece Rio was the test event programme for the Rio 2016 Games, which organised numerous events to test the individual competition venues as well as shared command arrangements to simulate Games time activities. As well as providing opportunities for athletes to familiarise themselves with outdoor sport climatic conditions and competition venue layouts, these test events permitted management to test security, cleaning, and transport arrangements from 18 to three months prior to the Games.

It is not uncommon in other major events, such as the Commonwealth Games, that a spectator-attended final dress rehearsal of the Games Opening Ceremony is held just two days before the actual ceremony. Obviously, the key celebrities and fireworks displays are omitted so as not to spoil the surprises of the official event. Dress rehearsal tickets are commonly sold through the event volunteers, just for their friends and families or for the other event volunteers not specifically involved in the Opening Ceremony. To the volunteers, this acted as an exclusive perk, creating considerable perceived added value, while to the event organisers it presented a final opportunity to refine the operational plans and systems of the event, as well as provide another income stream and promotional activity to sell the official merchandise.

Event management stage

Event phase

The second stage of the proposed event management lifecycle is the operational delivery of the event, meaning its staging and execution. Unlike a tangible building that can be handed over, an event is intangible, and therefore warrants a separate phase to implementation. Bowdin et al. (2012, p. 263) explain:

> The short time period of attendance of the major stakeholders, [such as the client groups] the audience and the participants, means that management cannot rely on the same management techniques that were used during the lead-up to the event … [but] move into 'operation mode'.

This is obviously the culmination of and justification for all previous work. As the prime indicator of event performance measurement it requires little explanation here, but will be developed more fully later in the book. The ideal event, in essence, will be the one that leads to total satisfaction of all internal and external stakeholders – a memorable experience, run in a smooth, safe, and enjoyable manner, in which all parties would wish to be involved again. According to Torkildsen (2005), this means a 'professional' presentation of the event, where class, flair, and imagination are truly evident; and this becomes possible only if the pre-event stages have been thoroughly planned, prepared, rehearsed, and executed.

As with any aspect of sport performance, even the most perfect baseline plan will not guarantee event success without some form of control. The interactive nature of people with their environment means that many uncertainties exist on the day of the event, and this is where performance measures need to be continually monitored and controlled. Monitoring, or 'formative evaluation', should take place throughout the event and not just during the event execution stage.

To eradicate risk and prepare for emergencies in the event delivery stage, key stakeholders are typically involved in many of the preceding phases of the event. This permits personal involvement and use of appropriate expertise in the agreement of respective role(s), task integration, and the formalisation of important communication and control practices that span the entire lifecycle of the project. At the event delivery stage, various control centres usually operate, minimally with a venue specific control centre established. Through closed-circuit television and radio communications, the event and facility multi-agency managers use instantaneous communication with each other, as well as their respective support staff, to manage the event effectively and efficiently. Control in this sense is about continuous monitoring of performance against baseline planned activity. Where differences are encountered, contingency plans are executed, or decisions quickly escalated up the line of control, which in the Games scenario could relate ultimately to the Olympic Coordination Group (OCG), a group of senior officials under the leadership of a government Minister. In essence, if planning is considered to be the route map of the journey, organising is the means to arrive at the destination. The controlling function informs management as to how they are progressing along the route, or, via deviations, can stay on course to successfully complete the journey.

Post-event management stage

Closure phase

This last phase requires a separate series of tasks, where management is scaled down and, as appropriate, is either returned to its pre-event format, decommissioned, or prepared for a future legacy plan. The phase of event closure therefore typically entails the on-site clear-away, the shutdown of operations as appropriate, feedback, and review, and in the case of the Games, legacy realisation including knowledge transfer. In some events, this final stage overlaps with the event delivery stage. For example, many world marathons start their clear-away processes literally minutes after the last runner starts the race.

Post-event feedback and review are often referred to as 'summative evaluation'. Given the significance of all types of evaluation (performance measurement) on future learning, this will be elaborated on in more depth in Chapter 11. Evaluation appears too often to be associated with negative connotations, such as coercion and blame, rather than the positive aspects of a continual learning process. Only when the evaluation is interpreted as constructive feedback by all relevant stakeholders will it be possible to begin to achieve the long-term aim of continually improving the efficiency of people and units, and hence the organisation.

Given the large costs of hosting major and mega-events, legacy has now become a central feature of event owner selection criteria (Bowdin et al, 2012). London 2012, for example, established a Legacy Action Plan (DCMS, 2011), and similarly Glasgow promised social, economic, and sporting legacies from hosting the 2014 Glasgow Commonwealth Games (Scottish Government, 2015). Entailing a 10-year robust research programme (2008 to 2019), 50 baseline outcome indicators are being tracked and the first summative report, published in 2015, reveals significant positive transformation from hosting the Commonwealth Games (Scottish Government, 2015).

From the host city and country perspective legacy plans need to be effectively funded and implemented, but increasingly from the event owner perspective, knowledge transfer systems are being introduced to retain, develop and share lessons learnt. Mallen and Adams (2008), for example, make reference to 'network activism', a conscious effort to expand networks and encourage contact between members, and in the Games scenario, the IOC has developed the innovative Olympic Games Knowledge Management platform (IOC, 2014). Specifically created to assist future hosts, such activities do not merely end the post-event management stage of an Olympiad, they begin to develop another event lifecycle, and more importantly professionalise the event industry of the future.

To recap: the purpose of applying the lifecycle concept to any project, in this case a sport event, is that it helps management to focus more specifically on the demands of each phase of development, clarifying the logical sequence and relationship between the interrelated components. However, the concept needs to be applied and intelligently adapted to the individual stakeholder circumstances.

Furthermore, and regardless of stakeholder perspective, management should place the lifecycle concept in context, meaning for example that it should consider its more strategic needs (such as the Games legacy) as well as other aspects of its portfolio. Sport organisations rarely operate as single-project entities, and in experiencing a multi-project environment they need to carefully consider the overlapping lifecycle demands of managing a portfolio of activities over time.

Such are the resource demands of some stages of sport event management that the lifecycle concept often includes many other projects and, in turn, their own lifecycles. From the perspective of Rio 2016, projects requiring completion before the Games event delivery stage were the bidding and hosting of the 2014 FIFA World Cup as well as the numerous international and national test events previously alluded to. Future event strategies will similarly mean building new or adapting existing venues. This will minimally involve other project lifecycles to consider.

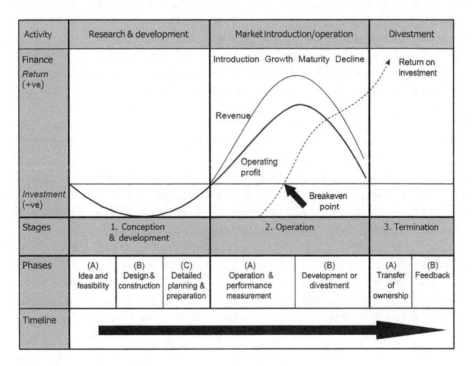

Figure 2.5 Lifecycle stages of a facility

Source: Adapted from Kerzner (2013, p. 72)

Given the focus of this text and case study presented in this chapter, let us now apply the lifecycle concept to a 'new build facility' environment, but obviously not in the same depth as the event example. Drawing on the previous lifecycle terminology and the marketing product lifecycle concept, Figure 2.5 illustrates an application to the facility environment – this time including financial details.

From Figure 2.5 it is apparent that the proposed stages can still be divided into three similar stages – pre-facility (conception and development), implementation (operation), and post-facility (termination) – from which seven phases can be identified. As many similarities exist with the event management lifecycle, these phases will not be elaborated on here but will be covered in more depth in subsequent chapters. An important difference to highlight between the two lifecycles relates to the component of time. While facility products and projects are likely to consume significant capital budgets, their lifecycle duration and hence earning potential is usually over a much longer time frame than that of an event. Events by their very definition may be one-off activities, whereas sport facilities are often built for a minimum operational period of 10 years or, in some cases (e.g. Lord's Cricket Ground), more than 100 years of use. But in both facility and event applications, it is important to realise that the early phase of development assumes considerable cash flow availability. As highlighted in Figure 2.5, the earliest return of investment and breakeven point is likely to occur in the implementation/operation stage of the lifecycle. Where short-term or political motives drive the project, and financial appraisals are superficially administered, 'white elephants' sometimes remain, which can become an embarrassing reminder to all of the ineffective management. One such example was the Montreal Olympic Games that nearly left the city bankrupt and for its taxpayers, who referred to the Olympic Stadium as the 'Big Owe', created a 30-year debt.

In fairness, hosting mega-events, such as the Games, is often a once in a lifetime unique experience and will always involve considerable uncertainty and change across the project lifecycle. The management of multi-organisation hierarchical partnerships and temporary involvement dictate that plans are iterative and are progressively updated as more detailed and specific information becomes available. Clearly, the analysis of the Games case study has demonstrated that managing a sport event or venue can be a particularly challenging project to undertake. The management experience can be highly rewarding and, on occasion, very frustrating. To minimise the latter and maximise the former, there is a need to be astutely aware of the individual and holistic demands of each stage of correlated projects, to fully understand the relationship between inputs, processes, and outputs, and to recognise that organisational integration is paramount to successful event and facility management.

SUMMARY

The central message of this chapter, which will be reinforced through subsequent chapters of this text, is that informed practice needs to be based on a clear understanding of the local operational context as well as on an insightful and appropriate breadth of awareness of management processes, systems, tactics, and techniques. As conceptual awareness and clarity are fundamental to operational success, this chapter has provided the broad analytical frameworks for planning, organising, leading, and evaluating a facility or sport event management performance. Through applying the lifecycle concept and systems theory of analysis to the multi-partnership complexities of contemporary sport, it is possible to simplify the real-world experience and be better able to manage the relationship between inputs and performance outputs or outcomes at any particular moment. Whereas lifecycle analysis highlights the important link between the present and the future, systems analysis provides the more immediate micro-management focus on the key drivers of operational success. In the case of effective and efficient sport facility or event management, the key to success, regardless of project scale and scope, could be said to be dependent on balancing the constraints of quality, cost, and time within the unique and complex environmental demands of both internal and external political pressures.

CASE STUDY

Time–cost–quality and their relationship to planning, organising, leading, and evaluating of the Singapore Sports Hub

The management functions of planning, organising, leading, and evaluating are central to the success of any project. Errors and oversights in each of these management functions will inevitably negatively affect at least one, and perhaps all, of the key drivers of project success – namely time, cost, and quality.

Underpinned by the Singapore Government's 'Vision 2030' sports master plan, the Singapore Sports Hub is a new stadium and events complex that was built to deliver a sustainable, differentiated, and competitive advantage for Singapore. With national government tender documents issued in 2006, the scope of the project was to design, construct, finance, operate, and maintain a sports, entertainment, and lifestyle hub over a 25-year term. The goal was to create the world's first integrated land and water sports and lifestyle complex with not only world-class sporting facilities but also extensive retail and commercial space. With construction delays and financial costs escalating, largely due to the challenging global financial crisis of 2007–10, construction contracts were finally signed in 2010 and the Singapore Sports Hub was opened on 30th June 2014.

Built at a cost of $1.33 billion, it now operates under a 25-year Public-Private Partnership (PPP) agreement between Sport Singapore (SS) (Government) and SportsHub Pte Ltd (SHPL) (Private). While the Government did not pay anything upfront, SS bears the construction and operational costs of the Sports Hub, making annual payments to SHPL, which manages the Sports Hub, over the 25-year terms of the agreement.

Promoted as an integrated sports, entertainment, and lifestyle hub delivering world-class sporting and entertainment events, it boasts something for everyone. For example, to replace the previous national stadium (July 1973 – June 2007; 55,000 seats), the primary venue of the precinct is the state-of-the-art 55,000 seat national stadium, which operates a retractable roof, localised comfort cooling for spectators, and retractable seating capability for hosting a multitude of events. Furthermore, this 35-hectare site includes an indoor stadium, aquatic centre, arena, skate park, water sports centre, sports information and resource centre comprising a library, a sports museum, and an exhibition centre, and even possesses 41,000 square meters of retail, restaurant, and entertainment space.

However, despite winning the 2013 World Architecture Festival (WAF) award for best future project in the leisure-led development category, and being named the third best stadium in 2014 by a jury of stadium architects (stadiumDB.com), the Singapore Sports Hub project has experienced numerous challenges across its short history as illustrated by the following headlines and reported problems:

- 14th February 2014: World's largest dome delayed – Planned delivery in April this year had to be delayed in order to thoroughly test all systems before the world's largest dome can open to the public.
- 25th May 2014: Dome opening postponed – The 'Causeway Derby' between Singapore and Malaysia was to inaugurate the new national stadium of Singapore. But the game was postponed indefinitely to give time for preparation.
- 13th October 2014: Shameful sell-out? The super-stadium with not so super turf – First few months of the Singapore National Stadium was not supposed to look like that. One of the world's most expensive stadiums was about to experience its first sell-out game, but the field quality had been disappointing since opening … Brazilian coach Dunga said, 'Most of it is sand, not grass … It is going to be hard to pass the ball. There is more chance of getting injured on this field.'
- 21 October 2014: Exhibition rugby match between the Maori All Blacks and Asia-Pacific Dragons in Singapore Sports Hub cancelled due to the poor state of the now world-renowned pitch. The pitch was universally

slammed by the Juventus football team, who played a friendly there two months earlier in August by both the Brazil and Japan football teams. Ex-national football captain Baihakki Khaizan also criticised the National Stadium with the hashtag #stadiumforconcerts.

■ With the stadium's much-publicised $800,000 Desso GrassMaster pitch unable to grow properly because of the stadium's domed design, the Sports Hub invested more than $2 million in growth lights and a 'lay and play' surface with warm weather grass to solve the problem.

■ 29th December 2014: Leaking roof, bad acoustics criticised after Sports Hub concert – New national stadium of Singapore failed once again. This time, problems surfaced during a concert at which fans were getting wet despite the closed roof, while the sound system offered poor quality. And the list goes on.

■ 16th January 2015: Singapore Sports Hub fiasco: The unspoken issue – Moving forward, it would be in SHPL's best interest to boost its communication with the government and public, perhaps by engaging a corporate communications expert who knows the ins and outs of Singapore's sporting scene ... But to succeed, the government needs to improve its monitoring and governance of the PPP. There's an unspoken issue it needs to address.

■ 13th December 2015: High rental costs said to be the reason for the National Stadium's threadbare 2016 schedule – As it stands now, only three big-name draws had been confirmed for 2016 to date ... Said Singapore Cricket Association CEO Saad Khan Janjua: 'Top teams want to come to Singapore to play, but promoters are finding it much easier and cheaper to stage cricket matches in Dubai or Abu Dhabi. Our National Stadium is going to be a white elephant if costs remain as they are.'

Questions

1 Using systems theory, identify the nature of the time, cost, and quality problems experienced in the Singapore Sports Hub project lifecycle. How are these problems associated with the management functions of planning, organising, leading, and/or evaluating?

2 How could Sport Singapore have planned, organised, led, and evaluated differently so as to have eradicated, or at least minimised, the losses of time, cost, and quality?

REFERENCES

Bowdin, G.A.J., Allen, J., Harris, R., McDonnell, I., & O'Toole, W. (2012). *Events management*. 3rd edition. Hoboken: Taylor and Francis.

DCMS (2011). *Government Olympic Executive London 2012 Olympic and Paralympic Games Annual Report February 2011*. London: Department of Culture Media and Sport.

Drury-Grogan, M.L. (2014). Performance on agile teams: Relating iteration objectives and critical decisions to project management success factors. *Information and Software Technology, 56*, 506–515.

Emery, P.R. (2003). Sports event management. In Trenberth, L. (Ed.), *Managing the Business of Sport*. Palmerston North: Dunmore Press.

IOC (2014). *Factsheet. Olympic Games Knowledge Management – 20th February 2014*. Lausanne: IOC.

IOC (2015). *Olympic Games Framework. Produced for the 2024 Olympic Games*. Lausanne: IOC.

Kendra, K., & Taplin, L.J. (2004). Project success: a cultural framework, *Project Management Journal, 35*, 30–45.

Locatelli, G., & Mancini, M. (2014). Controlling the delivering of projects in mega-events: An application on Expo 2015. *Event Management, 18*, 285–301.

London 2012 (2011). LOCOG concept of operations v2.0. Unpublished LOCOG working documentation.

Mallen, C., & Adams, L.J. (2008). *Sport, recreation and tourism event management: Theoretical and practical dimensions*. Oxford: Elsevier/Butterworth-Heinemann.

Meyer, M.W. (2002). Rethinking performance measurement: Beyond the balanced scorecard. Cambridge: Cambridge University Press.

Project Management Institute (2013). *A guide to the project management body of knowledge (PMBOK)*. 5th edition. Pennsylvania: Project Management Institute.

Rio 2016 (2013). *Sustainability Management Plan: Rio 2016™ Olympic and Paralympic Games*. Rio de Janeiro: Rio 2016.

Rio 2016 (2015). *Passada crise com o COI, Paes diz que obras da Rio 2016 estão 'na mão'*. Retrieved from http://g1.globo.com/rio-de-janeiro/rio-450-anos/noticia/2015/01/passada-crise-com-o-coi-paes-diz-que-obras-da-rio-2016-estao-na-mao.html.

Rio 2016 (2016). Rio 2016 Homepage. Retrieved from http://www.rio2016.com/en

Robson, L.M. (2008). Event management body of knowledge (EMBOK): The future of event industry research. *Event Management, 12*, 19–25.

Scottish Government (2015). *Legacy 2014 Commonwealth Games ... More than 11 days of Sport: The Legacy of the XX Commonwealth Games*. Retrieved from http://legacy2014.co.uk/

Silvers, J.R., & Nelson, K.B. (2009). An application illustration of the event management body of knowledge (EMBOK) as a framework for analysis using the design of the 2006 Winter Olympics Opening Ceremonies. *Event Management, 13*, 117–131.

Torkildsen, G. (2005). *Leisure and recreation management*. 5th edition. London: Routledge.

Watt, D.C. (1998). *Event management in leisure and tourism*. Harlow: Addison Wesley Longman.

Key success factors

CHAPTER 3

FEASIBILITY ANALYSIS AND MARKET RESEARCH FOR PLANNING NEW SPORT FACILITIES AND EVENTS

CHAPTER FOCUS

1 Introduction to sport facility and major event management
2 Key success factors of operating sport facilities and running sport events
3 **Feasibility analysis and market research for planning new sport facilities and events**
4 New sport facility development: planning, design, and construction
5 New sport facility development: preparing the facility management infrastructure
6 New sport facility operations: attracting events
7 New sport facility operations: planning the event management infrastructure
8 Attracting customers: marketing sport facilities and events
9 Running the sport event: event operations
10 Destination marketing, image, and branding through major sport events
11 Performance management: evaluating operations
12 Performance management: legacy and measuring impact

CHAPTER OBJECTIVES

In this chapter we will:

■ Demonstrate the importance of and need for feasibility studies.
■ Outline the process of strategic scoping in terms of a project charter and project action plan.

- Explain the external factors that directly influence the successful completion and implementation of a feasibility study, including geographic, financial, and legal/regulatory analyses.
- Exhibit the role market research and competitor analysis play in the overall planning of new sport facilities and events.
- Describe the importance of industry, external environment, consumer market, and competitive analyses in providing objective data for the sport facility or event project manager.

INTRODUCTION

The previous chapter focused on the key success factors related to operating sport facilities, as well as running sport events. Those concepts, while vital to success, are only attainable when a solid strategic planning process is employed. Strategic planning involves the creation of a comprehensive and integrated plan that is designed to look at the long-term projections of an organisation. It starts with gaining a complete understanding of the current situation of the organisation, and how that information has a direct effect on the overall strategic planning process. This includes creating a coherent mission for an organisation, assessing its internal operational strengths and weaknesses, evaluating their external opportunities and threats, generating relevant goals and objectives, crafting an appropriate organisational structure to move the organisation forward, and developing an action plan to implement the process.

The next step involves determining where the organisation wants to be in the future. This is accomplished through the development of key results areas (KRAs), and a re-evaluation of the goals and objectives to determine validity and allow for the creation of strategies. KRAs serve to bridge the current situation of the sport business to where the sport business wants to be. Goals are specific accomplishments to be achieved within a specific time period; objectives are the steps taken to accomplish those goals; and strategies are processes used to achieve goals and objectives.

Ultimately, the organisation will use the strategic planning process to optimistically implement positive change for the sport facility or sport event. However, there is a lot more to the planning process than just coming up with ideas internally within the planning function of the organisation. There needs to be internal buy-in across the organisation, as well as external validation of the planning process. Hence, the focus of the remainder of this chapter will be on the key concepts of feasibility analysis and market research/competitor analysis.

56

FEASIBILITY ANALYSIS

The planning process for sport and major events starts with a programme analysis. The purpose of this analysis is to determine what the needs for the facility or event are in terms of the organisational structure, the operational capabilities of the infrastructure, the human resources available, and the standard operating procedures that are the norm in the industry. This analysis not only looks at the current situation of the sport facility or event, but also towards a vision for the future of where the organisation wants to be.

This information is then used to conduct the feasibility analysis, which is a systematic process of determining the viability and practicality of a specific project. In sport facility management this may include determining whether a new facility is needed or if an existing facility can be modified to offer a programme. This could include investigating whether a sport event should continue to be offered, be cancelled, or be made either larger or smaller to meet the needs of spectators and participants.

The process of performing a feasibility analysis is more commonly articulated as conducting a feasibility study. The feasibility study starts with a project description that provides a general overview of the sport facility or event – including size, location, inclusions, and amenities. This is followed by looking into the scope and constraints associated with the project, considering the facility and event processes to determine the feasibility of the project in terms of definitions, controls, and restrictions. Once these processes are understood, a verification process is implemented to assess whether the project should continue – looking at both the current situations and trends, as well as how the project will have a positive and long-term impact. These impacts are often defined in terms of economics, societal needs, environmental impact, sport development, building brand, and enhancing positive image through marketing and media efforts. Once it is evaluated that the project is feasible, financial issues are addressed in terms of capital costs, revenue projections, and budgets – and timelines are set to create specific benchmarks and deadlines for accomplishing the tasks associated with the project.

Feasibility studies can be conducted by the organisation itself, but to ensure that the study is free from bias and analysed from an external point of view, a consultant is often hired who specialises in this type of work. However, it is also important that the internal organisation creates a planning committee to oversee the consultant and the project work, the development of the master plan for the project, and the selection of additional constituencies to ensure efficient and effective completion of the project. For a facility, this might include the selection of an architect and contractors to design and construct a facility or modify an existing one. For an event, this might include hiring specialists in food service or merchandising to manage those areas during events.

The need for feasibility studies

Performed correctly, there is no more useful tool for the prospective facility or event manager than a feasibility study. Between 3 and 5 per cent of the total budget allocated to a new project should be invested in its planning activities, the first of which is the feasibility study. This may account for as much as 20 per cent of the budget allocated to planning activities, as it yields the critical information concerning whether the project should proceed and, if so, in what form. While this might seem a large chunk of the budget required for a state-of-the-art facility or major event, it is much better to spend a few million on a feasibility study than spend a few hundred million on a facility that can never pay for itself, or on an event that requires enormous capital investment.

There has always been one problem with great new ideas for both sport and recreation events and facilities: more often than not, what people want to buy is not the same as what is being sold. Any product, including events and facilities, is only as good as its ability to provide a recognisably useful addition to an individual's experience. It is easy to assign usefulness, but the harsh reality is that useful means that someone is prepared to pay for it – usually the public sector in the form of local, state, or federal government. However, these bodies also expect a return on their investment. Each facility and event must return at least as much as it costs, either in financial terms or in its utility to the community. This is tempered by the reality that few facilities or events are so important to communities that they warrant full funding without any user-pays component.

The demand for new facilities is driven primarily by growth in the number, type, size, and attendance at sports and entertainment events. The need to redevelop or build new sport facilities – and the events hosted in them – is often a function of the physical suitability of a region (e.g. topography, climate) and the nature of its usage. This means that those undertaking a feasibility study need to be aware of the complexities inherent to determining the properties of a proposed facility or event, its location, and what its potential users might want. Often, there is insufficient overlap, as feasibility studies often find that the needs of the users, the broad expectations of public authorities, and the profit hopes of private partners are not the same. Excellent planning is predicated on sound information, which must be acquired through careful market analysis and the collection of consumer data. A clear link may be observed between the aspects of strategy, planning, market analysis and research, and feasibility.

A feasibility study is a critical beginning to the planning process, because of the following factors (Government of Western Australia, 2007):

■ It determines whether a community or owner can afford to build and operate over a period of time;
■ It radically decreases the risk of failure;

- It specifies the best fit of features of the facility or event to its prospective users;
- It is the first stage of balancing competing demands on facilities in an objective way;
- It identifies the revenue and expenditure opportunities, and burdens that need to be factored in to the capital and operational phases of the project;
- It begins to highlight the most appropriate management structures and marketing strategies required for the facility or event.

The feasibility study is the first serious stage of activity in the development of a sport facility or event project. It provides a comprehensive analysis of the costs and benefits of the proposed project, including a full consideration of its economic, social, cultural and political implications. The results of the feasibility study should determine the fate of the project. However, a positive result in a feasibility study is not a guarantee of success; it is merely a statement of risk: the more positive the results of a feasibility study are, the less the risk in proceeding with building the facility or hosting the event. If the project is deemed an acceptable risk, the feasibility study should provide much of the background information and analysis that is essential to the full planning of the project. Feasibility studies are decision-making tools, but they still require some interpretation. In addition, they can rarely be completed in less than several months; therefore it is worth taking the time to complete them properly. This is because even though the feasibility study is only a small percentage of the total cost of a project, the results determine how the majority of the budget is spent on the remaining costs for the planning, design, and construction/development of the facility/event.

A feasibility study is the first time in the development of a project that all the pieces are put together to see whether they can perform in unison technically and with anticipated economic outcomes. Hence, feasibility is concerned with the fit of alternative solutions to a clear set of problems. Almost every facility or event disaster has been preceded by a feasibility study that, despite assuring success, was either not undertaken correctly or unduly influenced by the political agendas of stakeholders. As a result, more information is needed to understand the feasibility process and to make informed judgements about the veracity of studies. This starts with the necessary strategic scoping that begins the study process, continues with conducting stakeholder analysis, and finishes with a look at external opportunities and threats related to the geographic, financial, and legal aspects of feasibility.

Strategic scoping of the facility or event project

Scoping the facility/event project requires a statement of exactly what the project entails, the project's objectives, and how these objectives are to be achieved. Fundamental agreement on the philosophical foundations of the project is therefore paramount. For example, is the project driven by a community need or is it simply an opportunity to be seized by a private provider seeking a profitable return? Subsequently, the industry or marketplace in which the project will be completed needs to be considered, along with the products and services to be offered and the potential users of the project. Ultimately, these uncertainties must be resolved in a project 'charter' that reflects the mission and objectives of the stakeholders involved.

The size of the required task comes to light during this scoping process. More often than not the project is larger than anticipated. As an example, consider the magnitude of constructing a new 18-hole golf course. Going from dirt to sculptured land is a massive task – it is not unusual for up to 750,000 cubic meters of dirt to be moved, including excavation for lakes/water hazards, sand traps/bunkers, and the planting of hundreds of trees.

The measurement of feasibility can be considered from a number of angles, ranging from the purely financial to the largely intangible social benefits for the users. Therefore, the return on capital investment and the profits that a facility or event can generate are only part of the picture. However, the reality is that feasibility is subject to an ultimate financial imperative because the money has to come from somewhere, and there are few facilities or events that require no ongoing financial support once the structure has been built or the initial event has been conducted.

In practical terms, there are more facilities and events that, when measured exclusively on financial returns, are economic burdens than there are those that deliver a net economic return. The type and form of returns (i.e. financial, social, environmental, etc.) require as much clarity as possible regarding the purpose of the project before an analysis of its feasibility can be undertaken. If, for example, we are concerned with an event that is to be run for the cultural benefit of a region, it may be inappropriate to constrain its feasibility to purely financial indicators.

A sound analysis will always reveal the financial situation clearly, but it should also highlight any non-financial benefits that might be worthy of the costs involved. The difficulty comes when users want a facility or event but are either unprepared to pay for it, if they consider the entry fees too high, for example, or feel they should not have to pay for using a facility or attending an event. As a result, other benefactors, usually bolstered by public funding, are then necessary to make the project a reality. These benefactors are rarely altruistic – and, as with any stakeholder group, have varied agendas ranging from acquisition of political support to the promotion of specific cultural values.

Not all motivations can be justified economically, or even rationally. For example, in the United States, the primary motive for constructing some stadia or arenas using public monies of a municipality is to attract a professional franchise to the city. Professional franchise relocations are not unusual, especially in recent years in American football, basketball, and ice hockey, and are usually a result of clubs wanting to capitalise on favourable lease arrangements. Cities substantiate their decisions on the basis of a combination of the enhanced economic impact that accompanies a professional sports team – a measurable value, and the social benefits that collective support of a team brings – an immeasurable value also known as psychic income.

In order for scoping to be completed, all stakeholders need to be consulted. While this is understandably a lengthy process, it is far less onerous than the management of important groups that perceive themselves as marginalised after the project is under way. Engaging stakeholders is a sensible investment to ensure that all stakeholders are identified and their perspectives solicited. These stakeholders are usually part of a planning committee, and may include individual investors, consultants, bank representatives, accountants, elected public officials, community members, agents from the prospective facility and/or event users, and the construction/design companies.

As with all large projects, those conducting the feasibility study have the added complication of determining not only who the stakeholders are and what they overtly seek but also what might be part of their 'hidden agenda'. Some of the objectives of stakeholders will almost certainly be contradictory. These issues must be worked through before the project proceeds. If these differences cannot be resolved, then the project becomes not feasible.

It is important to note that most feasibility studies report reasonably high economic risks, but do not discourage decision-makers from proceeding with the project on the basis of other benefits implicit in the project's completion. In other words, many stakeholder groups are married to the idea of proceeding before any objective data arrive, and these expectations are usually communicated to the feasibility team.

Scope management is primarily concerned with the definition and control of what is or is not included in the project. It encompasses the processes needed to ensure that the project includes all the work required to complete the project successfully. The processes of scope management interact within the context of the scope of the product and the project. Product scope refers to the features and functions that are to be included in a product or service, usually articulated through a master plan. Completion is measured against these requirements. Project scope refers to the work that must be done in order to deliver a product with the specified features and functions. Completion is measured against the plan, with the processes, tools, and techniques used to manage project scope as a key focus for success.

There are two distinct phases associated with scoping in any situation. The first – defining the project – occurs through developing a charter, and this is critical to project success. The second phase – planning the project – includes scoping the project by taking the outcomes articulated in the charter and using them to determine the project activities and deliverables, and defining the project plan by detailing the deliverables to produce, the resources needed, and how to operate with the defined constraints. This analysis takes into account the internal strengths and weaknesses of the organisation to ensure optimal success while addressing shortfalls in a timely manner.

The project charter

The purpose of the project charter is to provide an authorisation for the project manager to proceed with the project, and gives the authority to use organisational resources for the project. It is sometimes referred to as the project brief, the project statement, the mission, or the terms of reference. The charter describes the objectives, deliverables (products or outputs), and customers of the project, as well as the customers' expectations for the final deliverables. The charter should cover the business need or product description that is being addressed.

If the parameters of the project (including its goals and desired outcomes), rationale for the projects initiation and the constraints to be imposed, are incorrectly defined or unclear, then the project is heading for the dangerous realms of ambiguity. Without a charter, projects cannot establish a clear direction for their activities and are almost certainly heading for disaster. Charters should reflect the key content areas noted in Table 3.1.

The charter is then used to determine the future direction of the project in terms of scope, viability, and decision making. This is usually articulated in an action plan, which details what to produce (interim and final deliverables), what resources

Table 3.1 Key content areas of a project charter

Title page	■ Provides the project name and identifies the project owner and owner's representatives.
	■ The date signifies the beginning of the project.
Introduction, overview, or background	■ Gives a brief description of the project.
	■ This should include the business need, problem, or opportunity, and the events leading to the formulation of the project.
Goals, objectives, and strategies	■ Articulates the larger picture of what the project is aiming to achieve.
Deliverables	■ Denotes the outputs of the project that are designed to satisfy customer needs and requirements.
	■ Could be a good, service, process, or plan.
Key stakeholders and resources	■ Represents the people or organisations that have either influence or interest in the project.
Constraints and assumptions	■ Reflects on the factors that may limit the scope or viability of the project.
	■ May include related projects, corporate policy, or risks that will affect the outcome.
Planned approach	■ States how the project will be conducted, indicating main areas of activity, resources required, and steps in development.
Authorisation	■ Involves senior management signing off or giving written approval before proceeding with the project.

62

are required (human, financial, etc.), and how to go about producing the deliverables within the constraints established. Within that framework, a work breakdown structure (WBS) is generated to provide a graphic representation of the activities and specific tasks to be completed. With good organisation of details, resources can be managed effectively and efficiently.

External factors

Beyond the internal analysis related to planning the project, there are also external feasibility issues that provide opportunities and invoke threats to the organisation and the project. The three main areas of analysis evaluated during a feasibility study are geographic, financial, and legal in nature.

Geographic analysis

Feasibility issues from both an industry and market perspective are often directly related to the geographic distance of potential customers to the facility or the event. In addition, the breadth of the scope is directly proportional to the geographic areas to be targeted (i.e. the broader the scope, the bigger the geographic area to be incorporated in the analysis). Therefore, geography is an important part of the feasibility equation when considering the potential customers for a new facility or event.

There are numerous customer and operational issues of geography to be considered, including location; transportation philosophy and capacity; costs related to land, construction, and labour; climate; the natural environment; and the development of tourism. As far as location is concerned, the market value of a property is determined by location, and this holds true for the positioning of a sport facility or event. Facilities – as well as established events – cannot be simply picked up and taken to another geographic area, hence the decision of where to build them in the first place is an influential one. The 'location' decision drives decision-making and perceptions about the new facility or event, such as how to get there, visual attractiveness of surroundings, and availability of essential services. In addition, from a community and local and regional government perspective, addressing how the proposed facility or event fits into the overall site development plans of unused, reclaimed, or derelict locations is paramount.

In terms of transportation philosophy, a new facility or event immediately poses the question of how people will get there. Generally, city locations offer the benefit of existing and extensive transport infrastructure, but the downside is the heavy traffic and congestion common to 'downtown' city areas. Train, tram, or metro access to downtown areas is often of excellent quality, whereas access by car requires extensive parking areas, which requires land in city areas that is very expensive or has already been used for office or residential developments. In contrast, suburban or country locations for new facilities or events offer the benefits of easy access by car and plenty of parking spaces, but access by public transport is impractical. However, it is often difficult to get approval from the local government, as the anticipated social and economic benefits of the proposed facility or event may not in their eyes outweigh the social costs of air, noise, and visual pollution. In addition, if the government is championing the new facility or event, issues where some local residents may complain can arise, or there may be difficulties in acquiring necessary physical and human resources in the area.

As far as transportation capacity is concerned, a geographic population analysis of how many people live in the surrounding areas of the anticipated location must be included. Emphasis should be on issues of travel, such as travel time, access to transport systems, willingness to travel, and transport capacity considerations related to the size of the catchment areas the facility is likely to serve. Feasibility researchers must determine whether existing transport infrastructure is sufficient, and whether there are opportunities to work with the government or private transport operators to upgrade the number of available services.

The costs associated with land, construction, and labour can be significant based on the attractiveness of the geographic area. The closer a facility or event is to the largest cluster of potential users – the central business district (CBD) of a city – the higher the cost of the land to be built on and the more expensive the leasing of existing facilities for events. Also, proximity to a CBD increases the number of suppliers of services and goods in close vicinity to the facility or event – but the competition and cost also increase proportionally. At the same time, in areas where there is fierce competition for space, the demand for construction labour will most likely also be higher. From a government perspective, the questions that are most often raised include:

- Can the ground be used for sport facility development?
- Is the development to the benefit of the majority of the community?
- Should the expensive ground and labour be used for other community purposes (e.g. building an extension to the city hospital, including extra parking spaces)?

Climate as a geographic issue can be defined as a macro-variable, in that for local or regional feasibility researchers, climate will not vary enough to be a consideration. For example, average rainfall in particular geographic regions will necessitate incorporating simple or advanced drainage systems, especially when the grass is not artificial and gets heavy use throughout the year. However, on a grander scale, the choice of whether to build a new stadium in either Miami or Boston to accommodate a baseball franchise is dependent on climate and is in direct correlation to the continuously increasing service and comfort expectations of modern-day sport spectators. Typical weather in Miami during the summer is humid, hot, and rainy, which requires the incorporation of cooling systems and a roof covering all the seats.

In contrast, Boston can see a myriad of weather including freezing weather in early spring and fall, requiring the consideration of a retractable roof and heating systems as part of the plan.

Beyond climate, the natural environment has been an issue of great debate in relation to the planning and development of sport facilities throughout the world. Stadia in particular, because they are such large constructions, are sometimes considered visually unattractive or even pollutant to the natural surroundings. Planners now strive to optimise the location of proposed facilities by blending the facility and/or event into the scenery of the city in a way that it can be used for television and photographic purposes.

With regard to the development of tourism, 'designing a sport facility to fit in with the local area can help to make it an attractive distribution point, which is also useful for media attention' (Smith & Stewart, 2015, p. 168), hence the opportunity to create exposure through a sport facility is present at local, regional, national, international, and global levels. As a result, municipality marketers realise that bringing major sporting events to a city can result in wide publicity for the host city and host facility, creating a flow-on effect of people wanting to come and visit both. This entices planners to try to incorporate the facility and/or event into the standard 'tourist route' through the city, not taking visitors too much out of their way. Beyond convenience, facilities and events have the potential to contribute positive effects through tourism on gross domestic product – and across a wide range of industries including manufacturing, retail trade, personal services, finance, and construction. Therefore, any facility that can be used for a variety of events (multipurpose), including business meetings or conferences, one-off tourist events, and other major events that are likely to attract visitors from other geographic regions to the city, are most desired.

In summary, the most influential factors associated with the selection of a site for a sport facility or event are those related to design, accessibility to customers and participants, the size of the geographic catchment, climate, marketability, and potential occupancy or utilisation rates. All of these factors have revenue potential and inherent costs which must be weighed against each other. As with all aspects of project management, feasibility is a function of time, cost, and quality. The perfectly located facility or event may be possible, but it will come at a price. Better quality takes longer to construct and organise – and usually costs more. However, if the price is compromised, often so is quality, which might result in reduced opportunities for maximising usage.

Financial analysis

A financial feasibility analysis is a comprehensive study of all the potential and existing factors that may affect the likelihood of financial success of a proposed facility or event. The data obtained from the financial analysis are used to determine whether the development should be pursued, revised, or abandoned. This section highlights three principal questions that must be resolved in order to complete a reliable financial feasibility analysis.

1 How much money is needed in order to satisfactorily finance the design and construction of the facility, or develop the event concept?
2 Where is the money going to come from?
3 Do the benefits outweigh the costs from a purely financial perspective?

While at the feasibility stage it is impractical to precisely calculate design and construction or organisation costs, it is nevertheless essential to develop preliminary estimates. Expenses incurred during the design and construction phase are reviewed in the next chapter (Chapter 4), and collectively provide a comprehensive summary of the items to consider. The important decision at the feasibility stage is to determine approximately how much money will be required in order to plan and build the facility or lease and administrate the event. Pedantic decisions about specific architectural configurations are unnecessary at this point, but the broad strategic purposes of the facility or event need to be determined. In addition, some preliminary operational calculations are required in order to satisfy lenders and stakeholders. While it is logical to begin by calculating the amount of money required to develop and construct the facility or hire the personnel required to organise an event, the amount of money available for design and construction will ultimately provide the boundaries for specific decisions. Thus, the amount of money desired will be dependent on the funding available. Almost every project manager is forced to compromise their idealised design as a result of the limited financial resources that accompany the implications of certain funding strategies.

There are a variety of sources available for funding facilities and events, but also implications of each possibility. These sources fall into three broad categories: project costs, project financing, and borrowing.

Project costs: Project costs will be covered in more detail in the next chapter (Chapter 4); however, as a starting point, it is important to note that when developing a detailed checklist of design and construction elements it is necessary to develop estimates of these elements as part of a financial feasibility analysis. Further, if development is to be undertaken in phases, distribution of costs per phase should be identified. Costs should also be calculated at a macro-level using broad, generic categories that can readily be understood by non-architects. Typical headings may include: land acquisition, site preparation, permits and temporary facilities, road system, power system, communication system, water

66

system, sewerage and drainage, fencing, buildings, parking, landscaping, and architecture and engineering.

Project financing: The second category is project financing, which comes from a number of sources of revenues whose composition related to the design and construction of facilities has far-reaching implications for the financial feasibility of the project and its scope. The importance of where the money comes from is often underestimated in feasibility studies. Typically, all that is relevant is whether the money is going to be available at all. In reality, however, the ramifications of the choice of funding arrangements are substantial, and will affect the financial feasibility of the facility or event for the rest of its operational life. The most common funding approaches are considered below; they include public funding, government funding, private funding, and corporate funding.

Public funding involves raising money through selling shares to the public. The great advantage is that the revenue need not be repaid, and may be invested in the capital works of the facility without worry about interest repayments. However, public shareholders are demanding, and will expect the prompt payment of dividends and an increase in the value of their holdings, which are exposed to the vagaries of international money markets and volatile economic perceptions. In addition, public companies are subject to weighty regulations governing accountability and policy making. Some facilities attempt to circumvent the complications associated with public share offers and pre-sell reserved seating and other limited services such as memberships for life. While this approach can provide much-needed revenue during the early life of a facility, it tends to contribute insubstantially to the overall funding, and can limit essential operational income.

An alternative to this is government funding, of which there are several forms that are viable but are often accompanied by numerous conditions. Like all creditors, the government will lend money to finance a facility if it perceives sufficient reciprocal benefits. Governments tend to provide funding for three reasons. First, as its core stakeholder is the general community, government tends to be interested in facilities that can provide generic, low-cost services to the general public to furnish necessary sport and recreational infrastructure or provide events that a government deems to have benefits relevant to its constituency. Second, governments may see a proposed facility as a prudent consolidation of cash assets that may provide an attractive return, as long as they would receive a share of the profits and have a voice in the policy and operation of the facility or event. Third, the government may assess the facility or event as a possibility for providing a significant economic stimulus, in either or both of its construction and operation, hence providing financial support on a short- to medium-term basis in order to reap the economic and social benefits. While governments become involved for any one or a combination of these three factors, there are other more complicated options that reflect agreements between government, communities, and sometimes corporations. One such option is a general obligation bond, which works well when the facility or event is at least a partially government-owned project. In this agreement the local community, in the form of its local government, finances the facility or event, and recovers its investment slowly through operational profits and local taxes. Several other methods have been employed, many of which use a unique configuration of tax funds, grants, private investments, and in some cases donations, student fees, institutional contributions, and public subscriptions.

Private funding is where an individual, group, company, or consortium provides the full financial resources for their design and construction or operations. This is advantageous in facility development, where the capital required to build even a small recreational facility is easily in the tens of millions of dollars. For events, while they often do not have the burden of heavy capital investment, they can require significant sums of money well before any return is yielded. In addition, many events also demand significant alterations to the host facility. Where substantial, these are made at the expense of the event rather than the facility. The advantages of private funding are that all profits are returned to the owners, as well as the decreased likelihood that the stakeholders will seek competing or non-complementary goals. The disadvantages are that private ownership necessitates significant investment in a non-current asset, which is difficult to convert readily into cash for other projects, and that it forces all risk squarely on the owners.

Another version of private funding is corporate funding, which comes from private organisations that are enticed to provide a share of the funding necessary to design and construct a sport facility or support the planning and operational phase of an event until the first revenues arrive. Companies may become involved in financing sport facilities and events for two main reasons. First, the company may seek to provide a facility within which to deliver its own products or services, or its own major event – essentially a method of vertical integration. Second, companies may commit financial support for no other reason than as an investment opportunity in the form of joint ventures between the real estate developers involved in different aspects of the project.

Borrowing: The final sources of financial analysis fall under the category of borrowing. Many prospective facilities and events are forced to consider borrowing money. There are a number of critical issues associated with debt financing that must be understood before deciding on the financial feasibility of the facility or event.

The first consideration before borrowing money is the interest burden it demands. The relative implications of variable and fixed interest rates for loans should be assessed as part of a financial feasibility study. Variable interest rates are lower on a current basis, but are also subject to volatile movements. Fixed interest rates, while

Feasibility analysis and market research

higher, allow the borrower to 'lock in' interest expenses over the term of the loan. As variable rates are controlled by the market and can move unexpectedly, they are more difficult to define in the feasibility equation. Convention recommends conservatism, but this precludes the chance of discounted rates.

When considering loans, one must also consider equity requirements. Lenders are mainly concerned about risk, and if they perceive the likelihood of being repaid their money with high interest, then they will look favourably on a project. However, they will seek to assure themselves that if the facility can no longer meet the payments, they can recover their money through the sale of the facility and property. This is one of the reasons why events have more difficulty in acquiring loans: because they rarely have anything tangible to return to a bank until after the event is run and gate receipts, sponsorships, and broadcasting rights (if there are any) have been cashed in full.

One challenge to borrowing is depreciation, also known as amortisation. This is the process of decreasing the value of the facility on the balance sheet over time. Amortisation takes into account the theoretical effect of time on the life of the structure of a facility, inbuilt equipment, and fittings. It is important to calculate the amount that may be legally removed from the value of these assets because they can have a significant impact on the net profit of a facility. For example, amortisation is recorded as an expense, and can therefore be used to offset total revenue. The outcome can be a substantially more favourable tax burden, which must be accounted for in order to assess financial feasibility. Again, events without ownership of tangible assets are not hit with the concern of deteriorating facilities, but neither can they yield tax benefits from them.

In the case of facilities and events, since financing deals with significant sums of money, most lenders impose rigorous requirements for borrower liquidity. This is often determined by calculating the ratio of existing and anticipated funds available for debt-service payments due the lender from the borrower. So for example, lenders might expect that for each dollar that is owed to them, the borrower has a minimum of one and a half dollars, either already collected or expected to be collected, available to pay. This would represent a debt-service ratio of 50 per cent. The lower the ratio, the more feasible the project. This often poses a problem for events, which have no source of revenue until they are run. As a result, the more successful events have managed to increase their cash inflows by signing up sponsors early or by pre-selling television rights that provide injections of funding during the planning phase of the event.

Allied to the notion of debt-service ratios are working capital calculations. Lenders impose provisions for borrower liquidity, which is determined by the availability of current assets. Working capital can be determined by subtracting current liabilities from current assets. Providing the result is sufficient to comfortably cover debt payments, the facility or event may be considered feasibly liquid.

This often directly relates to the notion of collateral and security. Most lenders require some amount of collateral in order to satisfy themselves that the loan will ultimately be repaid, irrespective of circumstances. Collateral expectations may range from the minimum, anticipation of complete loan repayment, to the maximum, the opportunity for the first mortgage to the financed assets and other property. Lower collateral expectations make for a more feasible project.

Other considerations related to, but beyond the actual finances of the analysis, include the composition of the management team, the requirements imposed on contractors, and an appraisal of the market demand. In terms of the management team, many lenders use subjective criteria to evaluate project risk by carefully scrutinising the skills and experiences of the management team that will supervise the design and construction as well as operation of the facility or event. This also connects to the contractor, where lenders will impose their own requirements in terms of architect and contractor experience and construction contracts. It is essential to identify these requirements so that they can be built into the costs of the facility construction or the development of the event infrastructure. Contractor requirements imposed by lenders do not necessarily lead to a less feasible scenario; they in fact tend to be in the best interests of the facility or event owners. Finally, some lenders will ask the borrower to engage with an independent assessor to demonstrate that there is sufficient demand for the services to be offered through the facility or event. In some instances, it is the process of market appraisal that stimulates the feasibility study, and almost without exception, lenders will not provide financial support without a feasibility study showing a favourable result. Occasionally lenders commission their own feasibility studies when they believe the ones provided by facility or event owners to be excessively optimistic.

Operational financial ramifications In addition, there are financial ramifications of operational, technical, and schedule feasibility. Under the broad banner of financial projections fall four essential dimensions: (1) economic, (2) operational, (3) technical, and (4) schedule feasibility. Each has an impact on the overall financial feasibility of a project. Economic feasibility is concerned with the economic impact of the facility and is principally concerned with whether the outcomes of designing, constructing, and operating a facility or event outweigh the costs. The economic feasibility analysis should provide a range of estimates that explain the financial implications of developing and operating a facility. Operational revenues and costs then should be investigated to determine operational feasibility. Investors will expect to be provided with return on investment (ROI) figures, which indicate the amount recovered as a percentage of the investment. Then the technical feasibility refers to the relationship between design and construction, where the difficulty of building the facility or programming the events to meet its specified purpose is examined. Especially with sport facilities and events, this also considers the ability for specific sporting activities to be able to be undertaken within facilities that were not originally designed for such a purpose; and new events to operate appropriately in the location provided for them. Finally, the financial consequences of schedule feasibility must be accounted for. The probability of construction completion on time will influence the final financial feasibility of the project. Issues to consider in determining this probability may include control over timing, externally imposed deadlines and windows of opportunity, contractors and their track records, and the political landscape.

Operational financial planning and projections   Ultimately, all that is accomplished in terms of financial analysis will come back to the one basic point for all financial planning – the budget. A budget is a prediction of the financial arrangement of an organisation over a specific period of time – usually monthly, quarterly, and annually. As well as being a valuable administrative tool, the budget can be important when communicating with members and customers, particularly if there is a need to justify higher fees and charges, or to assess the financial implications of new development initiatives. The purpose of a budget is to provide a systematic estimate of future revenues and expenses organised by time and activity. It also provides a procedure for monitoring, controlling, and evaluating the financial resources of an organisation.

There are three principal elements of a budget: total revenue, total expenses, and profit. The total amount of revenue earned is the foundation of any budget. Common revenue sources for sporting facilities and events include gate receipts, venue hire charges, broadcasting rights, sponsorships, signage and endorsements, memberships, catering services, equipment hire, food and beverage sales, merchandise, gaming machines, government grants and subsidies, parking fees, vending machines, publications, bar trading, social functions, rent on leased premises, investments, and asset sales. Projections for each of these items need to be made over at least a five-year period.

Total costs include fixed and variable expenses. Fixed expenses remain unaffected by the amount of activity and revenue a facility or event may generate. Common fixed expenses for sporting facilities and events include rent, interest, 'core' personnel, licenses, and permits. While fixed expenses remain static, variable expenses are directly affected by the level of activity the facility or event experiences. For example, merchandise costs are directly affected by the number of items that are sold. The more merchandise sold, the greater the purchasing costs. Similarly, food and beverage costs and extra casual staff salary costs will rise proportionately with additional levels of consumption. Other common variable expenses for sporting facilities and events include cleaning, maintenance, and repairs. There is also a large range of semi-variable expenses typical for sporting facilities and events that make budget development more trouble-some. These semi-variable expenses have both fixed and variable components. For example, the fixed element represents the minimum cost of subsidising an activity or supplying a product or service. The remaining variable component will be affected by the level of activity (which must be estimated accordingly).

The final area is profit: positive profit is often also referred to as a surplus; negative profit is considered a loss. Careful consideration must be given to con-structing realistic and appropriate profit projections. On the one hand, the total profit must be adequate to make the operation of the facility worthwhile for its owners; on the other, it must be sufficiently modest to ensure competitive pricing to encourage additional customers. It is also unrealistic to expect that lenders are going to support a facility or event that does not return a reasonable dividend; on the other hand, lenders will have difficulty believing projections that demon-strate immediate and easily acquired profits. Furthermore, all projections need to be supported by the data collected earlier in the feasibility study, during the market and competitive analysis phase. This ensures that projections are credible and based on objective data, rather than on the whimsical guesses of the project manager. Past trends, inflation, and the conventional assumption of conserva-tism (under forecast revenue and over forecast expenditure) are relevant issues to remember.

In summation, a financial feasibility analysis should examine three issues. First, the costs associated with designing, constructing, and operating the facility should be estimated. Second, the quantity of financial resources available for the pro-ject must be established and the implications of the funding arrangements clearly understood. Finally, financial projections should be calculated that unambiguously demonstrate whether the benefits of the project outweigh the costs. As with all com-ponents of a feasibility study, the hard decisions culminate at the financial end of the process, with the operational feasibility coming down to budgetary projections. Therefore, it is essential to consider the location of a speculated facility or event in light of an economic equation. The nature of the facility or event will determine its revenue opportunities and its expenditure obligations. This is a formula that can vary considerably with scope and location. Organisers of an event designed for a television audience do not need to think so seriously about being located some-where inconvenient for commuters. Stadia designed as much for live attendance as broadcasting, where gate receipts are paramount, do have to consider such fac-tors as parking and accessibility to public transportation. And of course, the more individuals who utilise a facility and/or attend an event, the higher the revenues that can be anticipated in ancillary areas such as ticketing, food and beverages, mer-chandise, and parking.

Legal and regulatory analysis

One final area of feasibility that needs to be considered is the legal and regulatory requirements that are inherent to sport facility and major event management. Later in Chapter 7, more detail will be provided about the areas of risk management and legal issues. As a preview, it is important to note that there are a number of critical legal, statutory, and regulatory issues that must be considered before the facility or event becomes a reality. Many of these are items to be added to the projected costs of the project. The following checklist of questions should assist in this task:

- Will government approval at any level (local, regional/county, state/provincial, federal, international) be required? Assuming that it can be obtained, are there any fees or taxes associated with the activities proposed?
- Which licenses will be required for the activities proposed, both during preparation and construction, and during events?
- Will insurance be required, and at what cost?
- Are there any patents and intellectual property rights for design and ownership?

These legal requirements are locally specific. For example, a sport facility that borders wetland or conservation areas may require regulatory approval and the payment of a several-thousand-dollar fee for land studies, alterations to designs for additional setbacks, and potential mitigations of water to new locations. The legal costs associated with staging a major event can also be considerable. The feasibility study conducted to support an Olympic and Paralympic bid includes budgeted items amounting to several million dollars for insurance and the legal costs for establishing commercial, venue, and local authority contracts.

MARKET RESEARCH AND COMPETITOR ANALYSIS

While the feasibility study provides a complete look at the project itself, the pros and cons of implementing the project, the outcomes expected, the stakeholder analysis, and the external factors affecting feasibility, there is another important part to the planning of new sport facilities and major events. This is the market research and competitor analysis process.

It is imperative for owners and managers of sport facilities and events to invest time and resources into creating an overall sport management information system, where all aspects of the organisational structure are responsible for collecting, organising, analysing, evaluating, and providing feedback on all data utilised to make decisions and solve problems across the sport facility or event. The central part of this information system is market research, which involves the collection and analysis of information about sport consumers, market niches, competition, and the effectiveness of sport marketing initiatives. This focuses specifically on identifying and defining market opportunities and threats, and then designing, implementing, managing, and evaluating actions to address to effectively implement into the planning and implementation processes.

Beyond market research, there are additional capabilities all sport facilities and events should have in place to maximise the efficiency of collecting and evaluating information to improve the organisation. First is the internal reports system, which focuses on the collection and evaluation of information that is generated by the internal operations of the sport organisation. Usually reported through the accounting processes of an organisation, this includes the management of assets and liabilities, the evaluation of revenue and expense operations, and the administration of retained earnings, or owner's equity. Second is the sport management intelligence system, which assesses the processes and procedures that the sport facility or event utilises to obtain everyday information about developments regarding external opportunities and threats. Third is the decision support system, which collates the primary and secondary data previously collected, and integrates it with the tools and techniques used for interpretation by the organisation, and the implementation process by which that information is used towards creating positive change for the sport facility or event.

Previously in this chapter, it was established that scoping the project is necessary before the feasibility team can begin gathering data. A sound starting point for this data acquisition phase is with the simple economic principles of supply and demand. In the first instance, we must consider the available marketplaces that might be entered, including the other facility or event players that these contain as well as the consumers that constitute those markets.

The prospect of entering the planning process for a new sport facility can be quite intimidating. When committing to a capital-intensive and subsequently risky process such as constructing a new facility or organising a new event's infrastructure, it is critical to have a thorough understanding of the dynamics of the different markets that the proposed facility or event will cater for. In the context of planning new sport facilities and events, we will overview here the market analysis process by distinguishing between four components: industry analysis, external environmental analysis, consumer market analysis, and competitive analysis.

Industry analysis

When the idea to build a new sport facility or develop a new event is born, the first things that should come to the minds of the policy makers and planners are the issues of competition and demand. These two must be confronted early in the feasibility study because the viability of the project is directly dependent on the levels of competition and consumer demand.

An industry, as a collection of producers of similar goods or services, can be very attractive if few organisations are competing in it. In an industry that is very

Feasibility analysis and market research

competitive it is hard to earn profits. For the facility operator or event manager, it is important to gather data about the industries in which they seek to establish a presence before further resources are committed. Events in terms of their properties and offerings, and facilities in terms of their physical features, need to be designed and constructed to accommodate the opportunities identified. It makes little sense to choose to operate in unattractive industries.

This starts with defining the industry to determine the needs of and benefits for the stakeholders. For example, assume a sport stadium being designed in Europe is for football as the principal spectator sport. Therefore, the collection of elite soccer-producing organisations (as a spectator sport) can be defined as the football industry. However, from the perspective of the financiers of facilities, who in many cases may be local or regional governments, an analysis of this industry is important before any further planning pertaining to a new facility takes place. Beyond the football industry, other industries that might require investigation include popular elite sporting leagues, the international events and concerts industry, and the major sporting events industry. Also important are the intended beneficiaries of a facility or event, most often at the community level. This requires a superficial analysis of other international events as a starting point, as well as additional research on community sport, where the emphasis is on whether the facility or event will meet a need.

Just as with feasibility analysis, the next step after defining the industry and stakeholders is identifying the scope of the market analysis. The focus of this investigation will depend directly on the anticipated reach of the facility or event in terms of from how far away the potential customers are likely to travel. Market analysis when planning a new stadium for the local football club playing in the second division and competing in the regional soccer industry needs a completely different perspective from that when planning a new facility for an elite European Champions League team such as FC Barcelona, Real Madrid, Bayern Munich, or Manchester City, all of whom regularly compete in both the domestic and global football industry.

Porter's Competitive Forces Model

A widely used tool for analysing the competitiveness of an industry is Porter's (1985) Competitive Forces Model, also known as the Five Forces Model. The model is presented in Figure 3.1, and describes the five forces that facility and event planners should review when examining competition and the attractiveness of an industry. This model can be applied at different levels of analysis. For example, it can be used to assess the competitive forces between different sports operating in the sport industry as whole. One can also analyse the competition between different sporting leagues.

75

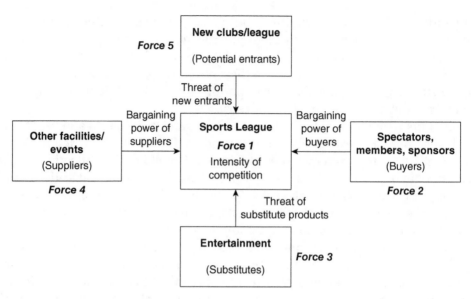

Figure 3.1 Porter's Competitive Forces Model

Source: Adapted from Porter (1985)

The Five Forces Model includes the threat of new entrants, bargaining power of suppliers, determinants of buyer power, the threat of substitute products, and the intensity of competition between existing firms within an industry. Quite often, the attractiveness of an industry is measured by profit potential, which is not always the principal goal of sporting organisations. For example, the number and location of teams in geographic (metropolitan) markets requires a feasibility researcher to assess the attractiveness of a market. In addition,'other questions indicative of industry attractiveness might include: (1) Is the economic base of a city or region large enough to sustain one, or more than one team?; (2) How many other professional sports already exist in this market?; and (3) What other recreation and leisure pursuits are potentially competing for disposable income?' (Shilbury, Westerbeek, Quick, Funk, & Karg, 2014, p. 28).

The first force concerns the intensity of competition within an industry. In the case of a football league, the location and the number of teams (both in code and beyond the specific code) is the first example of intensity of competition. The bargaining power of buyers constitutes the second force. The buyers are those parties who express interest in consuming the goods and services offered by facilities or events. Buyers include personal and corporate consumers of sport. In sporting terms, there is often a practical limitation given the finite number of teams located in each area. Attendance, membership, sponsorship, and media revenues provide most sporting clubs with their main sources of income.

The third force affecting the sporting industry is the substitutability of products. In other words, are there other recreation and leisure activities that offer substitute benefits for those provided by participation or spectatorship in sport (in this case, football). The bargaining power of suppliers is the fourth force, and in the sport industry increases with the ability of these suppliers either to form a united front or to become singularly important to the industry. In terms of facilities and events, they can often take the role of suppliers in the sport industry. They must fight for the opportunity to host events by providing the most attractive leasing or hosting arrangements. The bargaining power of suppliers is considered strong when few other options are available to event owners.

The final force is the threat of new entrants, which refers to the likelihood that new facilities or events will spring up to compete for the same consumers. This is a normal occurrence in business, but it is less frequent in professional sport. However, as related to community sport, if we were focusing on a new recreational facility proposed for a local community, we would be interested in the likelihood that another facility would consider the market attractive enough to enter, especially in markets that are underserviced or where certain niche services or goods are absent.

The application of Porter's Competitive Forces Model can be directly applied in the case of the city of Melbourne, Australia, which hosts two professional football (soccer) clubs – Melbourne Victory and Melbourne City FC. The Melbourne metropolitan market at the start of 2016 consisted of approximately 4.5 million inhabitants, so there should theoretically be sufficient consumers for two clubs. But beyond the soccer football market, the industry competition (Force 1) intensifies as a result of the presence of other sporting codes, including Australian Rules football (nine teams in the metropolitan market), the National Rugby League (one team), and Super Rugby (one team) – all seeking sponsor dollars, spectators, and members.

With all this competition in the football landscape alone, the bargaining power of buyers (Force 2) is fairly strong. In this case, the buyers are powerful enough to force prices down, demand higher quality, and play competitors off against each other, as they represent a competitive force to be considered by facilities and events. In other words, the bargaining power of buyers grows with the number of options they have to switch to other forms of entertainments such as the beach or going to wine country (Force 3), choose to spend their discretionary income at other facilities or events instead such as the Melbourne Formula 1 Grand Prix or Australian Open tennis (Force 4), or even look to new leagues and teams in the area such as the Big Bash League (BBL) in cricket, or the Australian Baseball League (ABL) (Force 5).

An industry analysis delivers the feasibility researcher a wealth of information about the specific products and markets in which the proposed facility or event seeks to operate. Depending on the five competitive forces, feasibility researchers can obtain a clearer picture of the viability of a new project and the potential contribution of operating in a particular marketplace delivering particular goods or services. The outcome of this analysis should be an assessment of the attractiveness of the prospective project as measured by competitive forces. It should also begin to make clear where the strategic opportunities lie for a new facility or event in terms of the functionality desired in a new facility or the experiences sought during an event.

External environmental analysis

The analysis of the external (macro) environment of an organisation focuses on those trends or changes in needs that not only have an impact on a new sport facility or event, but also influence operations of most other organisations in the vicinity. The analysis is aimed at identifying important changes in the macro environment that might influence the operation of organisations or provide new opportunities for businesses.

The scope of the environmental analysis depends on the definition of the industry. In the same way as the planning of a new stadium for the local football club playing in the second division determines the scope of the industry analysis, so it does for the external environmental analysis. Competing in the regional soccer industry is more likely to lead to the identification of domestic trends and consumer needs rather than when competing in the global football industry, which clearly requires a global scope of external analysis.

The different external environments to consider for this analysis are described with the acronym DESTEP, which stands for demographic, economic, sociocultural, technological, ecological, and political. These six environments are briefly described in Table 3.2 below.

Table 3.2 The DESTEP environment

Environment	Examples
Demographic	Average age, location, and makeup of the target market – both current and projected change over time.
Economic	The free flow of labour, money, goods, and services in an area.
Sociocultural	Changes in community attitudes towards sports or events, and the required social responsibility expected from facility and event owners/managers.
Technological	The incorporation of digital technologies and social media in all aspects of life, including the facility or event experience.
Ecological	The requirement about maintaining a healthy natural environment as a normal operational function by all sport facilities and events.
Political	Government policies affecting the offering of and support for sports and events from the professional level to grassroots and community offerings.

Feasibility analysis and market research

These examples emphasise the importance of taking both an external and an internal view of the new project. It cannot be assumed that the facility or event will thrive in isolation, ignoring the bigger picture of what is happening in the world surrounding it. Feasible projects have teams that anticipate the future and incorporate it into their design in order to exploit opportunities and counter threats when these arrive.

Consumer market analysis

Following the examination of the external environment and the competitive forces in which the proposed facility or event will be placed, a closer look at the people who make up the potential markets of the new facility or event may begin. A consumer market analysis focuses on the individuals most likely to attend events at the new facility, and the motivations governing their behaviour. The individuals can range from the general public as spectators to participants, sponsors, and corporate guests. Facilities and events can position themselves in several markets in order to maximise their revenue opportunities.

An industry can be understood as a collection of producers or sellers of products, where markets can be seen as the collections of people who buy these products. The people in the basketball market purchase the basketball product from producers in the basketball industry. The local basketball league will attract only regional customers, whereas teams in the Euroleague (Real Madrid, Olympiacos, CSKA Moscow) have an international audience mainly across Europe, western Asia, and northern Africa, and teams in the National Basketball Association (NBA) in the United States (Boston Celtics, Cleveland Cavaliers, Golden State Warriors, San Antonio Spurs) are likely to attract customers from all over the world. In the same way as the industry definition determines the scope of the industry analysis, so does the market definition determine the scope of the market analysis.

As a result of the variety of sporting opportunities and major sporting events across multiple product lines and geographies, researchers have to become involved in a number of different market analyses. Market analyses can range from simply describing the size and attractiveness of a market to in-depth data collection through interviews and focus group research, followed by mass consumer surveys, aimed at obtaining very detailed information about the consumer behaviour of people in those markets. Market analysis is a vital activity when planning a new facility or event, particularly because the construction of a facility is such a capital-intensive and irreversible activity. The size of potential markets, how much people in those markets are prepared to pay for a range of products, where they live, how they can be reached, how they can be motivated to buy, their interests and ambitions in life, and how much money they are likely to have in 10 years' time, is all information that planners need in order to optimise the physical design and construction of the facility. Market analysis will also deliver data that inform management how to accommodate activities to be hosted by the facility for which there is a genuine and financially healthy demand in the marketplace.

Demand is affected by the amount and quality of other events or facilities offering the same product(s) in the area. Research concerning the competition is therefore paramount. This competition may even go beyond the same goods or services. Alternative leisure, recreational, or sporting activities also need to be considered. In addition, demand is further determined by the existing population in the geographic catchment in which the facility or event is placed. Associated with this is the fact that demand is driven by growth. The building of new facilities needs to be justified either by an increase in the size of the catchment zone the facility is said to represent, or by an increase in population density within the zone. In some circumstances, where the facility houses potentially high-profile international events, it is important to consider overseas as well as domestic demand, whereas for local events research in nearby regions should be undertaken.

An estimate of the amount of usage or attendance the proposed facility or event is likely to attract is essential in consumer analysis. There are several ways to undertake this. The most straightforward is called the consultation method, where surveys and focus groups can be used to ask what specific facilities, programmes and services these groups would use, how often they would be employed, when they would be used, and how much the user groups would be prepared to pay for use. Another way to collect research is through the comparison method, which involves using an existing facility or event that is comparable to the proposed one as a benchmark for estimates of demand and interest. This approach works best when similar products are being compared for a marketplace with similar demographic characteristics. It is useful to benchmark against the existing competition, but one must be cautious not to expect similar outcomes given that the existing facilities and events are established and that the proposed one will more probably take some of their market share as well as attract new customers. A third method is known as the participation approach. This requires the examination of participation rates categorised according to demographic features. This information can be applied to the recreational or sporting products that are being offered. A final option is known as trend analysis. This method reveals consumption patterns across a range of facilities and events in an attempt to establish a trend that should continue into the future.

The best approach to forecasting demand involves the use of several or all of these methods in the hope of establishing the most reliable picture possible. It is also important to remember that any method may need to be undertaken for each of the target groups anticipated to be users of the facility or event.

Competitive analysis

While a consumer market analysis is important, it makes little or no sense if it is completed in isolation from external considerations. When a market turns out to be very attractive, there will probably also be a lot of competition for a share of

80

that market. Therefore, a competitive analysis needs to be performed to get a clear picture of how attractive a marketplace really is, and to feel reasonably secure that a facility can be operated viably.

The first step towards a competitive analysis was discussed earlier in this chapter through the application of Porter's Five Forces Model. The competitive forces analysis requires a basic insight into how many competitors operate in an industry, what their strategies and objectives are, how to expose their strengths and weaknesses, their most likely reaction to the movements of other operators in the industry, and how easy or difficult it is to enter or exit the industry. The goal is to use this information to move into a position of market dominance through detailed knowledge of competitors' marketing tactics and strategies.

Building on this knowledge, an organisation must make a decision based on their own market analysis as to whether they have the capabilities, ambitions, and resources to justify entering a market and working towards obtaining a share of that market. As a result, researchers define the market they wish to operate in, and determine who the main competitors are for the future facility or event. If they want to operate in the regional aquatic centre market, their main competitors are smaller regional facilities that can accommodate the needs of local swim clubs, and hence it makes little sense to look any further into broader domestic or international competitive environments. However, for the researchers of Levi's Stadium in California, they needed to have a broader scope as they wanted to be considered for hosting the National Football League's Super Bowl shortly after it opened in 2015. During their analysis, it was important that they considered operators of major stadia in New York, Dallas, Houston, Miami, Minneapolis, and New Orleans – as well as potential examples from international facilities such as Wembley Stadium in London – to ensure they could provide the maximum value to the NFL to bring the largest one-day sporting event in the United States to their venue.

Examples of other competitive analysis techniques utilised by sport facility and event project managers include conducting a SWOT analysis for each competitor (in particular determining their internal organisational weaknesses and the external threats they are facing), benchmarking other companies pertaining to issues that can deliver competitive advantage, market share analysis, maintaining a competitive intelligence system (collecting and compiling files with competitors' information), and the construction of a matrix that measures the industries attractiveness against the strength of the organisation/product (i.e. the GE/McKinsey Matrix) or a perceptual map to determine an organisation's position relative to competitors.

In closing, when it comes to market research and competitor analysis, one of the key questions is whether project managers will conduct the analysis fully, or outsource it to a consultant. In many cases, project managers will do some of the more basic parts of the market analysis themselves, and leave the more complex or less sensitive parts of the analysis to specialised feasibility research companies.

One area that is often outsourced is a competitive analysis because independent researchers are more likely than the organisation itself to be able to collect relevant and useful data on competitors. On the other hand, the external environmental analysis can often be done without having to access people in industries or markets because they concern macro-trends, and the information for these analyses is often readily available in nationally or internationally commissioned research projects either for sale or available through government agencies, universities, or libraries.

Two other key issues related to determining the best way to complete market research and competitor analyses are the timing and cost of research as related to the schedule and costs of the total planning and construction project. The longer it takes to obtain industry or market information, the longer it is before construction can commence, and in turn the more the overall cost of the project may be affected. The more research is outsourced, the faster results can be delivered, as the different analyses can run in parallel. However, outsourcing research is expensive. In the end, facility and event planners need to prioritise their research needs based on the relative importance of the scope of the research in terms of specific industries, markets, geographies, and scope. Based on whether the specific research is broad-based or very specific, choices will be made regarding who needs to complete the research, how much it will cost in money and resources, and how much time can justifiably be spent on it.

SUMMARY

Feasibility, as we have dealt with it in this chapter, forms the basis for the ongoing strategic planning of an organisation. From this viewpoint, the activities and analysis that are undertaken during the feasibility study are continuous and essential analytical techniques for the ongoing assurance of viability and prosperity. In order to get a new facility or event off the ground it is essential to scope the project first, resulting in a project charter against which the rest of the feasibility study is benchmarked, and culminating in a project plan that details what to produce, what resources are required, what various activities and tasks are essential to complete the project successfully, who will carry out the activities, and when the activities will be completed.

Another vital part of the feasibility analysis is a look at the external factors that will directly affect the successful implementation and completion of the facility or event project plan. Geographic feasibility issues related to the distance of potential customers to the facility or the event include location, transportation, climate, the natural environment, and the development of tourism, as well as the land, construction, and labour considerations. Financial feasibility centres on project costs, project financing, borrowing, operational ramifications, financial planning, and projections. Legal and regulatory issues also need to be studied to be certain that no legal barriers obstruct the development of the facility or event.

Over and above the feasibility analysis a sport facility or event project manager must engage in a comprehensive market and competitive analysis that provides objective data concerning the machinations of supply and demand. This research must focus on the analysis of the industry, the external environment, the consumer market, and the competition.

CASE STUDY

Feasibility studies for the 2012 and 2024 Olympic and Paralympic bids by Budapest, Hungary

In the first edition of this book, we reported on the preliminary feasibility study commissioned by the national committee responsible in 2003 for preparing Hungary's bid for the 2012 Olympic Games. According to GamesBid.com (2003), the report, conducted by PriceWaterhouse Coopers Kft (PwC), showed that Hungary would have to invest somewhere around US$16 million on the bid. In addition, the report, which cost US$1.6 million to produce at the time, highlights the developmental requirements in order to meet Olympic standards. For example, Budapest needed to construct about nine new covered stadiums, each with a capacity of 15,000 spectators. Locations needed to be found for 22 'special' sport events like mountain biking and sailing, each with their own specific needs, equipment, and viewing configurations. An Olympic village capable of supporting 16,000 athletes and officials was also required, along with hotel accommodation for another 18,000 people. The report also showed that all these additions would have to be built on a site of no less than 600 hectares. The report further speculates on the economic impact of the Games on the city. It was proposed that the Olympics could increase Hungary's GDP by up to 0.5 per cent, with final calculations to be completed to reach more definitive estimates of the economic costs and benefits of hosting the Games.

These feasibility study results, documented in over 1,500 pages, helped Hungary decide to not pursue the 2012 Games. Beyond the development cost, which could yield a substantial return on investment, the feasibility study articulated numerous risk factors that ultimately led to aborting the notion of a bid. This included a lack of consensus from the political and social infrastructures in Hungary, and the inability for timely legislative decision making and public procurement processes to meet the deadlines associated with the bid.

Fast forward 12 years to 2015, and Budapest again decided to conduct a feasibility study to determine whether to engage in the process of bidding for the 2024 Summer Olympic and Paralympic Games. Over the past decade,

Budapest as a city and region, and Hungary as a country, undertook a process of addressing the recommendations from the previous study to prepare for this current bid. The Organising Committee also noted changes in the Olympic bidding process through the affirmation of International Olympic Committee's (IOC) Olympic Agenda 2020, which created a new strategic roadmap for the future of the Olympic Movement – with 40 recommendations that included reshaping the bidding process as more of an invitation, new evaluation processes based on key opportunities and risks, and reducing costs of the bidding process, among others.

Prior to the commissioned feasibility study, KPMG – one of the leading auditing and advisory services firms in the world – conducted an independent assessment through their Global Sports Advisory group office in Budapest. They sought to answer three key questions: '(1) can Budapest realistically win the right to host the Olympic Games?; (2) can Budapest deliver such a global sporting event?; and (3) what are the benefits and risks for Budapest and Hungary?' (KPMG, 2015, p. 3). In examining each of these questions, KPMG had positive comments about the influence of the new Olympic Agenda 2020 guidelines allowing smaller nations to compete in the bidding process; the historical foundation of Hungary's success in the Olympics, Budapest and other cities having successfully hosted numerous other significant world championship events; and the ongoing development of world class sport facilities. They also articulated concerns related to transportation, urban infrastructure (especially as related to the Olympic Village), and the ability of the country and its residents to afford the financial commitments. Ultimately, KPMG concluded that 'Hungary should move forward with an Olympic bid only if the hosting of the Olympic Games is not considered as a goal in itself, but an important milestone in a long-term development plan for the country, reaching well beyond the event' (KPMG, 2015, p. 18).

Shortly after this report came out, and after discussion amongst government officials at the city (Budapest) and executive (Prime Minister and National Assembly) levels, it was determined to officially direct the Hungarian Olympic Committee to commission a feasibility study. The study, once again led by PwC, was conducted between February and May 2015 and reported to all relevant governmental agencies in May and June 2015.

In contrast to 12 years earlier, the feasibility study painted a very different picture. PwC provided a 1,300-page feasibility study that concluded Budapest had a realistic chance of winning the bid, and that they were also able to host a profitable Olympic Games. In fact, specific figures stated that the Games could generate HUF 1,100 billion (US$4 billion) in revenues to cover expenses and investments that were expected to be around HUF 774 billion (US$2.8 billion) (Mackay 2015).

Key points include the fact that Budapest had a vastly stronger facility infrastructure as compared to the previous bid consideration, and improved transportation capabilities that would allow for a number of venues from surrounding municipalities to support the bid by offering to host events. Local government also addressed the issues finding a location for the Olympic Village by targeting Csepel Island – the largest island on the Danube River (Mackay, 2015). The strongest conclusion by PwC was that 'the Budapest Olympics is a feasible and profitable investment and the Hungarian application has a good chance of winning the right to organise the 2024 Olympics' (Mackay, 2015).

As a result of these findings, both the Hungarian Olympic Committee and the Assembly of Budapest voted almost unanimously in favour of submitting a bid in June 2015. In July 2015, the Hungarian National Assembly followed suit and voted in favour, with over 80 per cent supporting the bid. A public opinion survey was then conducted later that month showing 49 per cent supported the bid with 42 per cent against. With the official backing of the government, the required documentation to bid for the 2024 Summer Olympic and Paralympics Games was then submitted to the International Olympic Committee (IOC) prior to 15th September 2015. A follow-up public opinion poll in December 2015 showed an increase in public support, with 60 per cent stating they would be happy to host the Olympics, and only 29 per cent against.

Questions

1   Once an initial decision to enter the bidding process to host the Olympics and Paralympics, a city usually has about two years to promote its bid and prove to the administration and the voting members of the International Olympic Committee they are worthy hosts of the Games. What additional feasibility studies do you believe a National Olympic Committee and Local Bid Committees will need to commission to ensure a successful bid process?

2   Relevant market research not only helps to prepare for actions in the future, but also provides a historical perspective regarding the bidding process and hosting the Games. What type of information could the Hungarian Olympic Committee glean from the following:

   ■ The most recent successful bids for the Summer and Winter Olympic and Paralympic Games (Beijing 2022 – Winter; Tokyo 2020 – Summer; PyeongChang 2018 – Winter)?
   ■ The most recent unsuccessful bids for the Summer and Winter Olympic and Paralympic Games (Almaty 2022 – Winter; Istanbul and Madrid 2020 – Summer; Annecy and Munich 2018 – Winter)?

- The most recent three cycles of Olympic Games hosts (Summer – Rio 2016, London 2012, Beijing 2008; Winter – Sochi 2014, Vancouver 2010, and Torino 2006)?

3 Of the four cities vying for the 2024 Summer Olympic and Paralympic Games, Budapest is the only one whom never to have hosted an Olympic Games (Paris – 1900 and 1924; Los Angeles 1932 and 1984; and Rome 1960). This potentially puts the Budapest bid at a disadvantage. How would you go about conducting a quality competitor analysis to turn that negative perception into a positive for Budapest?

REFERENCES

GamesBids.com. (2003). *Feasibility study approved on a Hungary 2012 Olympic bid.* Retrieved from http://gamesbids.com/eng/other-news/feasibility-study-approved-on-a-hungary-2012-olympic-bid/

Government of Western Australia. (2007). *Feasibility study guide: Sport and recreation facilities.* 2nd edition. Perth: Department of Sport and Recreation. Retrieved from http://www.dsr.wa.gov.au/docs/default-source/file-support-and-advice/file-facilitiy-management/feasibility-study-guide.pdf?sfvrsn=0

KPMG (2015). Olympics *in Budapest: Dream or reality.* Retrieved from https://www.kpmg.com/HU/en/IssuesAndInsights/ArticlesPublications/Documents/20150319-Olympics-in-Budapest-E.pdf

Mackay, D. (2015). *Budapest set to bid for 2024 Olympics and Paralympics after Hungarian Olympic Committee back plan.* Retrieved from http://www.insidethegames.biz/articles/1027896/budapest-set-to-bid-for-2024-olympics-and-paralympics-after-hungarian-olympic-committee-back-plan

Porter, M. (1985). *Competitive advantage: Creating and sustaining superior performance.* New York: The Free Press.

Shilbury, D., Westerbeek, H., Quick, S.P., Funk, D.C., & Karg, A. (2014). *Strategic sport marketing.* 4th edition. Sydney: Allen & Unwin.

Smith, A., & Stewart, B. (2015). Introduction *to sport marketing.* 2nd edition. Oxford, UK: Routledge.

CHAPTER 4

NEW SPORT FACILITY DEVELOPMENT: PLANNING, DESIGN, AND CONSTRUCTION

CHAPTER FOCUS

1 Introduction to sport facility and major event management
2 Key success factors of operating sport facilities and running sport events
3 Feasibility analysis and market research for planning new sport facilities and events
4 New sport facility development: planning, design, and construction
5 New sport facility development: preparing the facility management infrastructure
6 New sport facility operations: attracting events
7 New sport facility operations: planning the event management infrastructure
8 Attracting customers: marketing sport facilities and events
9 Running the sport event: event operations
10 Destination marketing, image, and branding through major sport events
11 Performance management: evaluating operations
12 Performance management: legacy and measuring impact

CHAPTER OBJECTIVES

In this chapter we will:

■ Move from broad facility considerations/analysis to specific design decisions.
■ Consider the importance of stakeholder involvement in design planning.

87

- Discuss multi-use flexibility in design planning.
- Review the temporary facility as an event option.
- Discuss the importance of the building brief.

INTRODUCTION

At this point in the book, we have outlined a range of broad, pre-development and event considerations for sport facility and event managers. This chapter takes the manager into the next phase of facility development – the final design and construction specifications. In many ways, this is both the most exciting and the most important phase in sport facility and event management. Many of the decisions made now are largely irreversible, and are likely to have a significant effect on the project's overall success. Having said that, this stage allows managers to incorporate their own vision and ingenuity into the project, and as such presents a stimulating challenge.

Up to this point, a need has been identified in the marketplace, key success factors outlined, and feasibility analyses and market research conducted. We now consider moving the project into the next stage, and converting that research into a 'tight' building brief that meets the project's desired outcomes, providing the blueprint for a high-quality facility. We commence with an overview of the design and construction process. This will include a rather extensive discussion of the most vital elements of this process, such as continued community consultation and site selection. Following the design brief, we will introduce some major design features, culminating in a discussion of sport-specific regulations and specifications. We conclude with an overview of a number of operational and service considerations and the optimisation of secondary spend areas and architectural identity.

THE DESIGN AND CONSTRUCTION PROCESS

According to the publication A Blueprint for Successful Stadium Development, published by KPMG (2013), there are five key stages to consider when planning, designing, and constructing a sport facility:

- development of a project vision
- planning and feasibility
- permitting and design
- construction
- operation.

This suggests, broadly speaking, that systematic planning, careful programme management, detailed documentation, and cooperative team–stakeholder relationships are the keys to developing a successful building solution.

88

The primary task of the project initiators (referred to here as the client) is to translate the needs of the facility into a detailed strategic and then design brief. The needs of the facility are derived from business, customer, human resource, environmental, community, and legislative concerns.

Even at this early stage, it is valuable to avoid a situation where the design and construction team operate in a fragmented manner. A construction consultant may add significant value to the design process. The design and construction process should be structured to facilitate collaboration between clients, designers, users, legislators, advisers, engineers, and contractors. Different members of the design and construction team have different agendas, and are often contracted separately with individual profit expectations. Architects, for instance, have been criticised for valuing design aesthetics well above cost, while structural and mechanical engineers have been criticised for making provision for safety and maintenance access at the expense of aesthetics. This tension was a key reason that the Japanese government changed the design plans for the 2020 Tokyo Olympic stadium in 2015. The initial futuristic Zaha Hadid design (costing around US$2.08 billion) was removed in favour of a smaller, more conservative Kengo Kuma designed stadium that was felt to be more in keeping with the local surroundings. Disciplinary (quality) fragmentation within design and construction teams has been worsened by tightening time and financial constraints on all industries. It is the pivotal and challenging role of the project manager to facilitate an integrated approach, where interdisciplinary disputes can be successfully negotiated. Once the project manager and design team have been appointed, they will coordinate the subsequent stages of design and construction, which are broadly summarised in Table 4.1.

CONTINUED COMMUNITY AND CUSTOMER CONSULTATION

As we have already indicated in Chapter 3, an estimate of the amount of usage or attendance the proposed facility or event is likely to attract is essential in the analysis of potential consumers. We have outlined several ways to undertake this, and the most straightforward way we have identified is simply through direct consultation with the potential user groups. In the context of establishing a design and building brief, this process can be extended. The process of consultation with the major stakeholders of a facility will, in that regard, yield significant benefits. Broadly speaking, it will help to ensure that the design of the facility meets the needs of the community. If the needs of the community are adequately met, then the facility has the potential to secure an ongoing customer base and operational cash flow. In addition, collaborating with the project's stakeholders provides the opportunity to positively resolve any conflicts between the needs of the facility managers and those of the community. Although collaboration can be criticised by some as delaying decision-making processes, in the long run it represents the best method for garnering community ownership of the facility, and for overcoming conflicts that could otherwise halt the project altogether.

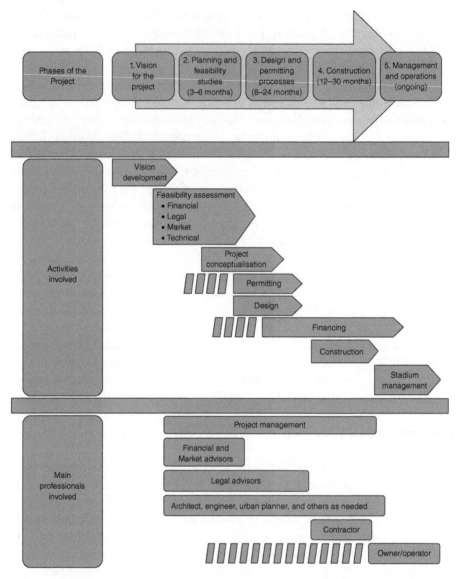

Figure 4.1 Key phases, milestones, timings, and the main professionals involved in the development process

Source: KPMG (2013, p. 7)

The *Community Design Collaborative* in Philadelphia provides an excellent example of tapping into the energy and expertise of community stakeholders to design urban active spaces for youth in the area. The project titled Play Space involves designers going beyond the 'token' gesture of inviting local stakeholders to a public meeting in order to hear their views. Instead, they opted for a model

Planning, design, and construction

of greater involvement, where local childcare providers, families, educators, and community members were invited to participate in a consultation and a design competition to design outdoor play spaces for three public sites in Philadelphia. In a city where play space is limited and outdated, this initiative offers an innovative solution to community and customer collaboration and consultation.

The apparent simplicity of open community consultation belies both their importance and the regularity of their omission. Such an omission can have serious drawbacks for any facility. For example, designers may miss an opportunity for input on cutting-edge trends, and the ability to create a sense of community ownership of the facility is lost. Such ownership feelings can be linked to such issues as usage and vandalism.

SITE SELECTION

The real estate cliché – that there are only three principles determining the market value of properties: location, location, and location – also holds true for the positioning of a sport facility or event, as observed in Chapter 3. The fact that (in the majority of cases) a building cannot simply be picked up and taken to another geographic area makes the decision of where to build it in the first place an important one. The 'location' decision drives further decision making. In a nutshell, the selection of a site for development should represent a win–win for all concerned – facility managers, the local community, potential customers, and the relevant government bodies. It should also be appropriate for the building application in terms of site and soil composition. In other words, as with all stages of the planning, construction, and design process, a collaborative and inclusive approach will ultimately yield the most successful outcome. But what does a win–win mean in practice?

In terms of the facility managers, a win–win would primarily mean that the facility is located in the hub of potential customers identified through the market research component of the feasibility analysis. The site will ideally be accessible to these customers through a public transport infrastructure, and adequate public roads and parking facilities. The existence of other sport and recreational facilities in the vicinity are also an important consideration, as it is undesirable to compete with similar facilities in the same area for the same customers. Given these conditions, the facility is most likely to receive patronage. This, of course, will supply the ongoing income stream required for the facility to be economically viable. Cost management may further be facilitated by considering the location of existing services to the site, such as electricity, gas (where applicable), water and mains drainage, and existing roadways.

For the prospective customers, transport accessibility is also a win. At the same time, the aesthetic wishes of these customers and the local community may influence the choice of site. Local residents, for instance, may not look favourably on the installation of a facility that blocks the sun from their backyard vegetable patch, nor on one which they believe contradicts a dominant architectural style that

91

characterises their neighbourhood. The planning of the facility layout may help to combat these issues, with the careful placement of parking, open park space, and screening vegetation.

The local community, as well as environmental groups, may be concerned with the potential environmental impact of the choice of site. In today's society, developers and facility managers are increasingly expected to be good custodians of the environment. A prominent example of this issue affecting the choice of site is Sochi, the 2014 Winter Olympics site in Russia. In the planning and design phase of development, several sensitive wetlands were 'relocated' in order to build the Olympic site on existing wetlands. Environmental groups campaigned for the preservation of the wetlands; however, the location of building structures and roads was not redesigned, and the immediate area of the wetlands was transformed into the Olympic Park. Although efforts were made re-establish artificial wetlands nearby, the 65 species of birds that frequented the original wetlands had been impacted by the newly constructed Olympic Park. The long-term impacts on the local ecology will be monitored; however, the move by Games organisers led to a community and environmental backlash against the Games.

As a representative of the local community, local government is likely to be concerned with the issues of local residents. In addition, it will be required to consider such issues as historical zoning classifications on any sites in question.

In response to the needs of local communities and their governing bodies, there has been an increasing trend to locate new venues in underprivileged areas or disused industrial sites. This is particularly true for larger, international-standard facilities that have suffered in the past from being located in areas where they have received little use after an international event. The Olympic stadium for the London 2012 Olympics, for example, has revitalised industrial areas in East London. Athens 2004 weightlifting stadium was formerly a disused quarry in a low-income suburb (Hope, 2003) The Homebush Bay area of the Sydney 2000 Olympics famously transformed an industrial waste and slaughterhouse site into a trendy new suburb. However, development and urban regeneration can often lead to urban displacements of marginalised and low socio-economic groups. The latter has been a particular concern for those living in East London and Rio de Janeiro, which has led to increasing prices for residents who lived in the areas regenerated prior to these major events.

Having obtained input and 'buy-in' from community stakeholders, particularly with regard to the selection of the building site, we are now in the position to consider the different elements of the design and building brief.

THE DESIGN AND BUILDING BRIEF

As with any architectural construction, the ultimate goal of a sporting facility is to be used – not merely observed. In other words, form should follow function. The design team should have an intimate understanding of how the facility will be used, when it will be used, who will use it, how it will be maintained, how it will be administered, and the many different kinds of equipment and services that it will house. For example, a stadium that needs to allow 50,000 spectators to flow into and out of the stands will need to incorporate different access features from those of a recreational pool facility that services 2,000 people per day. In addition, factors such as the budget, local regulations, and the aesthetic needs of the immediate vicinity will have a strong bearing on the design. The issue of regulations, in particular, is a complicated area. Sporting facilities are subject not only to national building standards and specifications but also potentially to the requirements of national and international sporting federations in order to allow the organisation of international sporting events and competitions. This, therefore, represents the kind of information that should be provided in the form of a design and building brief. The brief should also establish the processes for evaluating and modifying the design to ensure that it accommodates the needs of all stakeholders. In other words, the design brief should provide a clear picture for the designers of the needs and limitations of the project. The greatest testament to the creativity of a design team will ultimately be their ability to create an aesthetically 'appealing' design within these myriad logistical, financial, and political constraints.

A comprehensive design and building brief should therefore include information on the following parameters:

1 Introductory summary

    i   Summary of strategic brief, including mission, vision, and objectives of the facility
    ii   Overview of commissioning organisation(s) and key stakeholders
    iii Policy and funding context of the facility.

2 Design aspirations

    i   Desire/tolerance for innovation
    ii   Strategic branding concepts
    iii Local and/or sport-specific features to be highlighted
    iv Expectations of design quality.

3 Project limitations

    i   Budget (as informed by feasibility research)
    ii   Time, scale, and development deadlines
    iii Local ecological and community issues.

4 Operational needs of the facility

    i   Facilities and space required
    ii   Internal space arrangements

iii   All primary and secondary spend areas
iv   Staffing and administrative spaces
v   Media, technology, and broadcasting spaces
vi   Maintenance needs
vii   External spaces (parking, landscaping)
viii   Specific user and staff needs (as determined through market research and consultation)
ix   Technology requirements.

5   Performance requirements of the facility

    i   Sport-specific regulations

        a   Individual sport requirements
        b   National and international competition standards.

    ii   Government standards

        a   Building codes
        b   Sport playing surface and space codes
        c   Occupational health and safety
        d   Accessibility
        e   Services/energy efficiency.

    iii   Environmental sustainability

        a   Materials
        b   Sustainability
        c   Unique ecological issues.

6   Lifecycle plans for facility

    i   Life expectancy of facility
    ii   Planned schedule for refurbishment/development (e.g. 5–10-year cycle)
    iii   Potential future uses and flexibility needs.

7   Planning brief

    i   Site information
    ii   Site and soil surveys
    iii   Boundaries

        a   Ownership
        b   Topography
        c   History
        d   Urban context
        e   Pedestrian and vehicle access

  f Car parking and public transport
  g Services in place.

 iv Plans and other relevant documents included.

8 Project management and monitoring mechanisms

  i Anticipated configuration of the team
  ii Process for reviewing and negotiating design proposals
  iii Specific kinds of experts or consultants to be involved in decision making.

Ideally, the design team will respond to the above information with a careful analysis of the options, constraints and costs. Providing designers with sufficient funding to explore a number of alternatives at this stage may yield longer-term benefits with regard to problem resolution and design quality. Design responses should include a cost and deadline programme. Design responses will be presented to the project management team in the form of a report, in addition to outline specification drawings and potentially actual or virtual models. The opportunity should then be taken to creatively negotiate any alterations required before a more detailed brief is drafted. The detailed design brief will include the above information with further detail on all levels, for example details of products and materials to be used. For this reason, it is advisable that building and construction experts be involved in the decision-making at this early stage. In addition, the following should be included:

9 Additional detailed brief information

  i Revised programme plan

   a Costs
   b Deadlines.

  ii Specialised sports surface materials and equipment

   a Outdoor turf and track surfaces
   b Indoor playing surfaces
   c Specialised illumination
   d Seating
   e Scoreboard
   f Fitness and sporting equipment
   g Sport-specific equipment and outfitting.

  iii Other materials and finishes
  iv Temperature control and ventilation
  v Illumination
  vi Security systems and fire protection systems.

10 Detailed drawings and specifications.

MAJOR DESIGN FEATURES

Some of the features of the new facility are more important than others, principally because the major design features affect the core products of the facility directly. In this case capacity decisions and playing surfaces are important, and we discuss them below as the major design features.

Capacity and capacity allocation

To state the obvious, estimates of spectator capacity should be arrived at only after substantial consideration in the market research and feasibility stages of planning. Once determined, the anticipated spectator capacity of a facility has a huge impact on the overall size of the structure. However, the expected capacity of a venue is a much larger design issue than merely determining size. Maximum capacity projections have an enormous impact on other design features, such as access doors and ramps, choice of seating, support columns and bracing for the stands, spectator views of the playing area, merchandising and amenities, the need for media and broadcasting facilities, and optimising secondary spend and architectural identity.

An alternative way to look at the problem of capacity was proposed in the unsuccessful Japanese 2022 World Cup bid. As part of the Japanese bid, proposals were made for holographic projections of games in real time in empty stadia away from the 'physical' arena. These would allow spectators in an otherwise empty facility to watch the (holographic) sport event live whilst the (real) event was going on in another stadium hundreds of kilometres away. Capacity is only an issue for stadium designers insofar as people need to attend an event to receive the experiential benefits of their attendance. Holographic projections coupled with the more realistic (in the short term) virtual reality media devices that are able to project the experience of being in a game (via in-game cameras such as 'helmet-cams') remove the physical capacity constraints of stadia design.

Outdoor playing surfaces and turf

The selection of the playing surface presents venue managers with significant trade-offs that can render decisions far from 'clear-cut'. Like their indoor equivalents, outdoor surfaces can be selected from a range of artificial options or grass. There is, by and large, no one product solution that is applicable to any one venue. Different sports have different surfacing needs, while the vast array of products available confuses the decision even further. The unique climatic conditions in different countries may also influence the decision-making process. With regard to outdoor surfaces, the debate between natural and artificial options remains heated. While artificial surfaces can be praised for their durability and stability, they have also been criticised due to their initial expense, safety, and the replacement costs occasioned by their finite lifespan (Weber 2002). In contrast, a natural grass field can last a lifetime if installed with an appropriate sub-base and serviced by an appropriate maintenance programme. However, natural grass can succumb to wear and tear as well as weather conditions such as drought and heavy rain.

In the *Synthetic Turf Study in Europe, 2012* conducted by KPMG, natural grass pitches were found to be used between 30 and 70 days per year, while synthetic pitches were typically used more than 300 days per year. Furthermore, synthetic pitches were available for use all year round whilst natural grass was often only available for up to 100 days a year due to weather conditions and the time needed for the surface to recover from use. The increased frequency of usage available and reduced maintenance costs of synthetic turf meant that extra revenue could be generated and a broader range of facility utilisation strategies could be considered by stadium management (KPMG, 2013). Therefore, whilst the initial investment in synthetic turf is high, the long-term strategic benefits seem to outweigh the initial financial investment. In 2015, 16 out of the 31 National Football League (NFL) stadiums in the US (New York Giants and New York Jets share a stadium) use synthetic turf.

Technology continually contributes to improved design in artificial surfaces, but it is also radically improving maintenance systems for natural grass fields. This is because, away from the athletics track, natural grass still has its supporters. For example, for the 2016 Super Bowl in Levi Stadium, San Francisco, the entire 75,000 square foot field was replaced prior to the game (Belson, 2016). The surface was grown at a nearby turf farm 'West Coast Turf' and was trucked to the stadium in 536 rolls that were laid on top of sand, then stitched together by a special machine.

Indoor playing surfaces

The choice of floors for indoor surfaces will be heavily influenced by the requirements of the sport to be played on the surface. Where a number of sports are to be accommodated within one area, the final choice of flooring is likely to be a compromise for all codes concerned. Larger-scale facilities may have the financial resources to overcome this problem by installing flexible flooring systems. The Hisense Arena, for example (part of the Melbourne Park complex in Australia), accommodates a 250-metre velodrome circuit, which can be covered by retractable seating (10,800 retractable, removable seats) in order for other events to be staged, such as basketball, Australian Open tennis, or concerts.

Each sporting surface will need to fulfil certain sporting performance requirements. These can be measured using sophisticated methods, and must conform to the regulations for activities to be played on the surface. All sports will require the surface to be level and consistent, so as not to interfere with play. More specifically, the sporting performance requirements include provision for the ball–floor interaction and the person–floor interaction. For example, ball–floor interaction requirements include such properties as the spin, and angular and vertical rebound characteristics of the floor. With regard to the person–floor interaction, most sports will require a degree of friction to prevent slipping but enable controlled sliding and free foot movements. Shock absorbency is another person–floor interaction variable. Even the humble community facility must consider national standards when selecting flooring surfaces for indoor sporting applications. Most countries now have standards in place regulating the degree of impact absorption that should be offered by a floor surface used for sport. These may include the provision of a flooring surface that offers point elasticity (deflecting shock at a specific point of impact) or area elasticity (deflecting impact over a wider area). Some of these performance requirements are further explained in Table 4.3.

Sport England's guide, mentioned above, includes the performance parameters and British standards relevant to a wide variety of sports (Sport England 2007). The document also outlines useful information regarding types of indoor sport surfaces and the related construction methods. The materials and construction methods used

Table 4.1 General performance requirements of indoor sporting surfaces

Performance requirements	*Property*
Ball–surface interaction	▪ Spin characteristics ▪ Angular rebound ▪ Vertical rebound ▪ Velocity change of ball
Person–surface interaction	▪ Friction coefficient ▪ Slip resistance ▪ Peak deceleration ▪ Slip-resistant when wet or dusty ▪ Allows controlled foot movement
Durability	▪ Abrasion resistance ▪ Fatigue resistance ▪ Low-temperature impact resistance ▪ Spike resistance ▪ Resistance to indentation
Environmental resistance	▪ Resistance to temperature and humidity
Maintenance	▪ Ease of cleaning ▪ Tolerates spillages of a range of liquids
Other	▪ Sustainable sourcing of timbers ▪ Light reflectance value of 40–50% ▪ Visual contrast with floor marking system and walls

Source: Adapted from Sport England (2007)

Planning, design, and construction

for indoor surfaces vary greatly. Materials range from timber in a variety of forms (strips, blocks, composite boards, and composite tiles), sheet floors (rubber, vinyl, linoleum, and composites), in-situ polymerics (prepared and laid on-site without joins), and textiles (felt, heavy woven fabric, velour, and specialised carpets).

According to Sport England, sheet materials are generally inappropriate choices for multi-use areas unless they are combined with a support system that provides areas with elastic qualities to conform to the relevant sport standards. Similarly, the in-situ polymeric systems must have appropriate mechanisms to ensure area elasticity, such as support systems or synthetic meshes. Textile surfaces tend to be specialist surfaces for specific sports activities, such as weight training, gymnastics, and aerobics, as well as temporary facilities (Sport England, 2007). In other words, textile surfaces do not generally lend themselves to multi-use scenarios.

When using timber, moisture and expansion control mechanisms must be implemented. A damp-proof membrane must be installed between the subfloor and wooden floor, supplementary to that required by building regulations. In addition, a perimeter expansion gap must be provided to allow for lateral movement due to changes in humidity. The floor installed may also have specific ventilation requirements recommended by the manufacturer (Sport England 2007). Installation of subfloor heating or other facilities may be considered for the void between a subfloor and top floor surface, with provision for access panels. However, this should be thoroughly discussed with the floor manufacturer to ensure that any resulting heat and humidity do not interfere with the performance of the floor materials.

The choice of surface materials may also bear on the choice of marking system used. PVC tape may be appropriate for temporary surfaces, while painted or inlaid lines are used for permanent surfaces, depending on the base material. Markings must be accurately laid within a small error margin (generally 0.1 per cent) to comply with competition regulations (Sport England 2007). National sporting commissions may provide details regarding the recommended colours and widths of lines used for the different sporting codes.

SPORT-SPECIFIC REGULATIONS AND SPECIFICATIONS

Next to the consideration of more generic major issues, the design specifications need to take into consideration the regulations pertaining to a range of (sometimes smaller) sports. In other words, the facility needs to be designed from a multi-functional perspective, especially if this means that not much more design and construction money needs to be spent on accommodating a range of smaller sports. Activity spaces should be planned to accommodate the recognised dimensions and specifications for the sport that (potentially) will be played there. This may include requirements for the height of ceilings, the width and length of playing surfaces, the location of floor markings, and the depth of pools. Regulations for community club participation may differ from national and competition standards.

Liaising with the relevant provincial, state, and national sporting associations, in addition to government sports councils or commissions, will yield significant benefits in the planning stages. Not only will these sources have the capacity to provide advice on regulations, but they may also be able to offer wider expertise regarding the facility design and construction process. Sport England, for instance, publishes a number of documents to aid developers of community sports facilities. The documents, many of which are available through its website, include advice on disabled access, community hall design, and considerations for using natural turf.

Roofing

Unlike many other types of buildings, sport and recreation facilities do not necessarily require complete roofing coverage. Whether a roof is required depends largely on two factors: first, the types of activities and events the facility will host; and second, the prevailing climate around the site. For instance, big-budget stadiums that are designed for use as large-scale concert venues and sporting fields often capitalise on open roofing. This is particularly useful if natural grass turf is installed, given the benefits of natural sunlight and precipitation. If inclement weather is a feature of the location, a fixed or retractable roof requires consideration.

An example of a fixed, open roof within a new international facility is the Maracanã Stadium in Brazil, host to the 2014 football World Cup and 2016 Olympic Games. Originally built to host the 1950 World Cup, the official attendance at the final that year was a massive 173,000 people, making it one of the largest ever attended football games. However, multiple safety incidents reduced the capacity of the stadium and when Brazil was awarded the 2014 World Cup a new roof was installed and the capacity of the stadium was reduced to 79,000. The new roof, based on the principle of a horizontal spoked wheel, covers most of the crowd and gives the 'templo sagrado no pais do futebol', or 'the holy temple in the land of football' a new modern look that was displayed to the world in the two largest sporting events globally.

Contrary to the open roof of the Maracanã, where the minimum temperatures in winter reach around 18° Celsius, the retractable roof has become a widespread feature in many big-budget stadiums in temperate climate zones. The return of the Rams NFL franchise to Inglewood, Los Angeles has prompted the NFL and the local governments to begin construction on the world's most expensive stadium complex (predicted to cost US$2.6 billion and contain an NFL Disney World). The 80,000 seat capacity stadium that will host the Rams will include the next stage in roof design – a 19-acre transparent canopy that will cover the entire stadium. The transparent canopy thus makes the concept of a retractable roof redundant as it simultaneously lets in natural light whilst keeping out the other elements (Ponsford, 2016). The design and construction of a transparent canopy is obviously complex and expensive. Basic issues to be considered include the number and dimensions of each section, the design of the structures that will reinforce the material, the long-term structural integrity of the canopy material, and ongoing cleaning and maintenance costs.

Smaller-scale club or community recreational facilities are obviously faced with different demands when considering roofing options. The retractable roof is here not only financially impractical but generally unnecessary. In these cases, roofing choices will be influenced more by practical and financial needs than by impressive design mechanics. It is important to remember that the roof will function as more than a simple cover to waterproof the structure. The roof and ceiling cavity may also need to contain service infrastructure, such as temperature control vents and electrical conduits, and to accommodate the safe passage of service personnel. Acoustic linings can be considered for both walls and ceilings to facilitate sound absorption and control. The design and construction team should be able to provide recommendations regarding appropriate reverberation times for different sound frequencies. Ceiling colour should encourage the reflection of light back down to the playing area while minimising glare. Exposed ceiling and roof structures should be designed with few junctures and surfaces in which balls could become lodged.

Special building requirements

The function of some sporting and recreation facilities may necessitate the consideration of special building requirements. Indoor swimming facilities, for instance, must contend with such factors as rusting, vapour, and moisture, and need a vapour barrier not only within the walls but also in the roof. Metals chosen for ducts should have an appropriate coating system applied to ensure that expensive and awkward repairs are not required in the future. Similarly, the metals used for beams, joints, trusses, stairs, and seats should be chosen for their resistance to rust and corrosion.

Another example of special building requirements occurs in regions where seismic regulations are in place. The home of the NFL's New England Patriots (Gillette Stadium) in Foxboro, Massachusetts, needed to account for this variable. The design incorporates a framing system that results in biaxial bending, which is counteracted by cruciform columns. Splice plates connect deep trusses to the columns; during an earthquake these splice plates yield to ground motion before the trusses and columns. Seismic regulations also required the designers to consider the location of expansion joints, as swaying structures are not permitted to come into contact with them during an earthquake.

Determining the need to address special building requirements is important in the research and planning stage. Collaborations with building contractors, designers, and government agencies on this point are therefore essential. Networking with managers of other facilities may also yield valuable insight.

OPERATIONAL CONSIDERATIONS

A number of operational issues need to be specifically considered from the perspective of design and building specifications. Provisions such as amenities and offices, traffic flow to and from the facility, holistic approaches to designing for maximum safety, storage, and energy efficiency need to be considered first before we take a more specific look at service considerations.

Amenities

Provision of amenities should be made for male, female, and special-needs customers. Reference to local building standards will outline the minimum number of facilities required based on expected capacity, as well as specifications with regard to layout. A common ratio used in the industry of female to male toilets is 3:1. Unisex access will be required to nappy-changing facilities and nappy disposal. Mechanical air-extraction units are necessary for toilets, changing rooms, kitchens, and showers. A variety of options for hot water can be explored, ranging from individual water heaters to a multi-point heater and from storage systems to continuous supply. The choice of system will have implications for the cost of installation, type of pipes installed and ongoing utility costs.

It pays to consider indoor as well as outdoor access to changing facilities. This enables control of traffic flow, minimises maintenance and cleaning in passageways, and helps to reduce the risk of falls on wet corridor surfaces. Concealed entrances to changing rooms are essential and, surprisingly, often overlooked. The amenities area is likely to be a high-access and high-maintenance area. Careful planning for customer flow in and out, customer queuing, ease of refilling soap and toilet paper, and ease of cleaning will yield longer-term efficiency.

A pivotal consideration for the design of amenities is provision for customers who may have special needs, such as the elderly or disabled. Wheelchair-accessible toilets (and showers, if these are provided) require attention to many essential features, including:

- an adequate door width to allow the wheelchair to pass through,
- a door-opening mechanism that can be operated from a wheelchair,
- a floor without steps,
- an adequate circulation space that allows a wheelchair to enter and manoeuvre next to the toilet and basin,
- an appropriate height of toilet (usually higher than 'standard' toilet bowls),
- installation of grab rails at appropriate positions to aid customers in getting onto and off the toilet,
- an appropriate height of sink to allow access to a person seated in a wheelchair (usually lower than 'standard' sinks),

- space to allow the wheels and footplates of the wheelchair to slide under the sink,
- an appropriate mechanism for turning the tap on and off,
- appropriate heights and positions for other items such as hand dryers, toilet roll holders, mirrors, and doorknobs and locks.

As noted before, occupational therapists can provide expert consultation on access planning, particularly for elderly or disabled customers.

Administrative offices

Once the facility is officially opened, it is the administrative and operational staff that will be its lifeblood. It is at this stage that the ability of the infrastructure to support the administrative functions comes into question. In the worst-case scenario, operational and customer satisfaction difficulties can ensue if the needs of the staff are not accommodated.

Increasingly, stadia redevelopment includes scope for administrative offices of the sport for which the facility is designed. A case in point is the new administrative office for the national sport governing body of Tennis in Australia – Tennis Australia. Previously located within one of the main tennis stadiums (Rod Laver Arena) in Melbourne's sport precinct, the governing body moved into a new administration and media building in 2016. The building – designed by Hassell – will also house international media that come to Melbourne each January for the Australian Open Grand Slam tennis tournament. Melbourne Park collectively houses a cluster of facilities that offer tennis a competitive advantage in Australia, include hosting the Australian Open, elite training facilities, national administration offices, clay and synthetic courts, and various indoor and outdoor training facilities.

Traffic flow and access

Compliance with the relevant government standards for access to public spaces should be sought. These standards will outline the minimum requirements for physical accessibility to all areas of the building, including consideration for customers with disabilities. Areas for consideration include external access (pathways, stairs, railings, ramp gradient ratios, door width and door openings, hallways, height of reception windows), as well as access to toilets and showers.

The access pathways into a facility are not a mere ancillary feature. They are, in fact, the main arteries of the building. It has even been suggested that the design of a sports stadium is, in effect, the design of ways into and out of the facility (Canter, Comber, & Uzzell, 1989; Frosdick, 1997). Provision for disabled users is a legal requirement. This, in addition to indications that slips and falls are a major cause of facility accidents, means that ramps are often preferred over stairs. Signposting and a logical, unidirectional pathway will aid traffic flow, particularly when confusion is caused in cases of emergency. Non-slip, easy-to-clean, and even surfacing will further maximise safety and maintenance.

Safety design issues

The area of safety and risk management is significant and complex, with many aspects of this area discussed often throughout this book. Here we will introduce some of the broad safety and risk issues, noting the need for an integrated, ongoing strategic approach to safety management that includes expert consultation. In each country, there is specific legislation pertaining to safety in sports and entertainment facilities as well as events, and subtle differences may be noted internationally.

A good overview of the nature of international safety considerations is the *FIFA Stadium Safety and Security Regulations* (2012). Regulations are broken into eight areas: management procedures, stewards (safety personnel), maximum capacity, structural and technical measures, crowd management, emergency services, other requirements in extenuating circumstances, and provisions for violations of these regulations. Consistent with a systematic and strategic approach, a safety advisory group or committee should be established to consult on safety-related issues. While this is obviously pertinent to the facility when it is operational, there are advantages to using this kind of expert consultation in the design and construction phase. It will be the role of this committee to ensure the development, implementation, and review of the safety and security management. This will include ensuring that the facility complies with relevant legislation, conducting risk and safety management audits, and implementing procedures and developing other safety strategies as required in the context of the specific facility. All safety stewards should be regularly trained in emergency procedures, the use of emergency equipment, evacuation procedures, and pre-event checks. First-aid-trained staff and a core of emergency services workers (depending on the facility and event size) should be considered. Furthermore, contingency and emergency plans should be distributed and regular emergency training drills should be completed. In particular, emergency stewards should be aware of counter-terrorism measures and the level of associated risk with any given event.

The maximum safe capacity of a venue is considered by calculating the lowest capacity of a stadium that the stadium can seat (holding capacity) and can enter the facility considering the mode of entry and time taken to screen spectators (entry capacity), the time and method spectators must take to safely exit the facility, and the emergency evacuation capacity that considers the time and routes taken by patrons in an emergency. The lowest cumulative value for each section gives the maximum safe capacity of a stadium.

Structural and technical measures encompass several considerations, including but not limited to access control and accreditation to different stadium zones,

Planning, design, and construction

security checks, emergency lighting and power supplies, closed circuit television and the big screen, public address systems and stadium announcer, the venue operations centre, and the respective interaction of the above elements. More specifically, clear signage needs to be established to help manage the crowd. This includes safety and information signs as well as signs to concession stands such as food and beverages and the appropriate consumption of these. Furthermore, security should be readily available to respond to misbehaviour in the crowd.

Underpinning an appropriate response to an emergency within a stadium is the relationship stadium management and safety stewards have with outside support services such as fire, police, ambulances, and hospitals. In the event of an emergency evacuation, it is likely that these services will be needed quickly and must work within a crowded environment. In particular, events that cause panic amongst a crowd such as violence and fire should be key priorities of an emergency evacuation plan.

Employee access areas, maintenance worker/contractor zones, and player zones must also be considered. For example, the playing surface needs to be prepared as a safe working environment for professional athletes after the facility has hosted a rock concert in the main arena. In addition, there are safety issues to be considered during the construction process. The tendering process should ensure that contractors provide evidence of adequate experience, health and safety policies and procedures, a hazard identification system, and liability and employee insurances.

Energy efficiency

The introduction of energy efficiency measures during the facility planning process has the potential to provide both environmentally friendly outcomes and significant cost savings. The lighting of sport facilities, for example, has received considerable attention because of its capacity for 'bottom-line' benefits. Providing for optimal natural light in indoor facilities and installing automatic dimming systems are examples of such considerations. The LEED certification (Leadership in Energy and Environmental Design) is an initiative by the United States Green Building Council that began in 2000. As of 2015, there are nine areas in which facilities are measured on their energy efficiency and environmental design: integrative process; location and transportation; materials and resources; water efficiency; energy and atmosphere; sustainable sites; indoor environmental quality; innovation; and, regional priorities. Depending upon the fulfilment of these categories facilities are rated on a scale of certified, silver, gold and platinum. The NBA is the frontrunner in LEED certification with six stadia receiving a form of certification as of 2015. From these, the Portland Trailblazers' Moda Center was the first major sport stadium to receive the gold level certification of any US sport stadium. The initiatives that led to this achievement included: 60 per cent of their waste being recycled, highly accessible transportation to their central location in Portland, the purchasing of 100 per cent renewable energy, a focus on purchasing reusable commodities, serving healthy food options, and hosting the 2009 annual Green Games to raise environmental awareness (NBA, 2009).

Increasingly, (building) authorities are setting minimum energy efficiency standards that builders are required to meet. A commitment to a specified level of energy efficiency (such as a star rating), with consideration of greenhouse gas emissions and appliance use, may well put a sport facility in a position of world best practice, providing a marketing opportunity to put the facility 'on the map' and fix it in the minds of consumers. Energy efficiency standards should be made explicit to the design and construction team, and should become part of the building brief.

SERVICE CONSIDERATIONS

Having taken care of broader operational issues, we can now take a more specific look at design considerations that relate to optimising service delivery to customers. Issues such as seating, scoreboards, lighting, parking/transport, media/broadcasting, child care, and temperature control all have a direct impact on (end) consumer satisfaction levels, and can largely be prepared for in the design and building stages of the facility.

Seating

Issues to be considered when selecting seating options include cost, visual impression, ergonomic features, durability, ease of maintenance, and coordination with overall construction. Whether the seats are to be used for a corporate box or for public access stadium seating will, of course, dramatically affect these variables.

Durability can be facilitated by the use of corrosion-resistant materials, flexible plastics to prevent snapping, plastics that minimise UV radiation damage, and features to minimise the opportunity for vandalism. Other characteristics (particularly in stadium seating) may include ventilation holes and full back support to prevent the intrusion of feet from spectators seated behind. The ease of removing seats can also be an advantage in instances where it is required to replace damaged seats or to attach new sponsorship logos.

In addition to these variables, the choice of seating may be affected by more unusual features that are designed to delight the venue's customers. The materials and design of seating in the Denver Broncos' stadium, for instance, were chosen in part to enhance the stomping noise of spectators during a game (Gonchar, 2001).

Scoreboards

The scoreboard needs of the local basketball club and those of a state-of-the-art international- standard stadium are worlds apart. The greatest difference, perhaps, is the potential for the mega-stadium to broadcast streaming vision, such as replays and advertisements. However, both ends of the facility spectrum should consider the scoreboard as one of the prime spaces for sponsorship exposure. This is one of the locations where spectator gaze is guaranteed. The scoreboard at the Jacksonville Jaguars' EverBank Field appears to the spectator more like a movie screen due to its relative size. Opened in 2014 the scoreboard is an amazing 60 feet high and 362 feet long, and contains 35.5 million LED bulbs (van Bibber, 2014). In the case of large stadia where games are televised, the promotion of sponsors may require complicated arrangements with broadcasters serving their own corporate interests. In the case of the local club, the scoreboard provides an outstanding opportunity to garner support from local business.

Lighting

The lighting system for a facility includes three broad elements: the daylight system, the artificial system, and the controls. Maximising natural lighting facilitates energy efficiency, as previously mentioned. However, an artificial system and associated controls must still be selected. Evaluating artificial lighting options for a facility involves the consideration of disparate issues. For example, energy efficiency, uniformity of illumination, luminaire type, radiation of heat, placement and type of lighting poles, specialised broadcasting needs, visual comfort, initial and ongoing costs, and ease of cleaning and replacing lamps may all play a part in the lighting decision.

Lighting has come a long way in the past decade from traditional incandescent lighting to metal halide lamps, and in more recent times light emitting diode (LED) lighting. As metal halides emitted more light than their incandescent predecessor, LEDs produce the same levels of output with around an 80 per cent energy cost saving. LED lighting also produces improved lighting for night games, reducing shadows on the field and glare in the eyes of players. Furthermore, LEDs provide near-perfect lighting for broadcasters of sport to adjust colour within their broadcasts (Heitner, 2015).

Uniformity of lighting coverage is another important consideration in LED lighting design. Better lighting coverage leads to an enhanced uniformity – in other words, no dark areas. Uniformity can be measured as a ratio of the brightest to the darkest area of a field: the lower the number, the better. Greater lighting uniformity can be achieved by determining the best horizontal and vertical angles for all of the lights. Computer programmes are now available to aid in this process. Using different lighting patterns, including patterns that combine wide and narrow beams, can further decrease dark areas.

Sport England (2012) provides a summary of typical parameters for illumination of international and community sports facilities (Table 4.5). While this is not provided as a rigid guide for planning, it emphasises the complexity of illumination, ventilation, and temperature control systems through the different areas of a

Table 4.2 Summary of typical parameters for illumination for community facilities

Facility area	Illumination community (lux)*	Illumination international competition (lux)*
Swimming	300	1,500
Tennis	300	750
Basketball	500	750
Badminton	500	1000
Netball	750	1500
Volleyball	500	1,000–1,500
Fitness center	500	–
Table tennis	350	500
Archery	1,000–2,000	1,000–2,000
Darts	300	750

Source: Sport England (2012)

*Lux is a measure of illuminance or the amount of light falling on a surface.

facility. Numerous factors may further influence the levels required in a specific facility, such as local regulations, competition specifications, and the standard temperature range in a given region.

Parking/transport

Increasing ease of transport access to a venue is an important factor in encouraging repeat customer patronage. Whilst anomalies exist, for example AS Monaco's St Louis II stadium with a four-storey car park underneath the small 18,523 seat stadium, the majority of major sport facilities around the world attempt to reduce congestion by incorporating large public transport infrastructure into their design considerations. In the lead-up to the 2012 London Olympic Games, the Stratford Regional train station and nearby Stratford International station both received significant upgrades totalling around £339 million (Richter, 2012). Furthermore, some 1,738 new underground cars were ordered by the government from Bombardier in 2015. Although London already had an extensive rail network it was estimated that around 78 per cent of people travelling to the games would use rail and this justified the upgrades to the Stratford regional and international stations, both of which are within walking distance of the main Olympic stadium.

Media/broadcasting

Beyond the logistics of space and accessibility, accommodating the broadcasting and media needs of a facility demands consideration of significant technological issues.

At the time of writing, high-level sports and entertainment venues were address-ing the need to install wireless technology to allow for high-speed connection between media personnel and their outlets and publishers. In addition, major sport event organisers are concerned with providing impressive display screens for spectators and VIPs, as well as facilitating state-of-the-art coverage by commercial and pay-TV providers.

The installation of wireless technology for sport event photographers represents one of the continuing media advances. For example, in May 2003 Sydney's Telstra Stadium completed the installation of wireless technology for photographers using wireless LAN products based on the IEEE802.11b worldwide standard, running at 11 Mbps. The current standard at the time of writing is 802.11ay and allows peak transmission of 20Gbps. Traditionally, photographers were forced to transmit their digital files after the game, which is often a time-consuming process. Wireless tech-nology now enables the photographers to transmit their images instantly to their photo editors, while the game is still in progress. The photo editors are able to provide immediate feedback to the photographer, potentially resulting in improved coverage and higher-quality images.

The installation of broadcasting technology is usually a consideration for large stadia (including college stadia in the United States) and sporting events that occupy a temporary space. The technical requirements for this infrastructure are in a constant state of flux, and demand a great deal of flexibility and negotiation by facility and event managers. Zebra technologies partners with the NFL to use radio-frequency identification (RFID) technology to monitor everything from player movement to top speed and acceleration. Furthermore, the Hawk-Eye Innovations have become ubiquitous in most ball sports and particular tennis and cricket. By using high speed and carefully situated cameras, the Hawk-Eye technology is able to track the ball at speed and both assist the adjudication of the sport and enhance the viewing experience.

Establishing and maintaining a capacity for broadcasting involves a partnership between the facility, the broadcaster, and technology providers. The physical spaces required for on-site broadcasting include a studio or commentary booth, production control room, communication and control apparatus bays, a VT hall for editing of vision, off-tube booth, dressing room, editorial and production offices, and secure storage for cameras. The technological requirements, however, usually demand a flexible and collaborative approach, given the pace of innovations in this area.

Childcare facilities

The provision of, or access to, childcare or crèche facilities becomes an issue of increasing importance with facilities of growing size. The local football club is unlikely to consider this factor, given the nature of its use, but community-based recreational facilities, as well as large state and national facilities, often need to consider the childcare needs of their staff and customers. For example, a facility that plans to attract 30–40-year-old women to a fitness programme must consider the likelihood of the customers' need to accommodate young children. Larger employers may include child care as a component in their staff benefit and equal opportunity programmes.

Consultation with a state or national child safety information service may provide invaluable information on the physical design of the space, but the design of a physical space for crèche facilities is only the first step in this complex service area. The operational considerations of a childcare facility are substantial, with government regulations often detailing such requirements as training and accreditation, occupational health and safety, working with children checks, and staff-to-child ratios. In some instances, a facility may be able to accommodate these needs by establishing a relationship with a local childcare facility, without establishing its own service.

Temperature control

Surprisingly, the need for heating and cooling is often overlooked, due to budgetary restrictions. It is a false economy to ignore the provision of these control systems and expect that they can be accommodated at a later stage. Like all areas of construction and infrastructure, technology is continually extending the options available to facility managers. Engineering advice is invaluable in this area, as careful planning of natural ventilation can contribute significantly to cooling systems and therefore add to energy efficiency. Options for heating include underfloor systems, as well as ducted warm air and radiant panels. Insulation levels that create a well-sealed building envelope are essential. The location of master controls is another important consideration. (Energy efficiency issues surrounding control of temperature have already been discussed.)

SECONDARY SPEND AREAS

From the perspective of the sport facility manager and the sport event manager, areas for secondary spend are essential to the commercial success of the venture. Other avenues towards revenue maximisation need to be fully exploited, especially when the facility operators have only limited access to the revenue pie that is represented by event broadcasting rights. It will come as no surprise that how a facility is designed, taking into consideration how people (staff and customers) move through the facility, will determine where customers are most likely to spend money. Hence, service providers need to be located to present customers with opportunities to buy.

Merchandising

The scope of merchandising facilities should directly reflect the anticipated spectator capacity calculated for the sport facility. Small community facilities can usually accommodate merchandise in the front reception, which minimises space and staffing requirements. The dedicated shopfront, the temporary merchandise tent, and roaming sales staff are three additional options used in medium to large facilities. Market research conducted at the pre-design stage should determine how, where, and what potential customers will purchase. Like other secondary spend areas, such as food and beverage, merchandising may offer possibilities for outsourcing.

Food and beverages

Like many operational services, food and beverage facilities are increasingly likely to be commercial services provided by external companies that have successfully tendered for the privilege. The tendering process should be commenced well before construction in order to allow the successful company to collaborate with the design and construction teams. Infrastructure and design needs may be unique to the provider. The type of food and beverages available should reflect the needs of the customer as determined in the planning phase. Focus groups, for example, can be used to elicit ideas for the prospective facility users about the produce they are most likely to buy, and under what conditions. This approach can potentially be delegated to the service operators as part of the tender process, and will increase the likelihood of customer loyalty. However, it is important not only what people like to eat and drink but also when and how often, and why they leave their seat to buy food or drinks. This behaviour varies dramatically across a range of sports. For example, the US baseball leagues offer frequent 'time-out' opportunities for fans to leave their seat to get some food: it is part of the tradition of watching baseball to eat hot dogs and drink beer with friends in the stands. Soccer matches, on the other hand, offer few opportunities to leave the action because of the continuous play and few goal-scoring occasions. Stadium developers in the US-based Major League Soccer have started to build food and beverage stands facing the field of play in order to allow spectators to continue viewing the action while buying food and drinks. In other words, smart design, where designers and builders have put themselves in the customer's seat, leads to increased secondary spend.

ARCHITECTURAL IDENTITY

In order to put the new facility on the marketing map and position the facility in the minds of consumers, 'localising' a facility, be it a temporary or permanent venue, will greatly enhance the architectural identity of the place.

Localising a facility

Localising a facility design can be a useful adjunct to the overall marketing plan. This can be achieved by the use of unique design elements reflecting the character of the city, district, or country. Used as a promotional tool, a strong architectural identity can facilitate media coverage, local community pride, and even international attention.

The importance of localising a facility became apparent in the lead-up to the Japan 2020 Olympics when the Japanese government changed from the original Zaha Hadid design to a more traditional Kengo Kuma design. The original design was costly and did not easily fit in with the local surrounds. Criticism of the original design came in the form of its shape (critics said it appear to look like a 'bike helmet' or a 'turtle'), its height and modern look did not seem to fit in with its local surrounds, which include Tokyo's Meiji Shrine. Conversely, Kengo Kuma's eventual successful design was cheaper, lower, and used natural iron and wood materials to resemble traditional Japanese temples and architecture (Ap & Wakatsuki, 2015).

Similarly, the Denver Broncos' US$384 million, 76,000 seat stadium has been injected with the Denver spirit, thanks to its horseshoe-shaped design that opens towards the mountains. The upper seating bowl takes an undulating shape, mimicking the profile of the mountains as well as conveying the idea of a saddle. The designers have even enhanced the ability of fans to make 'Rocky Mountain thunder', the deafening rumble designed to intimidate opposition teams. This was achieved by selecting specific seating units where the 'rakers' and 'stringers' supporting each seat were sized to accommodate the frequencies created by stomping and rhythmic dancing.

The temporary facility

Temporary facilities are increasingly being considered as an option where research suggests that usage levels will not support a facility beyond the scope of a finite event. Major sport events are in some cases being managed like a travelling circus, with organisers erecting temporary event structures that reduce costs and improve location flexibility.

For one-off events, the maximum capacity projections pose a unique capacity challenge for organisers; the capacity for the given event (e.g. the Olympics) is significantly larger than the capacity required for domestic consumption after the event. Discussions around the challenge of capacity often use the language of legacy and involve leveraging stadia design to meet the short-term needs of the major event and the long-term requirements of the local community. As a result nearly every Olympics, and increasingly World Cups, has included stadia with flexible capacity via the use of temporary stadia. The 15,000 person temporary beach volleyball stadium for the London 2012 Olympics was constructed in the Horse Guards Parade in central London, less than 200 metres from 10 Downing Street, the Prime Minister's residence. In the 2022 FIFA World Cup bid, Qatar outlined that in order to meet the dual needs of high capacity in the short term and a much smaller capacity in the long term for domestic sport, the top tiers of several of their stadia will be removable and sent to developing countries to improve their sport infrastructure. If completed in such a manner, variable capacity and infrastructure development may be one of the lasting legacies of the Qatari event.

SUMMARY

The emphasis of this chapter has focused on the planning, design, and project management aspects of facility development. Clearly, there are myriad specific building and construction issues that are beyond the scope of this book. We therefore emphasise the need to collaborate and seek expert consultation throughout the design and construction process. As the client, the initiator of the project needs to understand the broad logistical, political, and conceptual issues, and to receive advice from experts. The client does not need to know how to install a retractable roof. What the project requires is a team capable of successfully negotiating the inevitable difficulties that will arise during design and construction. The team developing the new Denver Broncos stadium, for instance, faced challenges due to land acquisition delays. Because different parcels of land became available at different times, the project was unable to continue in the traditional sequence, where each project subcontractor works progressively around the field, race-track style. Instead, the stadium was constructed in the form of eight mid-rise buildings, the different sections being built from the ground up as the land was acquired.

CASE STUDY

Retrospective investigation of the London Aquatic Centre design and legacy

Having considered the switch by the Japanese government from a Zaha Hadid-designed facility, we shall now return to one of her successfully constructed facilities, the London Aquatic Centre that hosted the swimming and diving events at the London 2012 Olympic Games. The aim of this case study is to use both the online resources and the information detailed herein to determine the legacy of the London Aquatic Centre and value to Londoners.

London was awarded the Olympic Games on 6th July 2005. A year prior to winning the Olympic bid, Zaha Hadid had already won the bid to construct the aquatic centre in 2004 at a cost of £269 million. Given the timing, 17,500 temporary seats were incorporated into the design to host the anticipated crowds for the 2012 Olympic Games. Construction began in 2008 and was completed in 2011. The facility included two 50m Olympic-sized pools, a 25m diving pool, a dry diving pool, a 50-station gym, a café, and a crèche. During the Games, the facility hosted 32 swimming events and eight diving events as well as all of the associated categorisations during the Paralympics. Across the Paralympics and Olympics the £269 million facility had 27 event days – or approximately £10 million per event day if the Centre was going to be solely used for the Olympic Games.

The building has 628 panes of glass and eight external doors to allow plenty of nature light. It has two giant videoboards and a timing system that is able to record times of aspiring swimmers. Following the games the venue was converted into a community facility and welcomes up to 800,000 visitors per year.

Given these figures, it is obvious that legacy becomes a central concern for such investment. Following the Games, 14,700 of the temporary seats were removed to leave a total capacity of 2,800 to meet the domestic competition need for major national swimming events. In 2013, FINA awarded the World Diving Series (2014) and the European Swimming Championships (2016) to the venue, which would once again be used as an elite swimming facility.

In the meantime, however, the London Aquatic Centre operates as a central piece of community infrastructure in the Queen Elizabeth Olympic Park in Stratford. One of the catch cries of London 2012 was 'inspiring a generation', and as such the London Legacy Development Fund was created. Amongst other goals, the aim of the organisation is to 'promote and deliver physical, social economic and environmental regeneration of the Olympic Park and its surrounding area'; as such the operation of the venue was awarded to Greenwich Leisure Limited for a period of 10 years and 50 people from the local community were employed to operate the facility on an ongoing basis.

According to the London Aquatics Centre (London Aquatics Centre, n.d.), the facility has the following aims:

- London Aquatics Centre will achieve 700,000–800,000 visits a year (78,000 last month).
- 2,800 children and adults will have swim school lessons a week (140,000 lessons a year).
- 400 children and adults will take part in 'learn to dive' lessons each week.
- 4,00 school pupils will take part in London Aquatic Centre's new intensive school swimming lessons programmes per year (45,000 x one-hour lessons a year).

- 4,000 school pupils will receive one-hour taster sessions as part of the London Aquatic Centre.
- 300–500 people will undertake regular exercise each week that have come from a Health referral.

Furthermore, the London Aquatics Centre has the following commitments (London Aquatics Centre, n.d.):

- Host a range of Local, Regional, National and International events, and ensure community access is maintained where possible.
- Allow public access to swim from £4.95 for adults and from £2.50 for children during off-peak times.
- Our monthly (easy payment) swim membership will give you access to swim for less than a £1 a day.
- If your child is attending our swim school and has attended 25 hours of lessons but cannot swim 25 metres by the age of 12 you will receive 12 free swimming lessons to help achieve this goal.
- Pupils on our swimming lessons will be continually assessed so they can progress at their own speed and there are no waiting lists ensuring easy access on to lesson places.
- Our 'Kids for a Quid' scheme for members under 16 is available during all 'Swim for all' sessions Monday to Saturday all year round.
- A pool will be open for lane swimming at all times during public sessions.
- There will be a programmed fun session on every Saturday and family session on Sunday at all pools for swimmers to enjoy (Aqua splash, Extreme Aqua splash, Swim for families).

Questions

1 Considering the basic design and construction issues arising from building modern-day multipurpose sporting facilities, how would you rate the London Aquatics Centre in terms of its ability to cater for a range of events?
2 Knowing that aquatic facilities rarely deliver a profit to their owners, what would you have focused on when designing the facility and briefing the builders on the critical aspects of construction?
3 Are there any design features that you would consider to be vital in order to maximise the facility's multipurpose flexibility? In that context, who would you describe as the Centre's most important customers?

REFERENCES

Ap, T., & Wakatsuki, Y. (2015, 23rd December). Japan unveils design for 2020 Olympic stadium ... again. *CNN.com*. Retrieved from http://edition.cnn.com/2015/12/21/sport/japan-new-olympic-stadium-selected

Belson, K. (2016, 2nd February). Cue the new sod: N.F.L. plays Super Bowl on its own turf. *New York Times*. Retrieved from http://www.nytimes.com/2016/02/03/sports/football/super-bowl-50-nfl-turf-levi-stadium.html

FIFA (2012). *FIFA stadium safety and security regulations*. Zurich, Switzerland: Author.

Frosdick, S. (1997). Designing for safety. In S. Frosdick & L. Walley (Eds), *Sport and safety management*. Butterworth-Heinemann, Oxford.

Gonchar, J. (2001). Denver dares to give its new stadium a distinct local personality. *Engineering News-Record, 246*(13), 20–21.

Heitner, D. (2015, 18th December). How a shift to LED lighting is saving sports teams millions of dollars. *Forbes.com*. Retrieved from http://www.forbes.com/sites/darrenheitner/2015/12/18/ how-a-shift-to-led-lighting-is-saving-sports-teams-millions-of-dollars/#6c39d5624632

Hope, K. (2003). Capitals: An overview of current events and trends in Europe's capitals. *Europe, 422*, pp. 34–5.

KPMG (2013). *A blueprint for successful stadium development*. Budapest: Author.

London Aquatics Centre (n.d.). *History of the London Aquatics Centre*. Retrieved from http://www.londonaquaticscentre.org/about/history

NBA (2009). *Portland Trail Blazers Moda Center earns LEED gold certification*. Retrieved from http://www.nba.com/blazers/news/leed_certification.html

Ponsford, M. (2016, 19th January). Los Angeles Rams' stadium to be world's most expensive. *CNN.com*. Retrieved from http://edition.cnn.com/2016/01/19/architecture/new-nfl-stadium-los-angeles

Richter, R. (2012, 16th April). *Olympic Games: Transport infrastructure development*. Retrieved from http://www.transportnexus.com/olympic-games-3

Sport England (2007). *Design guidance note: Floors for indoor sports*. Wetherby, UK: Sport England Publications/English Sports Council.

Sport England (2012). *Design guidance note: Artificial sports lighting: Updated guidance for 2012*. Wetherby, UK: Sport England Publications/English Sports Council.

van Bibber, R. (2014, 27th July). Jaguars unveil world's largest scoreboards at EverBank Field. *SB Nation*. Retrieved from http://www.sbnation.com/nfl/2014/7/27/5941601/jaguars-worlds-largest-scoreboards-everbank-field

Weber, B. (2002). The new sports architecture, design, and technology. *Scholastic Coach & Athletic Director, 71*(7), 100–5.

CHAPTER 5

NEW SPORT FACILITY DEVELOPMENT: PREPARING THE FACILITY MANAGEMENT INFRASTRUCTURE

CHAPTER FOCUS

1 Introduction to sport facility and major event management
2 Key success factors of operating sport facilities and running sport events
3 Feasibility analysis and market research for planning new sport facilities and events
4 New sport facility development: planning, design, and construction
5 **New sport facility development: preparing the facility management infrastructure**
6 New sport facility operations: attracting events
7 New sport facility operations: planning the event management infrastructure
8 Attracting customers: marketing sport facilities and events
9 Running the sport event: event operations
10 Destination marketing, image, and branding through major sport events
11 Performance management: evaluating operations
12 Performance management: legacy and measuring impact

CHAPTER OBJECTIVES

In this chapter we will:

■ Introduce and discuss the concept and dimensions of organisational structure.
■ Provide an overview of the categories, functions, and personal expertise of staff within a sport facility.

- Discuss the issues related to outsourcing facility management labour.
- Outline the various processes inherent to human resource management systems.
- Explain the issues related to legal responsibilities, industrial relations, and occupational health and safety.
- Articulate the need for having experience in operational and capital budgeting.
- Review the role quality decision-making and problem-solving processes have in managing the facility management infrastructure.

INTRODUCTION

In the previous chapter, we looked at the planning, design, and construction processes inherent to new sport facility development. As those processes are ongoing – and especially during the construction phase – sport facility owners need to develop a facility management infrastructure that ensures the efficient and effective operation of the venue.

Executing the management and operational functions of a sport facility requires a well-developed facility management infrastructure. This starts with a quality organisational management structure that focuses on strong leadership and governance structures, combined with a clear understanding of human and organisational behaviour, to ensure optimal operational effectiveness of the infrastructure. To implement such a structure, strong human resource management practices and procedures must be employed, appropriate fiscal and economic practices applied, and quality decision-making and problem-solving processes integrated.

THE HUMAN INFRASTRUCTURE

No matter the size or scope of the physical infrastructure of a sport facility, it remains an empty building if it does not incorporate an appropriate human infrastructure to fulfil its intended purposes. The staff members of sport facilities are charged with the responsibilities of managing the physical space, physical structures, and the services and events that occur in the facility.

The staffing needs of a facility will be driven by a number of factors. These include the objectives of the organisation, its service quality philosophy, and its structure. The service quality philosophy of the facility operator, for instance, will drive staffing needs, such as minimum qualifications and full- versus part-time appointments.

Beyond that, there is a range of management functions that are specific to the preparation and operation of the sport facility. While this may be specific to individual facilities based on its functions, the goal of this section is to provide an overview of general functions that are common across sport facilities. This will allow for a broad understanding of the various functions, while allowing for selection of specific functions inherent to the context of a sport facility (e.g. specific human infrastructure).

ORGANISATIONAL MANAGEMENT

In order to fully appreciate the role of human infrastructure in running a sport facility, there needs to be an understanding of management functions and roles. The functions related to managing a sport facility include selecting and prioritising strategic objectives (planning), assessing and delegating resources to meet those objectives (organising), influencing human infrastructure to successful accomplish the required tasks (leading), and monitoring performance to ensure efficient and effective operation of the human infrastructure (coordinating/controlling/evaluating). This is accomplished through three major roles inherent to organisational management – social interaction (interpersonal), intelligence dissemination (informational), and dynamic collaborations (decision making).

Human infrastructure is made up of staff at multiple levels across a sport facility – from owners and operators ... to executive and top managers ... to supervisory and middle managers ... to administrative and operational staff. Regardless of the level, the need to understand individual differences in terms of personal characteristics is crucial to success in organisational management. This may include a myriad of considerations including personal characteristics, demographic factors, various levels of abilities and skills, personality characteristics, and even emotional stability in terms of stress management and well-being. In addition, employee perceptions, attitudes, motivations, values, and beliefs play a crucial role in effective organisational management.

Beyond individual behaviours, the interactions between employees also need to be considered as a part of the organisational management process. Understanding various formal and informal group interactions is crucial to developing a sense of collaboration across the sport facility and creates an atmosphere that encourages teamwork. The focal point for these interactions centres on quality leadership across the organisation. Leadership involves the process of influencing others to complete tasks, attain goals, and meet organisational objectives. Those in leadership positions need to provide direction to staff, manage conflict, promote an environment of trust and integrity, occasionally take risks, and promote success.

Organisational structures

As a result of the highly competitive global marketplace, there has been a proliferation of many different styles of organisational structure. According to Graetz, Rimmer, Smith, and Lawrence (2010), for an organisation to become profitable, it

119

must function flexibly, with high market sensitivity, and offer a participative work environment. In order to perform in this responsive and competitive manner, sport facility operators must evaluate the most appropriate organisational structure to adopt. This involves not only establishing structure and locations of responsibility, but also ensuring that the appropriate procedures, resources, and staff skills are in place to support the organisational structure.

The traditional hierarchical structure has been criticised in recent times for lacking market responsiveness and discouraging human resources from maximising their potential within an organisation. In addition, these types of structures have been shown to restrict creativity, frustrate organisational adaptability, and impede participative decision making (Culver, 2014).

Closely linked to the hierarchical model is the functional structure, a rigid, highly formalised organisational composition. This structure is based on the idea of organising according to specialised areas such as sales and marketing, finance, and human resources. It suggests that an organisation should be structured according to different functional areas from the bottom of the organisation to the top (Daft, 2012), hence the label 'functional structure'. While the functional approach facilitates efficiencies within each work function, the overall structure has been criticised for lacking responsiveness and flexibility.

An attempt to relax the rigid formalities of the functional structure is represented by the divisional structure. Separate divisions or departments are established to manage differing goods, services, groups, projects, business, profit centres, or even regions. Each division is serviced by its own units (e.g. finance or personnel). This configuration offers the advantage of allowing increased responsiveness within each division, but drawbacks include the duplication of resources within departments, the loss of specialisation, and a tendency for decentralised decision making (Bulander & Dietel, 2013).

Another structure that combined the efficiency of the functional approach with the responsiveness of the divisional composition, while also encouraging subordinate employees to participate in decision-making is called the matrix structure (Graetz & Smith, 2010; Graetz, et al., 2010). This structure is often used in organisations that deal with many non-routine tasks and where relationships and responsibilities constantly change in order to meet the needs of the particular project at hand. Reporting relationships are vertical (the traditional hierarchy), for example, to a departmental manager in finance or marketing; and horizontal, to what is often a project manager for a specific task. As can be appreciated, the project manager deals with all the specialists working on the specific task (left to right), whereas the departmental manager deals with all the specialists across all tasks (top to bottom). Predictably, the main criticism of this model is due to the increased likelihood of conflicts in lines of authority and responsibility, but it may not come as a surprise that many event organisations use matrix structures to manage the diverse needs of the event.

A more recent paradigm in organisational structure is the networked organisation. Also referred to as a 'loosely coupled system' (Shen, Hao, & Xue, 2012), this model aims to dismantle the barriers between divisions by establishing small, networked units where relationships are the key consideration. Widely used in facility management and maintenance, it is an integrated, service-oriented approach for managing data, information, and knowledge gathered throughout the lifespan of the facility – from planning to design to construction and eventually to management (Shen, Hao, & Hue, 2012). Depending on the resources and skills a work project requires, different units may operate autonomously, or pool resources as a project team. Hence, this is a form of project-based organising, as opposed to organising based on structure. This structure is of particular relevance for sport facility and event management organisations, as these require high levels of 'on the spot' problem-solving flexibility, in both preparing and hosting events.

There have been a number of recent innovations related to organisational structure. Despite the evolution of many forms of managing and organising in the recent past, this does not mean that the hierarchy has ceased to exist at all. It is more accurate to suggest that the hierarchy is one element of a complex organisation that includes other, equally important elements that play a vital role in its existence. In fact, Graetz et al. (2010) state that the concepts of relationships, processes, collaboration, inclusion, flexibility, creativity, and change are more effective in organisational structure development and management as compared to previous practices such as structure and control, functional hierarchies, size/scope/scale, costs and efficiency measurements, decision-making and planning.

This is not to say that the traditional organisational structural practices are obsolete, but rather to note a shift in emphasis from organising around the structure to organising around processes and relationships. Ghoshal and Bartlett (1995) initially suggested there are three core processes – rather than structures – that underpin successful management in the knowledge economy: (1) encouraging initiative via an entrepreneurial process; (2) linking and maximising competence as part of an integrative process; and (3) managing downsizing and regeneration through a renewal process. Kanter (1996) advocates the use of three key strategies – namely, building synergies, establishing alliances, and encouraging 'streams' of new information – in order to establish an organisation that is responsive and competitive. Synergies operate best in environments with a flatter (less hierarchical) organisational structure, where employees have greater involvement in workplace decisions and processes encourage integration across functional departments. Developing strategic alliances refers to building collaborative relationships with other organisations, such as suppliers to whom the organisation has outsourced non-core services (Whittington et al., 1999). The establishment of new information streams refers to the building of formal communication lines that ensure that new ideas do not become 'lost in the system'.

Since the turn of the century, another evolution of innovation in organisational structure has become evident. Innovation management in the service sector such as sport facilities operations and managing sporting events, where the delivery of the service is often a one-time opportunity to impress the customer, a rigid control-based organisational structure restricts employees in their ability to optimise the service experience. Free-flowing information combined with an empowered ability for most staff to 'act on the spot' are characteristics of a structure in which customer satisfaction can be optimised. According to Öberg, Adams, and Alexander (2014), innovation management capabilities allow an organisation to renew itself in a dynamic society in order to enhance the value for customers. This involves the integration of organisational processes, infrastructural resources, internal initiative, and external intelligence to enhance product/service offerings and positioning, operational processes, and potential a shift in the overall organisational structure paradigm (Tidd & Bessant, 2009).

HUMAN RESOURCE MANAGEMENT (HRM)

In concert with the development and refinement of the organisational structure is the development of the most important resource any organisation has – its people. Human resource management, as the function within an organisation that is responsible for the recruitment, training, and retention of personnel, plays a crucial role in not only ensuring the operational success of a sport facility, but also meeting the objectives set forth within the sport facility strategic plan.

Usually when one thinks about human resources, it is usually in reference to the employees of an organisation. Professional staff are hired to execute specific tasks in the form of job responsibilities in exchange for remuneration – either in the form of a paycheck or an agreed stipend/fee. Generally, there are four levels of professional staff within an organisation. The executive level has the most power and authority as it is made up of top/senior managers who are responsible for the overall strategic direction and conceptual management for an organisation. The administrative level is made up of middle managers who are responsible for the day-to-day management and operations of specific segments or groups of departments within an organisation, and are the communication bridge between the upper and lower levels of management. Supervisory level focuses on the management and operations of a specific unit or department who generally oversee the specialists within an area. General staff are the specialists within individual areas or departments who complete the individual tasks assigned by higher levels of management.

While the employees are the most important human resource to an organisation, there are other groups of individuals who are technically considered to be human resources. First are volunteers. Especially in the sport industry, volunteers play a crucial role in ensuring safe and entertaining experiences for attendees of events at sport facilities. Volunteers are technically not employees, but have chosen to become involved with an organisation by freely giving their time for little or no compensation. Volunteers give their time for a variety of reasons, ranging from altruism to building psychic income for their community to wanting to engage in a socially responsible activity. Regardless of the reason, volunteers are a significant human resource, and just as with paid employees must be considered in the development of human resource policy.

Developing sport facility staffing functions within HRM structure

Having established the broad parameters around which a sport facility organisation may be structured, it is important to determine its specific staffing requirements. Broadly speaking, each functional area of the facility will require specialised human resource skills. Table 5.1 provides examples of some of the major staffing functions and personnel expertise required within a sport facility.

Table 5.1 Summary of key staffing functions for sport facilities

Staffing functions	Personnel expertise
Executive	■ Board of directors and executive management ■ Expertise in strategic management, corporate law, risk management, performance management
Administrative	■ Programming ■ Contract management ■ Secretarial/personal assistance ■ Media liaison ■ Front desk/reception management
Finance	■ Bookkeeping ■ Payroll ■ Computerised account-keeping expertise ■ Goods and services tax reporting ■ Asset management and depreciation ■ Company taxation ■ Budgeting ■ Financial analysis ■ Auditing ■ Annual report preparation ■ Strategic accounting advice ■ Performance management
Human resources	■ In-house/contractor expertise in legal obligations of employers ■ Occupational health and safety ■ Industrial relations

Staffing functions	Personnel expertise
	■ Recruitment, retention, and performance management ■ Training ■ Incentive schemes
Maintenance	■ Grounds and parking ■ Mechanical/engine room ■ Machinery ■ Pool/spa operations ■ Water management ■ Fitness equipment ■ Utilities ■ Media technology ■ Security systems ■ Turf management
Custodial/cleaning	■ Customer and staffing zones ■ Shower and bathroom facilities ■ Major event cleaning (turnaround between events) ■ Health and safety standards/obligations
Catering/food service	■ Quality and variety of food and beverages ■ In-house/outsourced split ■ Corporate box services and policies ■ Health issues
Security	■ Standard operations ■ Special events ■ Crowd management ■ Vandalism ■ Terrorism ■ Alcohol/drug policies ■ Law enforcement policies and collaboration with police ■ Risk management
Programme delivery	■ Fitness ■ Personal training ■ Learn to swim ■ Aerobics ■ In-house sporting competitions
Ancillary customer service	■ Ticket/box office ■ Retail and merchandising ■ Relationship/communication with outside ticketing agency
Event management	See Chapter 7
Marketing	See Chapter 8

In consideration of the above tasks – and much more – one of the most important questions when considering staffing functions and personnel expertise requirements is 'Should I hire this staff member or outsource the responsibilities to another organisation?' Many industries and organisations have gone through a cycle of rapid economic growth and expansion, then into economic decline and rationalisation or even downsizing. The latter process in particular often leads to a broader question: 'What is the core business of the organisation?'

This is an important question because it makes management of the organisation focus on what it does best, and in which areas it is most likely to be successful and thus profitable. If the answer leads to the realisation that a lot of 'non-core business' is being conducted 'in-house' the issue of potentially outsourcing that part of the business becomes an important business consideration. In order to successfully outsource parts of the non-core activities of the organisation, well-defined specifications need to be established, and when the business is brought to the open marketplace for tender, the successful tenderer needs to be monitored in order to ensure the high-quality provision of outside services.

The process of 'competitive tendering' in a sport facility is often seen in the areas of security, cleaning/custodial, parking, and food service contracts. In these areas especially, tendering ensures that 'specialist' providers compete against each other to provide the sport facility with the best and most cost-effective service package. Competitive tendering also provides the range of tendering organisations with the stimulus to constantly review and upgrade their service offerings in order to remain competitive. This benefits the professionalism of the industry as a whole.

As the outcome of a successful tendering process, a comprehensive and specific contract will be drawn up between sport facility management and the outside provider in order to have a clear and agreed overview of service specifications and the requirements of both parties involved, allowing for quality monitoring and continuous improvement. There are a variety of ways by which to contract the full range of non-core services. Recent years have seen a dramatically growing emphasis on the benefits of outsourcing, in tandem with trends towards privatisation and tender management, because it offers the facility a number of key advantages, including higher levels of service specialisation and decreased complexity of internal human resources.

However, it is also important to recognise the drawbacks inherent in the outsourcing model. Higher variable costs for service delivery are likely, as well as higher administrative demands for contract management. The process of service specification and tendering, for instance, requires specialised expertise. In addition, drafting of a contract, including duration, terms of renewal, and conditions such as costs, profit sharing, incentives and alliances, must be performed. Further disadvantages include the relinquishment of control over service quality on the implementation of the contract.

Given the delicate balance of advantages and disadvantages afforded by outsourcing, not all functional areas of the facility will be served best by the approach. The decision to contract for services is obviously complex, and is aided by considering some key principles. As noted before, current best practice suggests that

Preparing the facility management infrastructure

organisations should focus on their core competencies, rather than look towards diversification (Graetz et al., 2002). Therefore, it is the non-core activities that tend to be considered for outsourcing rather than those areas deemed to be essential management and primary service delivery functions.

Developing HRM systems and processes

Establishing and maintaining a human resource infrastructure within a sport facility goes far beyond identifying the staffing roles that are necessary for the facility to function. As one of the key strategic staffing functions mentioned earlier in the chapter, recruitment procedures, performance management systems, reward systems, incentive schemes, and mechanisms for identifying and fulfilling training needs are crucial to successfully securing the best employees. It is also important to keep in mind the complex legal responsibilities an organisation has to its employees, as well as remuneration and benefits policies, industrial relations matters, and occupational health and safety management.

Job analysis and design

The starting point of developing a human resource management system is to analyse the job tasks that need to be completed and create the appropriate job descriptions to fulfil those duties. When completing a job analysis of tasks to be completed, considerations must be given to the current organisational structure and the other work activities that will be affected by a new hire. Through this process it is determined if other changes to the organisation need to be made, including shifting responsibilities of other employees; job tasks are assigned to groups; a title is given to the position; and organisational charts are modified.

This is followed by the development of a job description, which will list all of the job responsibilities and candidate competencies inherent to the position. These may include the commitment required in hours per week/weeks per year, salary, job summary, expected education and experience, contact information or method for applying, general information about the organisation, and any legal requirements or government standards required for job postings. This job description not only articulates the roles and responsibilities inherent to a position, but is also used as a job announcement for recruitment of new personnel.

Recruitment and selection

The recruitment and selection of appropriate personnel with suitable experience and qualifications will help the facility to fulfil its objectives. Recruitment, as a process, begins with identifying the organisation's human resource needs, and ends with the receipt of applications. It is at this point that the process of selection commences.

Once the job has been identified and defined, the decision needs to be taken as to whether internal or external recruitment is appropriate. It is important to note that some geographic regions and specific industries will be subject to laws regarding accepted procedures for internal and external recruitment. Internal transfer and promotion can offer a number of advantages, including lower recruitment costs, intimate knowledge of the employee's work capacity, reduced orientation needs, and improved morale among existing staff. It should be noted that internal recruitment can bring disadvantages, such as the promotion of personnel beyond their maximal capacity, limited opportunity to introduce new perspectives and skills, and the potential for conflict among existing employees applying for the position. In the case of sporting events, it is common industry practice to 'event-hop'. For example, numerous professionals who worked for the Organizing Committee for the London 2012 Olympic and Paralympic Games were subsequently recruited by the Glasgow 2014 Commonwealth Games organisers. Some of those employees will have moved directly to the Rio 2016 Olympic Games – and will continue on with the Winter or Summer Olympic Games upcoming in PyeongChang in 2018, Tokyo in 2020, and Beijing in 2022, or Commonwealth Games in the Gold Coast in 2018 or Durban in 2022.

In the case of a new facility, the option to recruit staff internally does not usually exist at this point. Recruiting from external sources may therefore be necessary, bringing with it different advantages and disadvantages. The new sport facility may go about recruiting externally through a number of different mechanisms, including advertising, employment services, recruitment consultants, and search firms.

The selection of appropriate employees cuts training needs, and there is a reduced likelihood of turnover and other problems as job dissatisfaction, absenteeism, and poor performance. Good selection practice is more likely to occur when relevant legislation has been observed (e.g. equal opportunity and affirmative action laws), the right match of the job description to the job specifications has been identified, and a selection policy clearly outlines a systematic selection process. The selection process should clearly outline the role of participants in the decision-making process, such as management, human resource personnel, and external consultants. It should also overview the selection steps and techniques to be used, such as screening mechanisms, type of interview, use of psychological and aptitude tests, and background investigations.

Identifying and fulfilling orientation, training, and development needs

The orientation, training and development function of the human resource programme plays a vital role in improving organisational performance, and in enhancing the career development of individuals. In order to fulfil these roles, it is vital that the programme be aligned with the organisational objectives and with employee performance through the performance management system. In this way, the corporate goals of the facility are supported, and the behaviours required of individuals to achieve them are facilitated.

Orientation is the first step for integrating new employees into the organisation. During this process, further human resource processes are discussed, organisational culture is explained, specifics about the role of the new employee in the organisation are covered, and a foundation of knowledge is developed to integrate them into the working environment.

Training is the specialised or extensive education an employee receives related to their job responsibilities. The level of training will often depend on the level of education and experience of the new employee. Training should also be a continuous process throughout the time of employment to ensure continued growth of the individual and the organisation. Training often takes the form of development programmes such as seminars, conferences, or even classes offered at a local university.

To ensure a cost-effective and successful training programme, a systematic approach should be taken. This should involve the logical steps of needs analysis, programme development and implementation (see Figure 5.1), and finally evaluation (Stone, 2013).

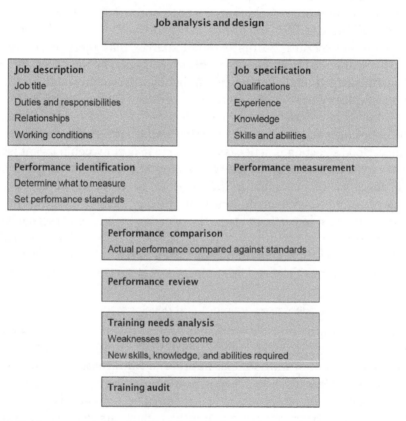

Figure 5.1 Performance appraisal and training needs

Source: Adapted from Stone (2013)

Preparing the facility management infrastructure

A needs analysis should determine the specific training needs of the organi-sation, including the specific skills or knowledge, where in the organisational structure these are required, and who requires them. Stone (2013) suggests an 'organisation, task, and person' model for evaluating training needs. The internal environment of the organisation, including its culture and overall objectives, will influence the kinds of skills and knowledge that are required of and considered appropriate for employees. In addition, the external envi-ronment of the organisation may indicate the need for training through legal, social, or technological changes.

The 'task' component of Stone's 'organisation, task, and person' model indicates the skills and abilities required by the incumbent or potential employee. The pro-cess of job analysis and design, indicated in the section 'recruitment and selection', will contribute to an under- standing of task components and competencies. Finally, the 'person' variable of the model indicates how an employee is actually perform-ing the job requirements. The outcome of evaluating each of the 'organisation', 'task', and 'person' variables should be a comprehensive set of behavioural objec-tives for the training effort. Behavioural objectives are clearly stated goals that can be measured. A comprehensive behavioural goal will include a series of elements, as depicted in Table 5.2.

It is evident from Table 5.2 that the training programme will flow logically from a clear set of objectives. Also, the development and delivery of the training pro-gramme should consider not only the content required but the methods and learning principles to be employed.

Finally, the effectiveness of the training programme should be evaluated. Evaluation may determine whether knowledge was learned, skills were gained, and job performance was improved. The programme can be further evaluated to determine whether the attainment of the skills and knowledge translated into the realisation of organisational objectives.

Table 5.2 Elements of behavioural objectives for training programmes

Who:	Indicating the personnel who will be receiving the training programme.
Given what:	An outline of what will be delivered in the programme, including content, learning principles and tools, motivation tools, and assessments.
Does what:	A statement indicating what the person(s) receiving training will be able to do on completion of the programme.
How well:	An indication of how the performance of the person(s) receiving training can be measured after the programme to determine if it has been successful. This may include completion of a knowledge test, or ability to perform a task to a specified standard.
By when:	Indicating the timeline of the programme.

Performance management can be defined as a set of processes for measuring, assessing, and providing feedback on the progress of individuals and the organisation towards stated objectives. Measuring usually involved the development of metrics; assessing is the process of determining whether objectives are met within specific parameters, and feedback is provided in the form of performance reviews.

While a number of variables contributes to the success of a performance management system, the overall match between the system and the organisational objectives, as well as acceptance of the system by employees, are arguably the most pivotal. A performance management system is implemented to achieve objectives; therefore it is vital that this outcome contribute to the overall objectives of the organisation. Similarly, a programme is more likely to be successful if representatives of all levels of the organisation are involved in its design and implementation. Employees are more likely to participate in a system that they understand, and that offers positive outcomes for both themselves and the organisation. As a result, successful performance management systems contribute to employee development and career management, in addition to succession planning. This process becomes more complex in event organisations that are characterised by relatively short-term committed staff in combination with a high percentage of part-time and sessional employees.

The focal point of the performance management system is the appraisal. Appraisals are conducted by collecting data that evaluates performance in terms of specific metrics. It is important that this evaluation is free from bias due to personality differences or differences of opinions. The ultimate goal is to use an appraisal as a developmental and growth tool for the employees rather than as a punishment – although the result may result in sanctioning for poor performance. Also to be considered is how the performance of the employee has helped and will continue to help the organisation move forward towards reaching its vision.

Generally, the results of the appraisal results in one of four actions: (1) rewards, (2) compensation, (3) incentives, and sometimes (4) termination. The reward system within an organisation is concerned with facilitating its desired outcomes through positive reinforcement. Remuneration is a key element of the package, but other factors may play a role, such as recognition, opportunities for participation and challenge, professional development, and career progression. Employee remuneration is an essential organisational function that not only underlines the values of the organisation but can also help fulfil its objectives (Stone, 2013). The remuneration system, for instance, can reward high levels of job performance, facilitate employee satisfaction, and reward desired behaviours and ideas including service innovations. Not only is remuneration a key feature of the overall reward and performance management systems, it can also be used to leverage change and to reward desired outcomes.

Compensation objectives should be established after careful consideration of the overall objectives of the organisation and of the human resource function. Compensation objectives may be to observe legislative requirements, attract and retain a core of quality staff, motivate employees towards improved performance, provide fair and reasonable compensation, remain competitive within the industry, and ensure an appropriate level of return on investment (Stone, 2013). In the sport, entertainment, and event industries, it has been quite common to be paid considerably less for the same or similar work than in other industries. Part of the reason for this is the inherent attractiveness of working in the major sporting event industry. Many people are willing to give up financial rewards and trade them in for the privilege of being part of, and hence associated with, high-profile, exposure-generating events and their stars. In other words, to be working in the sport event industry for many people is a reward in itself, which to a certain extent compensates for being paid less money.

The most basic compensation an employee will receive is a raise in base salary or basic pay, which many times is accompanied by a promotion to a higher position. In addition, additional employee benefits must be provided by law, including minimum levels of superannuation, leave entitlements, worker's compensation cover, and smoke-free work environments (depending on the legislation relevant to different countries and industries). Other monetary rewards may include bonuses/additional commissions, long-term incentives (such as pensions), equity in the organisation, and profit sharing. Other incentives may be considered at the discretion of the employer, guided by the objectives and philosophy of the organisation, such as fringe benefits, childcare, healthcare insurance, life and permanent disability insurance, and employee assistance programmes such as counselling. Again it can be noted that employee access to valuable tickets for high-profile events can significantly contribute to a sport facility employer being favoured by high-quality staff. Overall, these employee benefits form a significant component of the organisation's overall compensation costs and require specialised human resource skills and knowledge to administer.

It is important to remember that not all appraisals end up with a positive result. Poor performance appraisals can lead to the termination of an employee. It is important prior to terminating an employee that all appraisal documentation has been reviewed, all efforts have been made to remedy any deficiencies in performance, and all legal considerations have been taken into account. Again it is important that the termination is based on the facts of the appraisals and not the character or personality of the individual. Termination processes are very uncomfortable times, and no matter how uncomfortable all facts must be stated and provided in writing to the employee. Also at this time it is often the case the human resource officer or supervisor will need to collect keys and access cards, disable passwords, and have security accompany the employee to their office to collect their personal belongings.

Legal responsibilities

The aforementioned legal considerations related to terminating an employee are only a small percentage of the legal responsibilities inherent to human resource management. All aspects of managing the human infrastructure of a sport facility are now moderated by a complex system of legislation, different in every country or state. It is obviously beyond the scope of this book to detail the specific legal obligations of organisations in every state, region, and nation of the world. It is useful to emphasise, however, that legal obligations for the employer are complex. This complexity stems, in part, from the number of different sources from which legal obligations are documented, in addition to the relevant documents' size, density, and legal terminology. Once again this underlines the imperative to hire qualified human resource professionals to ensure that breaches of legislation do not arise from ignorance.

As mentioned, the legal obligations of employers come from a range of different sources. These can include common law precedent arising from court judgements of specific cases, as well as statutory law generated in both federal and state parliamentary forums (Stone, 2013). National and state awards outlining the obligations of employees are also common, and usually include conditions such as minimum pay, hours of work, types of leave, and appropriate termination processes. These awards may be generated and reviewed by industrial relations tribunals. In addition to these sources, employer obligations can be outlined in the contract of employment, and through enterprise bargaining mechanisms in certain countries.

Other aspects of employment that may be regulated by legislation include personal income tax; payroll or company tax; goods and services taxes; occupational health and safety; equal opportunity, antidiscrimination, and sexual harassment protections; superannuation requirements; maternity and paternity leave; annual leave; and long-service leave. Behavioural objectives are clearly stated goals that can be measured. A comprehensive behavioural goal will include a series of elements, as depicted earlier in Table 5.2.

Industrial relations

The term 'industrial relations' refers to the relationship between employers and employees conducted via their representative unions. Many times these interactions are mediated by an industrial relations court or tribunal. The function of industrial relations tribunals is not only to encourage observance of relevant legislation but also to arbitrate disputes that may in turn generate new or altered legislative requirements. Generally, negotiations centre on such items as rates of pay, hours of work, penalty rates, suspension and termination procedures, disciplinary procedures, leave entitlements, special allowances, and other employment conditions. Although the nature of union presence varies from country to country, as well as between industries, union influence is probably more significant in most Western and first and second world nations, and particularly in large organisations and industries. The need to accommodate union presence in employee negotiations is likely to be critical to the success of the day-to-day running of a sporting facility.

There are a number of different formats that direct industrial relations negotiations may take. These may include consent award, over-award, and collective bargaining negotiations (Stone, 2013). Consent award negotiations occur when the employer and union negotiate directly with one another and reach agreement within parameters set by the relevant government industrial relations body. Over-award negotiations occur when unions attempt to negotiate directly with employers to exceed the pay rates and conditions set down in an award, on the understanding that awards set a minimum rather than a maximum requirement. Collective bargaining can take many forms, but essentially refers to employer–union negotiation on all issues of employer–employee relations.

Given the reality of and complexity in industrial relations issues, the sport facility must have access to human resource expertise. It is the role of the human resource manager or consultant to fully understand the legal obligations of the facility and to manage industrial relations negotiations.

Occupational health and safety (OH&S)

Managing the complex occupational health and safety (OH&S) needs of an organisation is fundamental to providing employees (Nankervis et al., 2011), and indeed customers, with physical and emotional security. Today, organisations must negotiate a complex array of legislation in order to understand their obligations and establish appropriate policies and procedures.

Potential occupational hazards include both physical and psychological considerations, and can encompass a range of hazards:

- **Physical hazards:** thermal stress, noise, vibration, ultraviolet radiation, fire, electrical and machinery hazards; work practices arising from problems with manual handling, ergonomic, and overuse problems.
- **Chemical hazards:** poisons, toxins, corrosive substances, irritants, sensitisers, explosive/flammable materials, and asphyxiates.
- **Biological hazards:** animal and plant material containing micro-organisms such as viruses, bacteria, and fungi.
- **Psychological hazards:** cultural, interpersonal, and organisational factors, as well as work practices.

In order to effectively manage the risks presented by these factors, a comprehensive policy and procedure system is required. Generally, the occupational health and safety policy should identify the following information:

- General policy statement

  - Duties and responsibilities of employer and employees
  - Declaration of employer's intention regarding provision of safe and healthy working conditions
  - Indication of commitment to consultation with employees, consultation of experts
  - Relevant legislation for state/country
  - Compliance of policies and procedures with legislation.

- Mechanisms for risk analysis

  - Indicating consultative processes with employees
  - Indicating provisions for consulting experts
  - Indicating consultation with relevant government agencies and other pertinent sources of information
  - Use of appropriate audit tools.

- Allocation of responsibilities

  - Indicating clear lines of communication
  - Defining roles and accountability of management structure
  - Indicating means for allocation of human and financial resources
  - Indicating means of determining OHS priorities.

- Statement of procedures

  - Provision of information and training
  - Dealing with problem areas
  - Effective inspection and maintenance of facilities and equipment
  - Managing introduction of new facilities, machinery, equipment, substances, and processes
  - Dealing with identified hazards
  - Ensuring safe systems and methods of work.

- Mechanisms for monitoring evaluation

  - Indicating how and by whom policy and procedures are to be monitored
  - Indicating mechanisms and responsibility for evaluation.

BEYOND ORGANISATIONAL AND HUMAN RESOURCE MANAGEMENT

While the organisational structure and human resource planning are focal points of preparing the facility management infrastructure, there are numerous other factors that affect the development of it. Many of those processes are embedded across multiple chapters in this book, as the facility management infrastructure development process is continuous and dynamic. However, there are two areas of special note to mention in this chapter – fiscal management and the decision-making/problem-solving process.

Fiscal management

Fiscal management within the organisational infrastructure focuses on the areas of accounting, finance, and economics. Accounting is the function related to the recording, summarising, analysing, and reporting of financial transactions through balance sheets, income/profit and loss statements, statements of owner's equity/retained earnings, statements of cash flows, and budgets. Finance is the process of money management through the allocation of assets and liabilities via investments, in order to improve the financial position of the organisation in terms of profitability, leverage, activity, and liquidity. Economics focuses on the process of utilising scarce resources to drive the production, distribution, and consumption of products and services.

When considering a sport facility and its operational infrastructure, two main topics of focus must be considered. The first is operational budgeting, which focuses on estimating expected income and expenses over a specific period of time in the future. In other words, in consideration of the assets, liabilities, retained earnings, revenues, and expenses of an organisation, how do we forecast the financial operation of the business? Budgets are maintained and managed on a daily, weekly, monthly, quarterly, and annual basis – in other words always and continuously. The ability to project accurately the revenue and expenses related to how many people will come into the sport facility (admissions), how many memberships are sold, how much will be made on selling product and services such as merchandise or food, and what are the costs related to earning this revenue (cost of goods sold, salaries of employees, utilities expenses, etc.) is a crucial skill for any manager.

The second is capital investment appraisal – a unique type of budgeting process that involves planning for the short- and long-term investments needed to make capital expenditures on fixed assets such as sport facilities. To break this down a bit further, capital is the net worth of a business in terms of investments of the owners in a business and the profits that are retained by the organisation. Capital investment is the money invested in fixed (or long-term) assets that help further the business objectives over time. Capital investment appraisal is the planning process involved to maximise capital and make the most appropriate capital investments to meet the strategic objectives and vision of the organisation.

Decision-making and problem-solving

Ultimately, everything that is important to preparing the facility management infrastructure comes down to making the right decisions and solving problems in an efficient manner. In terms of decision-making, managers have to balance making programmed decisions based on precedent, policies, or experiences – and non-programmed decisions that have no guidelines. Regardless of the decisions to be made, there are challenges inherent to the process. Some decisions are easily made because of certainty of the manager due to being fully aware of all alternatives and benefits – and a best decision is evident. Others are rather risky because of only having partial information or not knowing all the benefits or consequences of a decision. Then there are decisions based on uncertainty, where there is no basis for a decision and there is no clarity on whether outcomes can be met. Regardless of decisions to be made, while some often have to be made ultimately by one person, the best organisational decisions are made with guidance from groups of pooled talent so that a wider range of knowledge and intelligence can be utilised to implement the best decision.

Group guidance is even more important with regard to problem-solving. While many decisions are about the functioning of the organisation and its infrastructure, many times it involves determining the best plan of attack to overcome a deficiency. Perhaps the best way to describe this in contrast to decision making is that problem-solving is an intuitive process, whereas decision-making is an action process. Hence problem-solving is a very systematic process that requires excellent critical thinking skills. There is a need, through critical thinking, to make clear, reasoned, and unbiased judgements by synthesising and evaluating information and choosing the best course of action. In addition to this intuitive process, there is also a need for quality communication amongst members of the problem-solving team so that the information exchange is clear, truthful, respectful, and non-confrontational. It is important to remember that ultimately the goal of problem-solving and the associated decision-making process is to enhance the facility management infrastructure.

SUMMARY

The structure and processes of managing organisations have changed significantly over the past few decades. The hierarchical model of management has ceased to be the overriding determinant of organisational functioning and has moved towards being one element in the mix. In recent years, there has been a shift suggesting that organisations are able to perform more responsively and competitively when structures are more synergistic, organised around project teams, and when decision making is decentralised. Processes that enable networking, and that empower employees to develop relationships, take risks and innovate, are processes that encourage contemporary organisations to flourish. It has also been observed that organisations today are seeking to develop strategic alliances with other organisations in order to leverage resource utilisation, and to collaborate closely with suppliers to which non-core services are outsourced.

The organisational configuration that is established for a sporting facility will influence the subsequent human resources profile. All functional areas of a facility require specific staffing expertise at the executive, administrative, supervisory, and general staff levels. General functional divisions include executive, administration, finance, human resources, maintenance, cleaning/custodial, catering/food service, security, programme delivery, ancillary customer services (box office, merchandising), event management, and marketing. The mode of delivery for these services may vary from permanent to casual, from full-time to part-time, and, importantly for the sport sector, from employees to volunteers. In addition, the organisational philosophy may support outsourcing of certain functions, on a contract or consultation basis. Given the delicate balance of advantages and disadvantages afforded by outsourcing, current thinking suggests that it is most appropriate for non-core activities.

Managing the human resource infrastructure of a sport facility requires a comprehensive and strategic human resource programme. This starts with a process of analysing the tasks that need to be completed, configuring them into a position, and creating a position description. From that point forward, the processes that need to be managed include recruitment and selection procedures; orientation, training, and development programmes; retention policies, performance review systems, and incentive-based reward schemes. Further, the human resource infrastructure must be able to negotiate a complex array of legal obligations, industrial relations interactions, and occupational health and safety regulations.

Beyond organisational structure and human resource planning, there are other factors that affect the development of facility management infrastructure. Fiscal management and the understanding of accounting, finance, and economics are crucial for managing the operational and capital budgetary processes that help maintain and advance the overall facility infrastructure. In addition, being able to intuitively solve problems and act to make decisions that will move the organisational infrastructure forward toward attaining the strategic objectives and vision are integral to the overall facility management process.

CASE STUDY

Outsourcing facility and event management operations and services: Comcast Spectacor

Spectra is the evolution of over 40 years of facility and event management of Comcast Spectacor Chairman Ed Snider. Comcast Spectacor, based in Philadelphia, USA, has been involved with sport team ownership, facility design and management, event production, broadcasting, food services, and ticketing.

Comcast Spectacor has a large portfolio of sport properties and business, including ownership of the Philadelphia Flyers of the National Hockey league (NHL) and the Wells Fargo Center in Philadelphia. The company formerly owned the Philadelphia 76ers of the National Basketball Association (NBA) and a regional sports network that has since been sold the NBC Universal.

On the operations side, three of its best-known divisions are Global Spectrum, Ovations, and Paciolan. Global Spectrum is the venue management arm of the company – providing event booking, management, marketing, and operations services to over 500 arenas, civic centres, convention centres, equestrian centres, ice facilities, stadiums, and theatres around the world. In addition, they provide event production services for international conventions and trade shows, as well as design and consulting services to new facilities.

Ovations Food Services is the food service and hospitality side of the business, contracting food, beverage, and hospitality services to many sport and recreation facilities across North America. The range of services provided varies from concessions (both food service and merchandising management) within facilities, to specialised hospitality offerings ranging from banquets and sit down dinners to corporate outings.

Paciolan focuses on ticketing and fan engagement, offering services including ticketing services, technological solutions, marketing and analytics, and fundraising. Paciolan's software offers multiple solutions to make it easier for customers to reserve, purchase, and re-sell tickets, as well as on-site technology that makes the purchase of merchandise and concessions easier through bar-code and pay-wave technologies.

In 2015, Comcast Spectacor decided to bring all three divisions under one umbrella brand called Spectra. The goal of this merging of capabilities under one brand was to be able to bring full-service management and operations experience across all operational areas to all of their clients rather than having to deal with each division independently.

Questions

1   What are the pros and cons of outsourcing services to Spectra if you were the owner of a 25,000-seat downtown arena or stadium?
2   What are the benefits and disadvantages of contracting with a full-service company such as Spectra vs. being able to work with individual smaller division such as Global Spectrum, Ovations, or Paciolan?
3   Two of the other major facility management companies worldwide are SMG and AEG. Assume you are the owner of a new 100,000 seat stadium expected to host major sporting events ranging from professional football to mega-events such as the Super Bowl or the Olympics. Evaluate each of the three companies and justify which you would hire as the management company for your stadium.

REFERENCES

Bartlett, C.A., & Ghoshal, S. (1995). Changing the role of top management: Beyond systems to people. *Harvard Business Review, 73*(3), 132–142.

Bulander, R., & Dietel, M. (2013). The consideration of organizational, human and corporate cultural factors in the implementation of business process management projects: Social factors to prevent failure of BPM projects. In *e-Business (ICE-B), 10th International Conference on E-Business* (pp. 1–9). IEEE.

Culver, E.M. (2014). The *Canadian Ski Patrol: Probing the potential for change*. Doctoral dissertation, Royal Roads University.

Daft, R. (2012). *Organization theory and design*. 11th edition. Boston: Cengage Learning.

Graetz, F., & Smith, A.C.T. (2010). Managing organizational change: A philosophies of change approach. *Journal of Change Management, 10*(2), 135–154.

Kanter, R.M. (1996). Beyond the cowboy and the corpocrat. In K. Starkey (Ed.), *How Organizations Learn*. International Thomson Business Press, London. pp. 43–59.

Nankervis, A., Compton, R., Baird, M., & Coffey, J. (2011). *Human resources management: Strategy and practice*. 7th edition. Sydney: Cengage Learning.

Öberg, C., Adams, R., & Alexander, A. (2014). Innovation management capabilities in the creative sector. In *ISPIM, June 8–11 2014, Dublin, Ireland*. Retrieved from https://www.researchgate.net/profile/Richard_Adams8/publication/264552963_Innovation_management_capabilities_in_the_creative_sector/links/53e5c6c70cf25d674e9c2b61.pdf

Shen, W., Hao, Q., & Xue, Y. (2012). A loosely coupled system integration approach for decision support in facility management and maintenance. *Automation in Construction, 25*, 41–48.

Stone, R.J. (2013). *Human resource management*. 8th edition. Milton, Queensland: John Wiley & Sons Australia.

Tidd, J., & Bessant, J. (2009). Managing *innovation: Integrating technological, market, and organizational change*. Chichester, England: John Wiley & Sons.

Whittington, R., Pettigrew, A., Peck, S., Fenton, E., & Conyon, M. (1999). Change and complementarities in the new competitive landscape: A European panel study, 1992–1996. *Organization Science, 10*(5), 583–600.

CHAPTER 6

NEW SPORT FACILITY OPERATIONS: ATTRACTING EVENTS

CHAPTER OBJECTIVES

In this chapter we will:

■ Present event application goals.
■ Outline the involvement of the facility and event manager in attracting events.
■ Identify the distinguishing features of the bid process.

- Consider the requirements of a bid application document.
- Develop the management lifecycle phases of a sport facilities and events from the perspective of the initial bid through to the evaluation of that bid.
- Identify network relationships between key actors in the event application process.

INTRODUCTION

Attracting events to a host location has become a major undertaking for host townships, cities, regions, and countries. Whether these events have a sporting, cultural, or arts theme, there is a strong emphasis by bid committees to seek to integrate these events into the community. The reasons for this are many and varied, ranging from the generation of a significant economic upturn, enhanced employment opportunities, and infrastructure development, through to an increase in tourist visitations that can accompany these events. While these more economically driven outcomes are considered important in hosting events, increasing emphasis is being placed on the social and environmental outcomes connected to events. These additional impacts provide community benefits such as programmes to aid sport participation and development as well as providing cleaner and user-friendly spaces for communities. Further to these benefits, many influential and interested parties from political figures and community members through to major corporate interests see benefits from associating themselves with events.

The attraction of major events to a community involves key stakeholder groups, from the sport governing body, the facility manager, relevant community interest groups, the media, politicians, government departments, and the building and construction industry, to name a few of the organisations involved. No individual or group in the community remains unaffected by the intrusion that these events bring. Understanding the how and why of attracting events into a community is of immense value to all the people involved.

This chapter discusses the attraction of sport events, from the perspective of the attraction to the community and the sport facility, with an emphasis on the event bid process. Identification of network relationships is included with a focus on the event owner and the facility. While events can range in size and prestige, an event host will seek to maximise the existing infrastructure, people, and support structures available. The impact of an event on supporting the facility, as well as the local community, can be determined in a range of economic, social, and environmental outcomes. Focusing on the major participants involved in the attraction process forms the basis of this chapter.

141

ATTRACTING EVENTS FOR GOOD OR FOR BAD

The attraction of events can be developed from the perspective of the community (comprising the country, region or city), and from the perspective of the actual facility itself. A facility must attract events in order to remain a viable and profitable business entity in its own right. The community attracts events in order to generate economic turnover, tourism, and interest in the region. The types of events that are attracted by both community and facility groups can vary in their size, structure, and global importance.

Events can extend to a broad range of activities from sporting fixtures through to unique cultural performances or even national celebrations. This broad definition of what constitutes an event was described by Getz (1997, p. 4), who referred to events by their context as 'one-time or infrequently occurring event outside normal programmes or activities of the sponsoring or organizing body', or alternatively from the point of view of the event organiser or customer as 'the opportunity for a leisure, social or cultural experience outside the normal range of choices beyond everyday experience'.

Events have further been categorised according to their size and scale (Bowdin et al., 1999), with common categories referring to events as mega-events, hallmark events, major events, and local events. Size and scale tend to be associated with importance and therefore tend to be aligned with major international events such as the Olympic Games (Getz et al., 2012). While size and scale are important factors in the mega or hallmark event categorisation, Getz et al. (2012, p. 50) indicated that 'even a small music festival can have "mega" impacts on a small town in terms of tourists, economic benefits or disruption'. The impacts of media coverage, image, tourism, prestige, and economic impact on the local community all have some bearing regardless of size, and while hallmark events can be large, they are often differentiated from 'mega-events', as most mega-events are one-time only (Getz et al., 2012). As a result, size is variable and not always the defining characteristic of an event. This is often true in terms of the iconic nature of certain events, as they may be of greater significance because they have gained mythic status within a culture; or they continuously attract media attention and enter into the realm of the popular (Getz et al., 2012).

Richards and Rotariu (2015, p. 90) focused on the alignment of cities in capturing events, referring to the contemporary 'eventful city'. They indicate that an eventful city does not just harness events to achieve economic, social, and cultural policy goals, but also manage a portfolio of events in order to maximise outputs and improve the effectiveness of event processes. As such, an eventful city can be defined as one that 'purposefully uses a program of events to strategically and sustainably support long-term policy agendas that enhance the quality of life for all' (Richards & Rotariu, 2015, p. 91).

The emphasis on major events generally is seen as a positive opportunity for a host community, bringing economic, tourism, social, and environmental benefits. While the focus on events tends to be positive, the hosting of major events has not been without some negative attention. The 1984 Summer Olympic Games was awarded to the only host city that applied, Los Angeles. Much of the negativity associated with hosting an event such as the Olympic Games at the time was as a result of the perilous financial state that Montreal saw itself plummet into as a result of hosting the 1976 Games. Even in 1999, the situation of attracting a host city for a major sporting event saw Melbourne emerge from a possible three-host city contest, to become ultimately the only city left standing in its bid to host the 2006 Commonwealth Games. The Australian Formula One Grand Prix has been plagued with a level of community negativity around the costs, location, and environmental disturbance for all of the 20 years that it has been held. Added to this is the impact of corrupt and improper bidding practices that have plagued the IOC, FIFA, and the governments of bidding countries around the world for a considerable period of the 2000s. There are significant economic, political, technical, and social consequences associated with bidding for and ultimately hosting major events. These consequences impact on a broad range of community groups that ultimately affect the capacity for an application to host major events to proceed, and must therefore be part of the event bid considerations made.

ATTRACTING EVENTS INTO THE COMMUNITY

Attracting events to a country, city, or region reflects a conscious planning process whereby specific rituals, presentations, performances, or celebrations are conducted to mark special occasions or achieve particular social, cultural, government, or corporate goals. While being iconic has been identified as being important, Getz et al. (2012) also refer to reputation as a key feature for attracting events. Reputation may need to be fostered over a longer period of time to be achieved, therefore requiring some permanence and tradition to be established. While a one-off mega-event such as the FIFA World Cup brings its own reputation with it, permanence and repeatability may be required by a hallmark event. Many hallmark events may require possession or access to permanent facilities, thereby garnering full support of the entire community (Getz et al., 2012). Hallmark events shift towards being 'iconic', either in terms of overall destination branding, community place identity, or social-world relevance (Getz et al., 2012).

An iconic event suggests attractiveness. 'Attractiveness' refers to the relative strength of attractions, which could reflect the number of people attending, the geographic spread of the market area, or its appeal compared to the competition (Getz et al., 2012). Having a sense of attractiveness will likely lead to a higher degree of attraction towards an event to various stakeholders ranging from public and private interests, venue operators, small business owners, politicians, media, and the general public.

In terms of attractiveness, Getz et al. (2012) introduced a 'Hallmark Event model' that developed goals and a planning process around hallmark events. While these authors applied this process towards hallmark events (which they defined as being iconic and continual) rather than being applied to all mega (one-off) events, the process has been adjusted here to apply to events within their broadest context. The emphasis is on the goals of attracting an event being applicable across a community. The outcomes identified by Getz et al. (2012) have been collected from a range of tables and identifiable comments and grouped together and customised for the purpose of identification in Table 6.1.

As a primary feature of this chapter is 'attracting events', the first aspect identified highlights attraction goals. These are viewed predominantly around attracting people. While Getz et al. (2012) refer to this attraction as often being built around tourism, the attractiveness to a wide range of people from a wide range of international and local communities is considered here. The emphasis on attraction extends towards developing an attractive and unique theme (A-1), which offers wide appeal, but within parameters of attraction to specific segments and groups. The event should be iconic (A-2) or have the potential to become iconic over time, ensuring people view it as a significant moment on their events calendar. The setting (A-3) for the conduct of the event(s) should be both appealing and functional, with infrastructure upgrades or reviews especially around venues (indoor and outdoor). Finally, the event should be of the highest possible quality/standard (A-4) achievable for the benefit of the community.

Image and branding goals relate to developing an iconic brand identity for the city or community and this can be achieved through positive media coverage (I-1), which highlights the strength and appeal of the event and community that is hosting the event. Having strong media support and media partners (I-2) goes a long way towards supporting the development of brand identity, and this should be built with equity (I-3) co-branding of the event with the local community. At all times a positive image (I-4) should be managed and maintained, with the management of this image leading to the development of a strong reputation (I-5) for the host within the local and wider international communities.

Community goals should 'endeavor to align the "fit" of the event within the community in which it is held, in order to establish and sustain an event that will directly benefit and be supported by residents, effectively becoming a tradition and a permanent institution' (Getz et al., 2012, p. 59). The event should provide benefits to the community (C-1) in areas such as employment, entertainment, infrastructure development, and broader integration, while also enabling the community to become actively involved through participation and volunteerism (C-2).

Communities should not be negatively impacted upon (C-3) by the event through aspects such as poor tourist behaviours, increased violence, and parking or transportation bottlenecks. Communities should be aware and supportive of the political and regulatory (C-4) aspects associated with the event, including the flow of benefits (or costs) to the community through fully accountable practices (C-5).

The management of marketing functions associated with events is variable and changing, with input and expectations from a wide range of stakeholders. This often requires a high degree of relationship building across these stakeholder groups. Whatever the relationships, the adherence to a professional approach to marketing is of utmost importance. This approach includes an understanding of, and adherence towards, marketing mix principles (M-1) to incorporate all product, price, place, promotion, people, process, and physical evidence aspects. Constant improvement through quality control (M-2) systems is important to ensuring appropriate practices and outcomes can be achieved, and these control mechanisms should assist in building relationships (M-3) with customers and partner stakeholders. The marketing activities should be customer focused (M-4) with an ongoing emphasis on quality and improvement.

There is a strong public ownership associated with events, many sport organisations and event owners having a not-for-profit emphasis. Yet even with this emphasis, the case for strong business fundamentals is strong, and business activities and practices are crucial for success. This business focus requires investment from commercial (O-1) sources, but also must factor in non-commercial sources of investment. Investment from an array of stakeholders (O-2) is crucial in maximising outcomes in the shorter and longer term for the event. It also enhances a sense of pride and ownership by the stakeholders towards the event. An additional component associated with the investment of key stakeholders is a sense of professionalism (O-3) that this can introduce – which can also encourage and reward innovation (O-4) across design and management activities. Ownership and organisational goals are aligned with stakeholders and the supportive networks which arise.

It is not simply enough to just provide a commercial outcome, but the need to be 'green' and add to the social responsibilities within a community has emerged as a critical measure of success. This requires an adherence by the event towards sustainable event standards (S-1), and being socially responsible (S-2) through entering into a contract with the community to provide transparency and accountability of sustainable practices. Resources (S-3) need to be allocated towards social responsibility either as financial or business planning processes, and this includes the monitoring of all risk factors (S-4) which will adversely affect the event as well as the community. Environmental targets (S-5) need to be clearly articulated and the event must be able to cope with a rapidly changing environment (S-6).

Getz et al. (2012) believed that their model could serve as a guide to communities, tourism organisations, and event producers, in terms of guiding the entire planning

Table 6.1 Summary of broad event goals

Attraction goals	Image and branding goals	Community goals	Marketing goals	Organisation and ownership goals	Sustainability goals
To attract people (tourists)	Iconic brand identity	Community institution	Professional	Strong business model	Social/environmental responsibility
A-1: Develop attractive, unique theme	I-1: Positive media coverage	C-1: Community benefits	M-1: Manage marketing mix	O-1: Capital investment	S-1: Sustainable standards
A-2: Iconic event	I-2 Strong media partners	C-2: Volunteerism/participation	M-2: Quality control	O-2: Stakeholder investment	S-2: Socially responsible
A-3: Effective community setting (venues)	I-3: Brand equity	C-3: Negate negative impacts	M-3: Build relationships	O-3: Professionalism	S-3: Resources
A-4: High standards	I-4: Positive image	C-4: Political/regulatory approvals	M-4: Consumer orientation	O-4: Innovation	S-4: Risk assessment
	I-5: Strong reputation	C-5 Full accountability			S-5: Targets
					S-6: Manage change

Source: Adapted from Getz et al. (2012)

and implementation process for hallmark events. With some adaptation, there is some indication that this is in fact the case, and the model outlined in Table 6.1 has applicability across the whole event process. The six goals apply across all areas and in the attraction, implementation, and conclusion phases of all types of events.

ATTRACTING EVENTS TO THE FACILITY

The event attraction process encompasses a broad range of potential groups comprised of interested parties representing national interests, the city interests, political interests, media interests, venue interests, and sporting organisation interests, to name but a few. The involvement of these groups is instrumental (and influential) in the success associated with attracting events. However, one of the core groups associated with this process are sport facilities. Sport facilities are crucial in presenting infrastructure support for a bid, as well as contributing in a major way to the operational outcomes of the event. Therefore, the presentation of a substantial facility option as part of an event bid can only enhance the way in which the bid is received. Equally important to the facility being included as an infrastructure support dimension of a bid application is the fact that in certain cases the facility must also present itself on its own merits to be considered as a host venue for major events. So, on the one hand, an event organiser can include the facility as part of their infrastructure support message, while equally, a facility can actively seek out to attract events directly.

A facility is often referred to as an 'infrastructure asset' in many bid application documents used for attracting hallmark or mega-events. The facility in this regard should be featured in these bid documents, with the support of a formal contractual agreement in place. The bid may refer to the 'outstanding' facilities that exist within the city to highlight to the event owner the level of infrastructure in place. This process is especially integrated into the bid where the facility has some community or local government ownership or affiliation.

Including a facility in the bid application is a significant consideration. It is not as simplistic as an event organiser advising the event owner that all facility infrastructures in a particular city are available to them. There must be clearly defined agreements in place prior to the final submission of documentation. For example, Australia's World Cup bid document to FIFA clearly outlined that 'unilaterally executed Stadium Agreements have been provided by all 12 proposed stadiums' (FIFA, 2010, p. 13). While this was supported within the final bid documentation, gaining full access to all facilities had not been without its problems. The Federal Government had to step in to alleviate concerns from Australia's other major football codes that a World Cup would not impact their competitions. Hosting a World Cup in cities that have limited stadium availability during the main Australian Football League (AFL) and National Rugby League (NRL) seasons created much media speculation about how these other competitions would react. Given that FIFA requires specific stadium configurations and shutouts of other events in a city for lead-up and during the tournament, this would mean access to stadiums for 6–8 weeks of the year in the middle of normal competition period would be denied to these major Australian football codes. Added to this was the dimension that long-term contractual agreements existed between these leagues and their facilities, covering a multitude of contractual obligations by all parties (Hall, 2009).

The World Cup example clearly indicates that it is not as simple as identifying interest in capturing a major event. The agreement from multiple stakeholders must be sought out and confirmed before any agreement can be reached and a professional bid presented. As identified, this process extends to the bid team including the facility in the bid application, while also ensuring that the facility views the attraction of key events to the community as a key requirement. This example displays the way in which the facility manager can be inadvertently placed in a compromised position where there are demands from a wide range of stakeholder groups. Each group wants to ensure they maximise their outcomes, as does each respective football league governing body. The facility is attempting to maximise its attendance and support the event, but needs to be mindful that the football league organisation and clubs will be their ongoing future tenants, paying the rent and supporting sponsors and spectators for many years to come.

The arrival of a major event could well disrupt these fixtures, coupled with the effect on existing agreements and introduced obligations such as signage removal or relocation, or even the requirement for a removal of all signage resulting in a clean stadium (as is the case for the Olympic Games where there is no signage allowed in the stadium). Other issues can also arise with respect to existing members or season ticket holders, existing (or even conflicting) naming rights obligations between the stadium and the event, and existing catering and pouring (food and beverage) rights' obligations.

The requirement for a facility to ensure it has a regular set of scheduled competitions or events, often ensuring weekly obligations which can then be disrupted by the attraction of a once only specialised event, requires significant negotiation, goodwill, and support from all parties involved in the process. The event bidding team must ensure the support of the facility, which in turn needs to ensure that the staff are well informed and receptive to hosting a new event. The facility manager presents the facility favourably to all customers and visitors, while being adequately compensated for the new event. This is not always a simple operation and the outcomes can often require intense negotiation.

MULTIPURPOSE NATURE OF THE FACILITY

Stadia are increasingly incorporating multipurpose facilities and audience-friendly environments. As a result of the influx of a corporate and entertainment culture within the facility and the movement away from being purely a home ground for one particular team, facility managers are required to assume the role of successful capacity management strategists. Managing a weekly fixture list over the course of a structured league season is of vital importance to the facility manager. Increasingly important is managing the 'down time' or 'structural wastage' associated with a facility. These concepts will be discussed in greater detail in Chapter 7. The requirement to attract new customers to the facility, comprised of both spectators and event operators, places additional burdens on the facility manager. The ability to clean the facility for a completely new event to be held on the following day, removing or relocating signage, changing and adjusting flooring and seating, ticketing, and security, coupled with the multitude of operational issues hosting a variety of events introduces, brings a unique set of challenges to the facility manager.

Ensuring that the facility can present a sufficient case to be considered suitable to host events is a critical initial step in ensuring the success of an event. If the facility is presented as part of the city infrastructure during a bid application, then it must be in a position to be available to undertake this responsibility. The facility must also be in a position to support the bid fully and be physically and operationally able to meet the demands placed on it by staging the event. Equally, a facility manager may seek to bid for host events in the facility's own right, again being mindful of the total application process.

A critical role that is played by the facility in attracting events is to provide a clearly developed infrastructure framework. This infrastructure is vital in supporting the event bid team in convincing event owners that the city or country can meet the demands associated with hosting the event. Vital to the success of any event application process are facilities of a significant quality to meet the scrutiny of minimum standard (international or national level) tournament requirements. Facilities must be able to provide a suitable competition platform, which must include a playing surface of an appropriate standard, areas for participants and officials to prepare and warm-up, and the capacity to cater to a range of spectator and media needs.

Major sport stadia have moved from a simple 'home ground' for the local football team into a multipurpose facility offering a wide range of services. While some stadia have traditionally been offered as host to more than one sport, such as Australian sport ovals playing host to cricket in the summer months and football in the winter months, the context has become far more encompassing in the modern stadiums. While by no means alone in stadium development, Stamford Bridge, the long-term home of Chelsea Football Club, offers experiences beyond fan attendance at a football game once or twice per week. On-site restaurants, hotel accommodation, tours, fan shop, and museum are all part of the services available for people, whether fans or not, at any time of the day (Chelseafc, 2016). Most major facilities are adding facilities that can open up the business well beyond the traditional match-day offering. These new stadia are also being configured to allow for concerts and other events beyond their purpose-built activities.

CONCEPTUALISING THE EVENT APPLICATION PROCESS

Much of the existing information available on the value of hosting hallmark events has focused on the staging of the event and the post-event analysis. There has been limited insight into the preparation of a bid and the submission of the bid documents. Information available in these areas mainly focuses on technical requirements, such as location, equipment, facilities, and personnel. The underlying factors that improve a bid organisation's chance of securing an event, such as community support, the support of media, and the formation of relationships have been largely neglected in the literature.

A successful bid is one which addresses the technical (facilities, budget, location), support (personnel, transport, accommodation), and cultural (entertainment, television, ceremonies) elements (Wilkinson, 1988). The International Olympic Committee (IOC) has a number of criteria for the bidding process which include controlled lobbying, evidence of government and community support for a bid, and a wide range of candidature documents which highlight the technical capabilities to stage the event. These elements are in turn supported by a visual presentation. The process of bidding to host the Olympic Games is presented in detail in the section on bid application documents later in this chapter.

Given that the limited research available stresses the need for technical competency in a successful event bid, an important question arises. If two bids are identical in technical aspects, how does one city succeed over another in gaining the rights to stage the event? It appears that there are other factors beyond the purely technical components that play a critical role in the selection process. Events must reach across a range of sporting, business, or cultural fields in terms of their potential attractiveness in order to be successful.

BIDDING CONSIDERATIONS

There are a number of important criteria that need to be considered when bidding for major events. For a bid to be considered, these criteria, as identified by the event owners, must be met. Many event owners, such as the IOC, have specific guidelines which must be adhered to by the bid committee as part of lodging a bid. There is a limited supply of hallmark-status events that exist, while the demand for events worldwide has increased.

For every bid there are a variety of considerations perceived as being an important part of the bidding process. Westerbeek, Turner, and Ingerson (2002) developed key success factors for bid teams. These key factors are listed as:

■ **Accountability** presents the reputation, legacy components, technical expertise, and facilities of a host city. Event bidding organisations are accountable to the public in relation to the need to show where tax money has been spent and how the local community will benefit from the event being held in their city.

- **Political support** offers the stability and economic contribution, as well as government support for a city. Political support is important from the perspective of securing vital resources (financial, physical, human resources), as well as the political and financial stability of the city and country in relation to the formulation of (longer-term) policies of government that will clearly contribute to the quality of the event. Economic contribution is also important in convincing stakeholders to host the event.
- **Relationship marketing** creates key relationships, whether political or event decision-oriented, in support of the event. Building relations is supported by general relationship marketing theory, which maintains that building and enhancing interactions with key stakeholders (decision makers) can develop long-term satisfaction and mutually beneficial partnerships. Aligned with this relationship marketing process is the capacity to build brand equity.
- **Ability** provides the sport-specific technical expertise, equipment, and event capabilities of the bid team. Sport-specific technical expertise, the event management (administration) expertise, the event equipment available, and the ability of the event organisers to fund the event (public and private) are all base requirements that directly relate to the actual event being hosted.
- **Infrastructure** provides the accessibility, transportation, and community support for the event. A well-integrated infrastructure plan can reduce costs, improve spectator and athlete convenience for staging events, and provide long-term benefits for the community after the event has gone. Attention to the infrastructure requirements of an event enables the event organiser to convince the event promoter that the event host has the capacity to successfully host the event personnel and competition activities.
- **Bid team composition** offers the level of support, mix of personnel, and selling capacity of bid team officials and ensures a wide variety of skills and approaches are available to tackle a range of complex tasks. Bidding experience and bid team composition reflect the need to recruit, train, and develop individuals with specific bidding skills.
- **Communication and exposure** both presents the capacity of the city to develop media exposure opportunities, and the capacity for communication systems to support the bid.
- **Existing facilities** provides the current facilities available, construction dates, and accommodation capacity.

The key success factors highlight those elements required within the bidding framework in order to achieve success. Each criterion identified can be reflected upon as being more or less important depending upon the circumstances of the bid, the critical significance, and the size of the event. Event bid committees may concentrate their strategies on all or some of these elements to distinguish their bid from other competitors. These strategies are highlighted in the next section, which introduces bid application requirements.

THE BID APPLICATION DOCUMENT

A successful bid application requires significant time, energy, and financial and personnel resources in order to ensure that it meets the standards and criteria required to achieve success. While the key success factors identified previously are of crucial importance to achieving success, the standard of the final application must represent a document which identifies and supports the required components that are requested by the event owner. This section examines some of those crucial components, through an in-depth analysis of the IOC bid application prerequisites.

Successful bid application documents obviously need to attend specifically to the requirements as defined by the event owner. The submission needs to clearly examine all required aspects and present the required information in a clear and concise manner. The IOC developed a bid framework as part of Olympic Agenda 2020. It was designed to be an open invitation to all National Olympic Committees by creating more flexibility that would enable more cities to aspire to host city status. This process represented a method to decrease the costs associated with bidding for and staging the Games, and to ensure that the Games would deliver lasting legacies for the host (IOC, 2015). This new process evolved from the previously cumbersome submission of information via a 'candidature file', which represented a master plan for organising the Olympic Games. The candidature process for 2024 was split into three distinct components, beginning with the 'Invitation Phase', introduced to assist potential candidate cities to identify a vision that best matches their sports, economic, social, and environmental long-term planning needs. During this stage, the IOC discusses with potential candidate cities possible solutions to deliver a great Olympic Games and leave a positive, long-term, sustainable legacy. The second stage ensures that cities have the necessary legal and financial mechanisms in place to host the Olympic Games. Stage three involves candidates submitting their file detailing how they will deliver the games and ensure a sustainable legacy (IOC, 2015); with the 'emphasis placed upon operations to ensure successful delivery, legacy planning and Games experience for all stakeholders with a focus on the athlete experience' (IOC, 2015, p. 19).

Table 6.2 indicates the key framework requirements required to be considered by interested host cities. The elements in this framework form the key success factors considered important in the delivery of an excellent Olympic Games (IOC, 2015). The framework elements are:

- having a clear vision,
- effective engagement,
- delivering a great experience,
- operational excellence,
- achieving a balanced budget,
- leaving a great legacy.

Added to the framework elements is a list of key functional areas to be considered. These are:

■ product and experience,
■ venues and infrastructure,
■ Olympic Games services,
■ commercial and engagement,
■ governance.

Alongside the framework elements, the core functional areas identified are listed in Table 6.2. The document clearly states that this list should not be considered exhaustive, but constitutes key cost and organising drivers when planning and delivering an Olympic Games (IOC, 2015). Each framework element and functional area is developed in turn in Table 6.2.

Table 6.2 Olympic Games bid framework requirements

Framework considerations (for 2024 applicants)

Clear vision: All stakeholders from each city should have a clear vision of why they are bidding, based on what they want to achieve and how it fits into the city's long-term development plans, from an urban, social, sporting, environmental, and economic point of view, with a clear focus on sustainability.

Effective engagement: In order to meet their full potential as a catalyst for sustainable change, the organisers should engage the entire host nation and beyond. Full community participation through volunteering, ticketing programs, culture and education programmes, live sites, and the torch relay could be considered.

Deliver a great experience: the groups of key people and stakeholders who ensure success.

■ **Athletes:** consider world class venues; training/preparation/recovery facilities; high-quality village; premium food meeting nutritional and cultural needs; transportation; full stadia; international flavour.
■ **National Olympic Committees (NOCs):** clear, transparent, timely, and consistent communication; Olympic village; transport; venue policies and procedures; knowledgeable and empowered team; well-trained NOC assistants; well-timed problem resolution process; administrative support; NOC support grant assistance.
■ **International Federations (IFs):** venue and equipment meeting technical needs; sport legacy plans; effective collaboration with the Organizing Committee of the Olympic Games (OCOG); full stadia/sport presentation; high-quality broadcast coverage; accommodation; transport; administrative support.
■ **General public (including spectators):** fair/equitable access to tickets; volunteer opportunities; inspiring ceremonies and events; transparent governance; minimal disruption.
■ **Media:** freedom to report; reliable services; secure, fast, accurate services; international standard technology; accreditation process for visiting media; logistical support including transport; accommodation.

- **Marketing partners:** early, clear, and open communication; appropriate brand activation; strong brand; brand protection; accreditation; access to tickets; transport and accommodation.
- **Olympic family and international dignitaries:** operational, working, and hospitality; security.
- **Workforce:** inspiring leadership and management; effective recruitment and staff retention; clarity of roles and responsibilities; briefing and readiness; transport, uniform; accommodation; timely procurement of suppliers.

Operational excellence:

- **The Olympic Games concept:** developed to guide feasibility analysis. Key elements include a Master Plan, sport and venue (stadia) viability; infrastructure (telecoms, technology, energy, mobility) considerations; village considerations; accommodation availability and requirements; transport operations; security.
- **Government support:** specifically focusing on urban cleaning and waste; security, transport; medical services; business continuity planning; legislation and regulatory support; brand protection; immigration; taxation; importing of goods.

Achieving a balanced budget: the operational budget (OCOG budget) used to cover expenses related to running the Games; the governmental or infrastructural (non-OCOG) budget which covers venues (which in turn provide a legacy to the community); operational services of public authorities to support the Games.

Leaving a great legacy: refers to physical improvements (new venues, infrastructure, public amenities, and green space); socio-economic benefits (increased resources for sports development); social progress (jobs, skills, education, health, and accessibility); tourism; business development and inward investment; intangible intellectual and emotional benefits (new methods, standards, knowledge, and experience, as well as community cohesion, increased national identity, and sense of pride and well-being).

Product and experience:

- **Sport:** sport and the athletes at the heart of the OCOG focus; moving from a sport-based to event-based programmer enabling OCOG selection of additional events; event schedule.
- **Ceremonies:** should reflect the overall vision of the Olympic Games.
- **Olympic Torch Relay:** primary asset to showcase country and advance promotion of Games to build excitement.
- **Olympic Truce:** 'sport for peace' activities undertaken through education and activities.
- **Culture:** programme of artistic, musical, and cultural activities to promote mutual understanding and friendship.
- **Education:** Olympism to embrace education, respect, human dignity, mutual understanding, solidarity, and fair play, while rejecting all forms of discrimination.
- **City activities and live sites:** promote engagement across the host city and host country.

Venues and infrastructure: important elements in financial, operational, and legacy considerations. Requirement across 'competition', 'training', and 'non-competition' venues.

- **Olympic Village:** suitable accommodation located near the venues to host athletes and support staff.
- **International Broadcast Centre (IBC):** suitably sized venue with appropriate infrastructure available 12 months prior to Games.

- **Main Press Centre (MPC):** suitably sized venue with appropriate fit-out available 24/7 6 months prior to Games.
- **Energy:** sufficient utility access and quality for all periods of the Games.

Olympic Games Services:

- **Accommodation:** guaranteed availability of 42,000 hotel rooms within venue accessibility.
- **Accreditation:** mechanism supporting management of large numbers of people and accessibility.
- **Medical services (anti-doping):** compliance, support, and laboratory testing accessibility.
- **Medical services (healthcare):** medical care available to all athletes and support staff.
- **Security:** multi-agency approach to ensuring safety for all.
- **Technology:** data and technical requirements in place.
- **Transport:** transport solution for safe, reliable, efficient, and accessible movement into and around the host city.
- **People management:** workforce recruitment and retention strategies in place.

Commercial and engagement:

- **Brand identity and look of the Olympic Games:** unique, unified, and comprehensive look for the Games.
- **Commercial:** three areas: domestic sponsor programmer; ticketing; licensing.
- **Communications:** selection of distribution platforms especially through digital media.

Governance:

- **Sustainability:** environmental, ethical, social, and economic considerations.
- **Finance:** financial systems in place and guarantee of any shortfall covered; procurement procedures in place.
- **Legal:** compliance; protection; agreements; commercial arrangements all in place.
- **Operational readiness, including test events:** learning process through simulations and rehearsals.

Source: Adapted from IOC (2015)

The list of items is extensive and relevant to the preliminary requirements of the IOC. It is clear that most items would appropriately match those sought by other event owners and is not far removed from the goals identified in Table 6.1. The differentiating factors would largely be reflected only in the size of the event. A smaller single sport activity may not require quite the extent of information across all areas required by the Olympic movement. Rest assured, however, that the requirement for the key attributes should be considered as a minimum when developing a bid application document. A bid application document should, at a minimum, consider many of these requirements and include those that are relevant to the event owner. The inclusion of as many of these factors as possible presents the bid in the clearest and most concise manner.

THE EVENT APPLICATION LIFECYCLE

A bid application is largely representative of a two-part life cycle (the bid and post bid outcome), reflective of a seven-stage process contained within the event bid procedure. A bid process envelops a clear time frame from conception to announcement and ultimately implementation through to evaluation of the actual event. It also represents a lifecycle that considers an unsuccessful bid, and this has received greater attention by event organisers over recent years.

Initially, when considering to bid to host events, key stakeholders must be identified and assembled (into a bid team) to provide support and direction for the bid (phase one). These people will represent the key stakeholders of the city, state, or region in preparing and planning for the bid. A bid team that will identify the key elements and attributes that must be presented to the event owner will be created from the initial identification of key stakeholders.

The bid preparation phase follows the initial bid team establishment (phase two), and involves various steps in acquiring knowledge about the bid, ensuring that the documentation meets the minimum standards and requirements sought by the event, through to establishing contact with key partners and officials. This preparation process will culminate in a submission of the relevant bid documents (as exemplified in Table 6.2), lobbying of key decision makers (phase three), and ultimately a final decision announcing the success or otherwise of the bid (phase four).

Phase four is most often referred to as the final element of the process, with the achievement of a final outcome being the conclusion of the bidding phase. Reality suggests that if the bid is successful, then particular components of the bid process will extend into the remaining phases connected with the event itself. The preparation (phase five), hosting (phase six), and post-event (phase seven) phases will ultimately require some input from the bid team or relevant partners to ensure success. This is due to the initial commitments that have been made during bidding being a distinct part of the process. If the bid is unsuccessful, then the bid team completes its work and the process would seemingly end.

While the process from bid to event delivery is somewhat cyclical in nature, as depicted in Figure 6.1, there is one component associated with an unsuccessful bid process that needs to be noted here. While phases one and four, in which the bid team forms and then creates and submits the bid application, are somewhat standard in approach taken, if the bid is unsuccessful it can be argued that the process enables the expertise already in existence within the bid team, and the knowledge gleaned from bid documents, to be redeployed for future bid applications, or redirected into developing alternative programmes in the host nation/city.

Attention on event bid teams maximising the knowledge and insights, as well as supporting future legacy endeavours and projects, is highlighted in the IOC Bid Framework document (IOC, 2015). The framework suggests that all interested host cities, even if unsuccessful, use the bid framework to help drive public engagement, tourism, and city profile. They present the example of New York, which failed to win the right to host the Olympic Games, but used the bid to drive a series of urban development projects across the city, particularly in areas that were considered to be relatively underutilised. Seven key zones were identified within the city and comprehensive plans targeted aspects such as new affordable housing, mass transit enhancements, new parks and amenities, as well as other infrastructure projects (IOC, 2015).

It can be clearly established that the process of bidding for events is not simply a one-off, hit-or-miss technique, but one which involves a great deal of thought, a gathering of key teams and expertise, and a process of improvement and development of the approach and techniques adopted by a bidding community. This approach is being seen as crucial in identifying a best practice approach to bidding for key events and activities.

Within the bid lifecycle framework presented, coupled with the factors required to achieve success and the bid application document inclusions, it makes sense to form event networks and stakeholder groups that are equipped to deal with, or even better still, integrate all the recurring elements. The formation of a network should include groups representative of political, host city, the media, the community, and the facility interests, all of whom are key contributors towards achieving a successful bidding outcome.

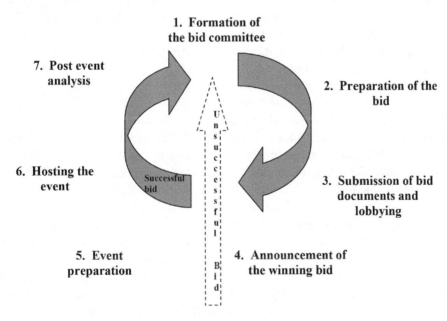

Figure 6.1 The cyclical bid process

Source: Adapted from Ingerson & Westerbeek (2000)

NETWORK RELATIONSHIPS IN THE EVENT APPLICATION PROCESS

Events serve a multitude of agendas reflecting government objectives, regulation, media requirements, sponsor needs, and community expectations, amongst others (Bowdin et al., 1999). A number of stakeholders are present in the event, all with various needs and conflicting demands. The success of an event can be achieved through the way in which these needs and demands are balanced. The event application process is also faced with this range of stakeholder expectations, as often agreements and arrangements need to be determined well in advance of bidding for or running an event. These include understanding that throughout the process community values need to be central to all decision-making processes; various stakeholders including community interest groups need to be involved with strategic activities related to event bid, management, and legacy; collaborative action should empower local communities to be the agents of change; and open communication across all strategic activities must be maintained throughout the process (Misener & Mason, 2006). Faced with this diversity of stakeholders, there are a number of ways in which the event application team can be presented, developed, and structured. Details in relation to different structural types such as simple organisations, functional or divisional groups, matrix organisations, networks and other configurations were examined in the previous chapter.

Although event application teams may be formed with particular structures that suit one of the above possible types, it is worth looking at the event bid team process in more detail from the perspective of the network. The reason for doing this is that major events predominantly epitomise a virtual corporation in which, though they may be ongoing, relationships remain more informal, less structured, and thus more dependent on consistent performance to ensure re-contracting in the future. Some events can be seen as an extreme form of virtual organisation because the participants come together literally only once a year to stage the event and then immediately part ways until the following year (Erickson & Kushner 1999; Turner & Westerbeek, 2004). At the more extreme end, the participants come together once and then disband the organisation completely (for example this occurs in the case of the Olympic Games). This virtual corporation relationship is true of event bid committees, where the level of interdependence between partners is substantial, with organisations coming together to support and enhance the bid, ensuring a high degree of resource and competency sharing. Following the bid process, these organisations disband the relationship formed and develop or seek new arrangements.

It is clear that events involve a comprehensive network of partners as a key requirement for success. Given the expense involved in establishing facilities and putting on an event, and the public risks involved in delivering the one-off final product, the total risk to event participants is magnified far above levels generally considered in standard network theory. Consequently, the circumstances involved

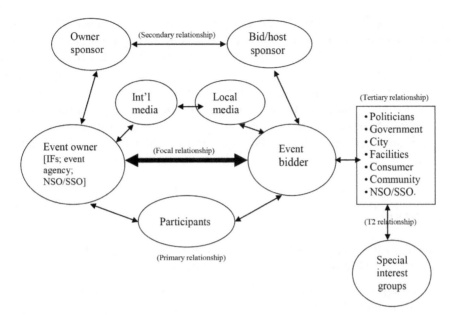

Figure 6.2 Network relationships in the bidding process

in putting together a network for a public event will provide even stronger incentives to prospective participants to seek out partners with extended track records in such events (Erickson & Kushner, 1999; Turner & Westerbeek, 2004). An example of the event network is presented in Figure 6.2.

Convincing the event promoter that the event host has the necessary infrastructure enabling the event to be successfully held in that country or city plays an important role in the success of the bid. In the network, the relationship between the host and the existing infrastructure that it provides and the bid team is an important component. A strong relationship is of significance during the period of the event to ensure that all parties are working together to ensure the success of the event. The greater the support between all parties in the network, the more influence the event host will wield on the outcome.

SUMMARY

This chapter emphasised the complexities and considerations that must be taken into account by facility and event managers in the event application process. Attractiveness is a key consideration in determining whether an application will achieve success, and represents the first concern an organisation encounters in hosting events. Attraction goals should be considered alongside other broad event goals. Following the event goals, a cyclical bid application process is one in which the members of a bid team must ensure that they have sufficient expertise and experience, support from other personnel, and a suitable infrastructure in place. There are a number of key issues that face the bid team in presenting information but the critical components surrounding political support, contracts and obligations, finance and financial management, safety and security, stadia and support infrastructure, media, accreditation, ticketing, sport support services, and community support services must be addressed in order to present and develop a successful bid.

CASE STUDY

'Influencing the influentials' and getting attention: support of 'bid stars' and 'bid slogans' in seeking an advantage

> Certainly no(t) ambassadors that command the football pedigree of the likes of David Beckham or Zinedine Zidane, but Hollywood stars Nicole Kidman and Hugh Jackman are instantly recognizable and universal faces that are not to be scoffed at.
>
> (goal.com, 2010a)

While the bid document represents the primary focus of the host nation, there is ultimately a point in time when the message has to be front and centre in winning support for the bid. This requires the event host to present their documentation and credentials to the world. Australia applied to host one of the 2018/2022 editions of FIFA World Cup and produced a strong bid application. To add 'star power' to the bid application, Australia utilised the support of mainstream global personalities Hugh Jackman and Nicole Kidman as part of the final presentation.

On the other hand, Russia involved President Vladimir Putin and presented a unified bid encompassing the whole nation, but the whole nation as a continent rather than one country or as a part of Europe (goal.com, 2010b). While not including specific high-profile sport or movie stars, the powerful people within business and government were front and centre of the Russian bid. Qatar incorporated many people who had lived and worked in the region, with Zinedine Zidane a key ambassador, representing his Arabic origins (goal.com, 2010c).

Alongside these high-profile ambassadors, each nation introduced a slogan to develop the message further. The slogan 'Come Play' was presented to invite nations to come to Australia for the World Cup. While the Australian bid for the 2018/2022 FIFA World Cups faltered in the end, the motto of 'Come Play' with its colourful imagery and two kangaroos playing football was considered very novel and reflective of the national culture. The message came across that Australia was a nation that does not take itself too seriously, and is prepared to have fun.

While the slogan itself was seemingly harmless, the global media and others perceived the message of 'World Cup? No worries mate' as indicating somewhat that Australia would be a nice, safe, laid-back place to come and experience a major event.

Considering the competitive global market for major events, presenting a message that may not be seen as being serious could work against a nation's bid. While the message supports a stereotype of Australia being the land down under, offering a friendly environment for people from many different cultures, 'Come Play' supported a message of Australia being a safe, welcoming nation for supporters from all nations, located within a time-friendly global marketplace (Asia).

Questions

1   In contrast to the Australian slogan, the winning bid nations Russia ('Ready to Inspire') and Qatar ('Expect Amazing') employed different slogans. How do they compare? The comparison may be part of the attraction for the selection of these host nations.
2   What is the importance of ambassadors and slogans for success in the bid process? Do the message and personalities involved even matter?

REFERENCES

Bowdin, G. A. J., McDonnell, I., Allen, J. & O'Toole, W. (2001). *Events management*, Oxford, UK: Butterworth-Heinemann.

Chelseafc (2016). *On-site facilities.* Retrieved from http://events.chelseafc.com/on-site-facilities/

Erickson, G.S., & Kushner, R.J. (1999). Public event networks: An application of marketing theory to sporting events. *European Journal of Marketing, 33*(3/4), 348–364.

FIFA (2010, May 14). *2022 FIFA World Cup Bid Evaluation Report: Australia.* Retrieved from http://www.fifa.com/mm/document/tournament/competition/01/33/74/50/b3ause.pdf

Getz, D. (1997). *Event management and event tourism.* New York: Cognizant Communication Corporation.

Getz. D., Svensson, B., Peterssen, R., & Gunnervall, A. (2012). Hallmark events: Definition, goals and planning process. *International Journal of Event Management Research, 7*(1/2), 47–67.

goal.com (2010a, Nov 22). World Cup? No worries mate. Retrieved from via http://www.goal.com/en/news/3512/20182022-world-cup-host/2010/11/22/2228301/bid-profile-australia-2022?ICID=AR

goal.com (2010b). Football's sleeping giant. Retrieved from http://www.goal.com/en/ news/3512/20182022-world-cup-host/2010/11/22/2228305/bid-profile-russia-2018

goal.com (2010c). The heat is on .... Retrieved from http://www.goal.com/en/news/ 3512/20182022-world-cup-host/2010/11/22/2228299/bid-profile-qatar-2022

Hall, M. (2009, 8 December). Melbourne: Sporting capital of the world (except for the World Cup). *SBS Home*. Retrieved from http://www.sbs.com.au/blogarticle/114887/Melbourne-Sporting-capital-of-the-world-except-for-the-World-Cup/blog/Open-Season

IOC (2015 May). *Olympic Games framework*. Lausanne, Switzerland. Retrieved from http://www.olympic.org

Misener, L., & Mason, D. S. (2006). Creating community networks: Can sporting events offer meaningful sources of social capital?. *Managing Leisure, 11*(1), 39–56.

Richards, G., & Rotariu, I. (2015). Developing the eventful city in Sibiu, Romania. *International Journal of Tourism Cities, 1*(2), 89–102.

Turner, P. & Westerbeek, H.M. (2004). Network relationships in the bidding process for major sporting events. *International Journal of Sport Management, 5*(4), 335–356.

Westerbeek, H.M., Turner, P., & Ingerson, L. (2002). Key success factors in bidding for hall-mark sporting events. *International Marketing Review, 19*(3), 303–322.

Wilkinson, D. (1988). *The event management and marketing institute*. Canada: The Wilkinson Information Group.

CHAPTER 7

NEW SPORT FACILITY OPERATIONS: PLANNING THE EVENT MANAGEMENT INFRASTRUCTURE

CHAPTER FOCUS

1 Introduction to sport facility and major event management
2 Key success factors of operating sport facilities and running sport events
3 Feasibility analysis and market research for planning new sport facilities and events
4 New sport facility development: planning, design, and construction
5 New sport facility development: preparing the facility management infrastructure
6 New sport facility operations: attracting events
7 **New sport facility operations: planning the event management infrastructure**
8 Attracting customers: marketing sport facilities and events
9 Running the sport event: event operations
10 Destination marketing, image, and branding through major sport events
11 Performance management: evaluating operations
12 Performance management: legacy and measuring impact

CHAPTER OBJECTIVES

In this chapter we will:

- Highlight the complexities of preparing for a facility in event mode.
- Identify the effective capacity management principles associated with facility management.

163

- Outline the requirements behind a successful facility and event project management structure.
- Identify the distinguishing features of contract management applied to the sport facility.
- Identify the distinguishing features of risk management applied to the sport facility and major events.

INTRODUCTION

The facility is built, staff are in place to run the facility, and now the facility is ready to host its first event. This moment reflects the outcome presented by the feasibility study, and through the design and construction process. The first event may involve a competition game of a host sport tenant or alternatively a special event that has been included in the planning process. Hosting the regular home fixtures of a tenant, who may pay rent to the facility, or who may be an owner of the stadium, places the facility in a slightly more enviable position than that faced by the facility manager who must attract a range of events without relying on a sequence of regular fixtures. A critical consideration no matter what the circumstances faced requires that the facility manager must seek to maximise the usage of the facility in order to maximise financial returns for the facility. Where multiuse operations have been built into or are expected of the facility, then there will be an expectation that a wide range of events will be forthcoming to the facility. The facility manager must respond to this condition of operations and must seek to maximise usage through attracting events.

If the conditions surrounding the facility involve no permanent tenants using the facility, or a lack of scheduled activities through the major spectator sport leagues, then the facility must present itself as a viable option for attracting key entertainment options. These options might range from a variety of sport, arts, or cultural activities through to other radical approaches for meeting the entertainment demands of consumers. A visit by a politician or dignitary, a conference or corporate event, Movie-Night-Under-the-Stars, or arts and crafts fair could be the types of activities that enable the event to fulfil its occupancy requirements. The facility manager must be mindful of the conditions around ownership, tenancy, government demands, accessibility of the region to events, size of the facility, services that are offered, dimensions of the arena surface, and current sponsorship/licensing agreements in place, just to mention a few of the wide-ranging usage responsibilities.

Under consideration are the multiusage capabilities that are present in the service delivery. This chapter outlines the considerations that must be made both by the facility manager and by the event manager in order to ensure that successful outcomes can be achieved. Identification of all those aspects that will ensure success, such as the operational, marketing, financial, and staffing issues, and from these issues contract, structure, and risk management responsibilities are also addressed.

THE FACILITY IN EVENT MODE

The preparation of events from the perspective of production and staging is not dissimilar, whether viewing it from the position of the facility manager or that of the event manager. Critical to either perspective is the attention to detail that is required. Every aspect pertaining to the event must be considered and designed to meet the needs of every relevant stakeholder group. The quote from Graham, Goldblatt, and Delpy (1995, p. 43) – 'Gather as much information as possible. You can never ask too many questions and if you assume that you know what your client is talking about, you may find yourself in big trouble' – never rings truer than in the case of event management operations.

All events have a similar lifecycle and organisational elements, which can be categorised in very different ways depending on the actual event itself. What is not in doubt is that these elements must be considered in order for an event to be successfully coordinated and integrated into the facility operations. For ease of reporting, the categories have been identified within three phases. These phases are the concept and planning phase, the operational phase, and the post-event phase. These phases reflect the actual running of the event within the facility and are not aligned to the phases necessary in the feasibility, design, and build aspects that have already been outlined.

Concept and planning phase

The concept and planning phase requires all the details surrounding the event to be identified and enacted by all parties. Meetings between facility management and event management should be conducted with the conditions and requirements being clearly stated. If a special surface is required to be in place for the safe conduct of the event, especially if it is a requirement for compliance with international guidelines, then this must be clearly understood. For example, the sand used for indoor beach volleyball events is of a particular salt-free consistency (Graham et al., 1995). The requirements associated with this playing surface must be clearly advised to the facility management, who must ensure that it is readily available and that it can be laid over the existing surface. There also exists a need to ensure that the associated costs with this surface must be included in the relevant negotiations. All necessary logistical elements should be identified and determined, with solutions outlined at this stage in proceedings.

Aspects for consideration during the concept and planning phase are not limited to, but include:

- **Event date/usage schedule:** The event date must be identified early with arrangements made to ensure the facility is available on that date. The facility will have bookings with tenants and special contractors that may extend years in advance. It is necessary to identify the availability of the facility with sufficient lead-time to ensure that a booking can be made. This date should be checked and double-checked to ensure there are no problems or misunderstandings.
- **Information exchange:** It is crucial for efficient management of an event that the parties responsible for running the event meet with facility management and exchange ideas and information. There may be the opportunity for the facility experts to provide a better way of achieving the event objectives given their experience in running similar events. Equally, the event organisers will be better placed to ensure that their wishes are met if there is a consistent and regular exchange of ideas.
- **Research:** The more knowledge that all parties have about the event and the operations, and support available, the more successful event organisers and facility managers will be in ensuring a successful outcome.
- **Negotiation:** Each party involved in the event will be keen to maximise their respective outcomes. While negotiation will occur during the contracts phase, it is important that this process results in a fair outcome for all parties. If this does not occur then there is likely to be resentment felt and the potential for a less than desired effort put in by the parties who may feel aggrieved. Once negotiations are finalised then it is important that all parameters are included in the written contract.
- **Contracts:** A standard contract between the facility and event organisers should be drawn up and enforced. It is important that this agreement clearly states what each party will deliver. For example, there is no point in coming back to the facility to request that they open up the press room after the event if there was no mention of this in the original agreement. All conditions and requirements should be identified during the information, research, and negotiation stages and included with the contract.
- **Budget development:** The development of the budget should occur simultaneously with the other phases. The facility may have different policies associated with its hiring charges depending upon the type of event and the number of spectators in attendance. This may involve an initial flat-fee charge and then a percentage of the gate receipts over and above a certain number of spectators. Again, the specifics need to be clearly outlined and recorded within the contract. There may also be associated costs and charges with respect to the special requirements on flooring, concessions, sponsor signage, merchandise, ticket sales, and many other elements connected with overall operations.
- **Retail policy/rates:** There needs to be clear agreement between all parties on the policy around sales and the way in which the income from sales will be distributed.
- **Staff selection:** The staffing of the facility and the event need to be clearly delineated. The event staff should be responsible for ensuring that the activities surrounding the event are managed and coordinated, while the facility staff

should ensure that those aspects connected with the facility are clearly identified. Again, this should be clearly agreed upon with specified conditions in the contract. Policies and procedures for hiring, retaining, and dismissing staff need to be stated, whether staff are permanent, contractors, or volunteers.

A significant level of financial and economic success is dependent upon the successful implementation and management of the core aspects and contract development activities identified during the concept and planning phase. Following the initial planning requirements being met, the operational aspects should be considered.

Operational phase

The operational phase occurs at the completion of the planning phase and is when activities surrounding the event begin to occur. The facility moves into operations phase, ensuring that patrons have access to all required services. The event organisers ensure that the event activities are undertaken in a smooth and efficient manner.

Aspects for consideration during the operational phase can include:

- **Promotional/PR campaigns undertaken:** Advising people of forthcoming events promotes both the event and the facility. This process can occur in conjunction with the event, in conjunction with sponsors or stakeholder groups, or independently. Whatever the approach, at the very least as a courtesy, all promotional activities should be agreed on by the parties involved. The facility and event management teams should jointly approve the way in which the facility is included in any promotional materials or publicity campaigns.
- **Ticket sales/box office operations commence:** Establishment of a ticket sales regime occurs at this time and ticket sales for the event should begin. Again, as with promotional campaigns, all parties should agree to the policy surrounding ticket sales. This should include whether sales will be made available to the public at the facility or only through agents. At the very least, answers to queries and access to information should be readily available both through the facility and event agency. Presenting a clear and transparent ticketing policy ensures that misunderstanding and frustration for customers is minimised.
- **Facility preparation occurs:** At this stage all activities and undertakings relevant to the event should occur, such as the checking of access to specific facility areas, validating surface conditions, equipment checking and erecting, facility cleaning, and monitoring of concessions and merchandise. Adequacy and availability of changing rooms, practice areas, medical areas, and other specialist athlete requirements need to be considered. Ongoing inspections, updates, and testing should occur on a regular basis.
- **Concessions and catering commence:** The purchase, supply, and storage of all food, beverages, and merchandise to be ready for sale to patrons.

- **Parking:** Conditions associated with parking and access, including athlete, officials, and VIP parking, should be identified and determined. Remaining conditions for spectators should be identified and clearly communicated to patrons.
- **Signage:** All sponsor and directional signage conditions and requirements must be erected at this stage. Facility and event staff should be fully aware of the requirements for placement and maintenance of specific directional signage at the venue, as well as the conditions for placement of sponsor signage. This is especially important if the event signage is to override or replace current facility sponsor signage.
- **Media/communications:** Clear access, location, and equipment services need to be provided for the media. The provision of printing and copying services, Wi-Fi, phones, and computer connections is an important requirement at this point. Media access to the arena needs to be clearly delineated, as well as access to the participants. Prior access to the facility is likely for communications set-up to occur, especially for specialist broadcast or communications services.
- **Spectator facilities engaged:** All requirements for the comfort of spectators need to be checked and rechecked to ensure that sufficient restrooms will be available, access to concessions runs in a smooth and orderly fashion, and the accessibility and supplies for the expected number of attendees are adequately met.
- **Emergency services enacted:** Emergency plans and procedures should be known by all staff, with policies and procedures implemented.
- **Cleaning/sanitation measures initiated:** The facility should be cleaned ready for spectators and participants, and clean-up should occur as soon as possible both during and following the event. Procedures for removal of hazardous waste need to be enacted. Also, many events are now incorporating more environmentally friendly practices into their cleaning policies.
- **Maintenance monitored:** Ongoing checks should occur of the facility and equipment utilised to ensure a safe environment for all spectators, participants, staff, players, and officials.
- **Safety and security implemented:** Staff responsible for security should be integrated into key areas of the facility, ensuring they are fully equipped and accessible through the communication mechanisms in place.
- **Administration activities in place:** Clear guidelines and activities reflecting financial management, staffing, and operational aspects of the event should be in place and being enforced.

The operational phase is followed by the post-event phase.

Post-event phase

The post-event phase is concerned with close-down activities and the evaluation of the event. All activities associated with the event will have concluded, spectators and participants will have departed, and the final undertakings need to be initiated.

Aspects for consideration during the post-event phase include:

- **Box office termination:** Final arrangements for auditing box office operations need to be made to ensure that the correct financial and administrative outcomes are achieved and reported.
- **Event settlement:** The facility and event management teams must ensure that all contractual obligations have been met, final spectator numbers tallied, and all agreed costs are finalised.
- **Clean-up:** A thorough assessment of any damage to the facility and equipment is required to ensure that payment for such damage is covered by the party responsible.
- **Evaluation:** An evaluation of procedures, operations, and outcomes should be conducted, including a review of aspects for future improvement to ensure that all parties are satisfied with the activities undertaken.
- **Staff redeployment/severance:** Staff should be redeployed to a new event, transferred, or paid-out for their services. Any volunteer staff appointed to assist with the event should be thanked and rewarded for their involvement.

STRUCTURING FOR MAJOR EVENTS

Organisational management reflects the philosophy surrounding the facility as well as staffing, servicing, and event implementation components. The quality of management and service staff can determine the ability of the facility to attract and retain tenants and supporters, ensuring profitability and income for the facility owner, and making it a successful venture for the event owner. Organisational management reflects the development of an organisational structure incorporating all key staffing requirements, and the needs of contract versus in-house management and staffing components.

It is important to consider how the facility or event management processes are structured in order to achieve the best possible outcomes. Understanding the required tasks ensures that the facility manager can respond to organisational management needs. Included in this structural approach is the critical element of determining activities that will be contracted out and activities that will be conducted in-house. The management structure is important, and enables the key divisions within a facility to be clearly identified. Facility operations managers have a variety of departmental responsibilities ranging across areas such as engineering, event coordination, security, maintenance, and housekeeping. They must possess suitable knowledge of budgeting, cost control, negotiation, and motivation in order to complete their job effectively.

The parameters of the event structure circumscribe the requirement for facility-dependent events to move from an event-related structure to a venue- or facility-oriented structure prior to the event being run to ensure the smooth operation of a large facility-dependent event. This is particularly crucial to those large events that operate from large spectator facilities, as many of these activities are performed by facility management through its regular staffing arrangements – but always under the watchful eye of the event organiser, who needs to ensure extensive checks have been conducted that provide assurances the event will run smoothly. If anything were to go wrong with the event, media and spectator dissatisfaction would be targeted at the event managers. The facility might also be criticised, but not necessarily so severely.

An example of this formalised approach took place as part of the 2000 Summer Olympic Games in Sydney, Australia. During its early planning phase, staff were appointed in event-specific roles with a clear emphasis on planning and preparing for the broad requirements associated with the event. Their initial role was to be responsible for their assigned sport. As the event date moved closer, many of these same staff were relocated to the facility in which their events would be held to work more closely with the facility management staff. Much of their job description shifted from an emphasis on the sport towards a closer alignment with the facility and the facility staff. The Sydney Organizing Committee for the Olympic Games (SOCOG) staff were responsible for checking and double-checking with the facility staff to ensure that the facility was clean and ready for each day of competition; that the playing surfaces adhered to international standards; that the spectators were seated in their assigned seats with the minimum of fuss; that the athlete areas were clean, accessible, and available at the required time; that the media had access to required equipment and accredited areas; that concessions were supplied to meet demand; and so on. This approach is one that organising committees have been encouraged to develop since the Sydney Games.

INFRASTRUCTURAL CONSIDERATIONS

A proforma organisational chart is presented in Figure 7.1. Although this chart does not do justice to the broad range of divisions that would occur within a facility or event, the inclusion of two key functional areas of maintenance and merchandise sales, one being maintained by facility management as an in-house arrangement and one as a contracted activity, makes for ready discussion.

Whether either or both of these functions should be undertaken by the facility itself or by alternate specialist contractors is the first question. Will there be economies of scale associated with incorporating a contract approach? Will there be a level of specialisation achieved by appointing a contractor to deliver a particular outcome? Will the appointment of a contractor reduce the need for full-time appointments to the facility (thereby reducing wastage as already identified)?

Identifying the different divisions, and their reporting pathways, within a facility or event management structure is an important initial stage. Determining whether these divisions will be integrated into operations in an in-house or contracted capacity is the next important consideration. Then there are specific areas of

Planning the event management infrastructure

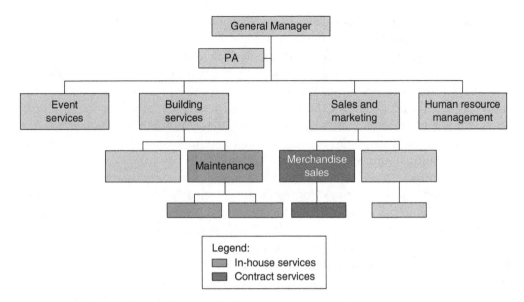

Figure 7.1 Sample organisational structure for a sport facility: separating in-house and contract operations

consideration that need additional attention including contract management, attracting events to the facility, capacity management, and scheduling/timing of events.

Contract management

Contract management presents a management tool that enables the facility to manage the areas of sales, service, equipment, and maintenance. The use of contract services helps management to better control the costs, responsibilities, and liabilities involved in operating a facility. Contract services can range from a simple one-area agreement in which, for example, merchandise services might be provided, through to the more complex arrangement of contract management applying to the entire facility.

Contract management decisions usually document explicit expectations of performance standards and associated costs that relate to key operational activities. Expensive equipment involving a large capital investment may be better employed through a contract provider than through purchase. Equally, a large catering firm might bring significant economies of scale in purchasing and catering management, not to mention a wide range of experience and expertise, and therefore provide a better option than that of any in-house arrangement.

In Figure 7.1 the organisational chart has four divisional areas associated with the facility management structure. Across the whole structure, some divisions will be contracted out or managed in-house. One such area, merchandise sales, is presented as a contract opportunity only. The other, maintenance, is presented as an in-house management operation.

Given the approach to retain maintenance as an in-house operation, the facility management must ensure that appropriate personnel (numbers as well as skills) are appointed to meet the required tasks. Having contracted the area of merchandise sales out to external expertise, the facility manager must ensure that the appropriate controls and standards are applied. Contracts for service must be enacted and management should meet and coordinate on a regular basis with the contractor to check that quality controls meet agreed standards.

Having contractors provide these services means that a contract will be in force over an agreed period of time. Contracts should clearly stipulate the obligations of all parties included or named in the contract. This can create a dilemma if an agreement with an event owner using the facility does not wish to enter into agreed contracts with existing contractors. For example, the event owner may refuse to have its merchandise sales undertaken by the facility's contractor, creating a situation in which the facility may have to compensate its current contractor for not being the official supplier of merchandise. The facility manager must agree to allow an alternate merchandise operator access to sales within the facility. Changing the contract will involve some additional costs to the existing merchandise contractor if they have an exclusive arrangement. That may involve some compensation to the existing contractor. Similar situations can arise with sponsor signage or food/beverage concession when a one-off event may hire the venue but require existing event sponsors to be granted prime sponsor sign placement around the facility. The facility manager must attempt to meet the demands of the event owner, but also be mindful of existing agreements with other contractors.

Attracting events to the facility

Circumstances surrounding the facility such as design, location, capacity, leasing arrangements, and staffing are all elements critical for an event manager to consider when seeking a venue. The facility manager has to ensure that the facility is relevant to meet the needs of the event manager. The fit of an event from the perspective of spectator and tenant needs, the frequency of event hosting requirements, and the capacity to run the event in an economically viable manner all need to be determined. Developing stadia with more multi-purpose practices in mind places more pressure on the facility manager to be more than just a specialist basketball, baseball, or football operator. For example, a stadium must be able to be transformed with short lead-times from a football stadium to a rock venue. Etihad Stadium at Docklands in Melbourne, a fully functional 50,000+ seat arena with retractable roofing, has been transformed from a football stadium (AFL, Rugby Union, Rugby League, and soccer), to a cricket oval, to a World Wrestling Entertainment (WWE) ring, to a concert venue, often being reconfigured to meet a new occupant's demands within

172

the space of a few days. This capacity to cross seasons (football is traditionally a winter sport, while cricket is played over summer), and incorporate both sport and entertainment options makes it a highly sought-after arena among event owners.

Being able to attract a variety of events provides good cash flow while displaying a versatility and capacity to accommodate many needs, a feature which is attractive to key event decision makers. Accommodating a variety of events limits the downtime experienced by the facility. But being able to meet a variety of tenant and entertainment options, often at short notice, has a potential downside. Hosting too many events can affect aspects such as the competition surface for major sporting tenants. This can detract from the desirability of the facility for future tenant agreements. On the positive side, an abundance of interest in events being hosted by a particular facility can reduce wastage (i.e. times when the facility is not in use). A suitable balance must be achieved. Maximising usage is a crucial consideration for facility management, and must be viewed from the perspective of capacity management (wastage) and scheduling issues.

Capacity management

Capacity management is the process of measuring the amount of work scheduled and then determining how many people, machines, and physical resources are needed to accomplish this work. There exists within this framework an assumption that there will be capacity surpluses or shortages, and that the way in which these are managed will affect the organisation's profit (Watts, 1999). While capacity management would seem to be an important feature of facility management, there is limited research into the area. Iversen and Cuskelly (2015) suggested that utilisation of sports facilities is a common aim, and that a nuanced approach to measuring utilisation is often required.

There are many ways to view capacity. Iversen and Cuskelly (2015, p. 531) defined utilisation as 'minutes of activity on the outdoor turf, sports hall floor or swimming facility'. They indicate that while their definition focuses on minutes of activity, it could also be relevant to consider the number of active persons using a defined space within a facility at a given time, or even the proportion of the space in use. Whatever the measure applied, whether it is applied to time, participants/spectators, or space, identifying the most appropriate measure is important to the facility manager.

A core issue in capacity management is the identification and elimination of wasted resources, or what could be termed 'idle capacity'. Watts (1999) presented the structural wastage associated with a hypothetical sport stadium, highlighting that there are obvious wastage components within any utilisation of a facility. This extends largely to the physical facilities surrounding the ground, functions, seating, equipment utilisation, and office utilisation aspects of the facility. The crucial aspect is how to maximise utilisation and minimise wastage. While eliminating wastage is an admirable achievement for the facility, there actually exists

Planning the event management infrastructure

a requirement for some downtime, in order to enable maintenance or repairs to be undertaken. Downtime should be factored in to occur around the event schedule, and in particular around peak usage periods. While maintenance and repair time is required, it can be commenced in stages, enabling parts of the facility to remain open and functional while other parts are being attended to.

Table 7.1 displays a framework for presenting usage and wastage in terms of time (minutes/hours). The starting point is to calculate the number of hours in any year (8,760 hours), and then to determine what is the most appropriate method to employ in order to calculate wastage. Table 7.1 identifies that in terms of ground capacity only 3,500 hours are utilised, which represents a wastage of 60 per cent. In truth, however, this is far too simplistic a measure to undertake. The reality may be that the while the facility might be operational for 24 hours every day of the year, events cannot feasibly be held at that rate. A better measure may be to determine whether events can be held every day. Measuring activity on a per day basis is also fraught with error in that there would be some requirement for setting up and packing up events which could account for some of the time. A better measure of usage, therefore, could be based on attendance figures, or simply the number of events using the ground space across a period of time. If there is a regular tenant for example, then the tenant playing games three times per week over a nine-month period (108 games = 108 days of usage) may maximise the capacity of the facility during this time. There may be no more opportunity for a facility to prepare grounds and amenities for any other events. The ground facilities would then be operating at near capacity (100%) even though this may only equate to 108 days out of 270 (40%). It would be an even worse calculation if considering an hourly measure given that the facility may only be open for 4–5 hours each day an event is held (i.e. 540 hours [108 x 5]

Table 7.1 Examples of structural waste

Resources	Total Capacity	Utilised Capacity	Waste
Ground facilities	8,760 hours per annum	3,500 hours per annum	60%
Function facilities	8,760 hours per annum	3,000 hours per annum	66%
Seating capacity	40,000 seats	22,000 seats	45%
Ground staff	1,750 hours per annum	1,050 hours per annum	40%
Grounds equipment	8,760 hours per annum	1,050 hours per annum	88%
Office staff	1,840 hours per annum	1,200 hours per annum	35%
Office equipment	8,760 hours per annum	1,200 hours per annum	86%
Management	2,400 hours per annum	2,400 hours per annum	0%
Supplies	bought as required	100%	0%

Source: Adapted from Watts, 1999

of a possible 6,480 hours [270 x 24], which equates to a measly 8 per cent usage). These measures indicate that the facility manager must ensure that their method of calculation and justification for the way it is undertaken should be very clear. In the above example, while 108 days is provided over nine months for competition dates, there are another three months of the year where there may be an opportunity to attract other events.

Table 7.1 lists some aspects that should be monitored by facility management in order to minimise wastage and ensure that the facility is operating at maximum output. The approach taken to minimise wastage needs to be carefully considered on the basis of what can physically be undertaken by the facility management. Tied in with the attention on capacity management is the schedule around events.

Scheduling/timing of events

Although scheduling has been discussed in previous chapters, it is worth briefly revisiting the concept from the perspective of scheduling events. This is a critical area for an event manager, and it must be taken into consideration within the constraints of the entire facility calendar.

In order to maximise the usage of the facility, facility management must put together a clear timeline of availability. All the known events within a particular period should be included in this event calendar. These known events will include competition games of permanent tenants, as well as special pre-booked activities. The calendar of known events can then be assessed in line with opportunities that may arise to attract other events that are available or potentially forthcoming. Scheduling of events is crucial to the success of any facility. Events generate revenue and exposure, which in turn have the ongoing impact of generating membership and formulating media interest.

An event schedule proforma is presented in Table 7.2. This includes the identification of the major commitments as part of the arrangements for a hypothetical multi-purpose 40,000-capacity stadium within one year of its operation. The schedule includes the sporting competitions and entertainment activities scheduled throughout the year.

Table 7.3 extends the list of events in Table 7.2 to include future events that could be staged at the facility. The facility manager must identify and determine which events (selecting from the current and potential event schedule) should be considered part of a viable event schedule. Consideration should then be given to the opportunity costs of including one event over the other in the facility schedule, as well as the costs of altering existing league commitments.

Determining the event schedule should include an assessment of the facility's current calendar, noting strengths and weaknesses in its programming, and including possible opportunities and threats that need to be considered. This analysis

Table 7.2 Event planning schedule proforma (current agreements)

Event / Month	Jan	Feb	Mar	Apr	May	June	July	Aug	Sept	Oct	Nov	Dec
Intl. Cricket one-day series	10–14	22–23	3				8–11					
Domestic cricket one-day series		4–6, 18–21	8–10	7–9								
Football Division 1			18, 19, 25									
Football Division 2			28	1, 2, 9, 16, 30	7, 8, 15, 23	4–6, 13, 20, 26, 27	3, 17, 18, 25	2, 11, 12, 26	3, 9, 11, 13, 18			
Domestic Rugby union									30	8, 11, 14, 21, 28	5, 12, 19	
National Basketball League		2–3, 7–9, 16–18, 27–30	4–6, 16–18									12–16, 28–30
Concert / entertainment bookings			14–16		3–5			4, 18–20			21– 26, 25	

will lead to a justification of current event scheduling. Key information reflecting on individual events – such as lead-time, cost range, breakeven capacity, profit margin, ability to attract alternative events, and date of scheduling – must be considered. This information can then be used to justify either retaining certain events or replacing them with other potential events at the same time of the year.

The final annual schedule needs to reflect a longer-term outlook, in which ongoing tenant relationships should be maintained, new relationships developed, and old ones potentially terminated. For example, the inclusion of domestic cricket in the schedule as identified in Table 7.2 would need to be considered by the facility. Domestic cricket does not attract significant spectator interest and is conducted either over a period of a full day (6–8 hours) or multiple consecutive full days. Given the time required to conduct cricket competitions, a facility needs to consider both its relevance and importance to the schedule. It may be that there is a long-term contract in place, or it may be

Table 7.3 Event planning schedule proforma (future interested parties)

Event \ Month	Jan	Feb	Mar	Apr	May	June	July	Aug	Sept	Oct	Nov	Dec
Soccer Int'l.	7–9				23		31					
Domestic / Club cricket competitions										12–16	18–22	18–22
Division 3 Football finals			20–23						22–24, 29–30			
Domestic Soccer league + finals	12	18, 25	7, 14, 21, 28	12	1							
Intl. Rugby union (+ Super league comp)		12, 19, 25	8, 22	1, 14 22–24	20–23	8–12						
Domestic tennis finals	11	12– 18, 25– 28	6– 12									12–16, 28–30
Concert / entertainment booking opportunities	11–16		1	9– 12						15–22		30

that the facility was originally purpose-built with cricket in mind. At the very least, the facility management would need to discuss the current arrangements of providing a venue for domestic cricket. Terminating the contract, assisting the cricket association in relocating to an alternative venue when clashes occur, or working together to make the domestic cricket programme more entertaining and capable of attracting greater audience numbers may form possible solutions. Having a clearly identifiable breakdown of the schedule enables a longer-term analysis of events and tenants to be identified.

RISK MANAGEMENT

Risk management reflects the potential for exposure to harm. The Australian and New Zealand risk management standard has altered the definition of risk from 'the chance of something happening that will have an impact on objectives' to 'the effect of uncertainty on objectives' (Australian Government Comcover, 2010). The standard advises that while consideration of risks occurring should happen, the application of risk treatment options to ensure that the uncertainty of an agency meeting its objective can be avoided, reduced, removed or modified, and/or retained, is paramount (Australian Government Comcover, 2010). The most predominant problem experienced by sport facility managers is minimising financial loss and liability exposure resulting from injuries to patrons. The primary goal of risk management is to reduce the possible losses and exposure to danger, harm, or hazards.

The Australian and New Zealand risk management standard presents 11 principles of risk management. These are considered to be important aspects that all organisations should adhere to in order to ensure they are serious about managing risk situations (Australian Government Comcover, 2010). The 11 principles may be broadly described as:

- **Understanding and reviewing risk:** Ongoing review of processes and systems contribute to the organisation's objectives.
- **Ensuring that risk is considered as an integral part of the organisation:** Risk management should be integrated with the organisation's governance and planning processes, at an operational and strategic level.
- **Including risk in organisational decision making:** Identifying risk management processes assists in identifying priorities, allows for informed choices to be made, and the most appropriate actions to be determined.
- **Addressing uncertainty:** Organisations can implement controls and treatments to maximise gains while minimising losses.
- **Being systematic:** Risk management processes should be consistent across the organisation, enabling efficiency, consistency, and reliability of results to be determined.
- **Being tailored:** The organisation's risk management profile needs to be established across its internal and external environments.
- **Reflecting good information:** All available information should be understood and considered to inform the risk management process.
- **Being transparent and inclusive:** Communication and consultation with stakeholders forms key parts in identifying, analysing, and monitoring risk.
- **Being responsive to change:** The risk management process needs to be flexible, adaptable, and contextual, with new risks understood and managed while those risks that no longer exist are discarded.
- **Including people management:** Risk management needs to consider the people within the organisation, including their contribution, culture, and impact on achieving the organisation's objectives.
- **Being part of the ongoing development of the organisation:** Organisations which invest resources over time and demonstrate continual achievement of their objectives most often display a mature risk management culture.

The exposure of an activity to risk is its exposure to the uncertainty of outcomes. Due to this uncertainty of outcome, risk must be managed or it can have devastating consequences. The approach to risk management in sport facility and event management should be considered an integral part of good management practice.

As a result, the facility or event management team is responsible for defining and documenting their policy for risk management. The organisational context or rationale relating to risk should reflect the range of financial, operational, political, social, legal, and market aspects that will be affected by the occurrence of a risk-related event. Criteria should be developed against which risk is to be monitored. Risks should be identified, analysed, assessed, and treated as required. Incorporated into this monitoring process is the development of risk management personnel and the ongoing evaluation and redefinition of risk factors.

Some of the common risk areas in sport facility and event management are identified below. There are the various injuries sustained by athletes, which may be in part attributable to the competition surface; the injuries sustained by spectators at Association Football stadia (as a result of some of the infamous English stadium disasters in the late 1980s and early 90s); the Monica Seles stabbing incident at a tennis tournament in Germany; tit-for-tat political disputes over attendance at Olympic Games in Moscow 1980 and Los Angeles in 1984; and the Munich air disaster in 1958 in which many of the Manchester United football team lost their lives. These are all incidents that have exposed sporting organisations to a significant degree of risk. The key is how those organisations responsible for running the event manage these risks and other occurrences. Aspects relevant to risk in sport facility and event management include (but are not limited to):

- sport participation itself
- spectators
- legal issues (legal liability, contracts, insurance)
- athlete protection
- loss prevention
- storage
- accreditation
- facilities/equipment/property
- hiring
- training
- transportation
- safety/security
- environmental factors (natural events)
- economic circumstances
- political circumstances
- management activities and controls
- human behaviour
- terrorism.

The sport facility or event manager must clearly assume responsibility for and be prepared for risks. There are many aspects related to this level of preparedness, including the following:

- Constantly update and review risk management plans.
- Undertake emergency 'drills' to ensure all staff understand and acknowledge how to react in an emergency situation.
- Ensure key personnel are familiar with all requirements and aspects associated with the risk management plans and procedures.
- Constantly refine strategies and incorporate new technologies and methods of risk management.
- Clearly determine a chain of responsibility and ensure that all staff are aware of the requirements. Key managers must be immediately notified of an emergency or crisis situation, regardless of the time of day (or night).
- Expertise needs to be recognised and experts included in risk management policy development and support when an emergency arises. This expertise should reflect medical, legal, and financial knowledge as well as operational and technical expertise where appropriate.
- Reviews and recommendations should be documented, regularly updated, and acted upon.
- All incidents should be reported on and practices and outcomes reviewed.
- Senior management must have a clear knowledge of the requirements and procedures and be immediately informed of any emergency that arises. This is particularly important as they will be identified by the media for comment.
- Those directly involved in the emergency need to be debriefed immediately after the incident, and need to understand the actions required and the reporting of those actions.
- Staff should be briefed on the emergency as soon as possible following the incident so that they are aware of what has occurred. This should extend to ensuring that they are aware of what is being done about the situation.
- The media will most likely be interested in the incident and the organisation should have a clearly identifiable spokesperson, who is well briefed and able to present a sufficiently developed organisational response with updates available as news comes to hand.

The process of risk management, in order to be effective, involves understanding eight key components: communication and consultation; establish the context; risk assessment; risk identification; risk analysis; risk evaluation; risk treatment; and risk monitoring (Australian Government Comcover, 2010). Communication and monitoring occur throughout the risk management process, while context, assessment, and treatment occur in sequence. Each component is identified and explained below.

Communication and consultation

Communication and consultation can be considered as continually occurring in the risk management process, and should occur regularly with internal and external stakeholder groups in order to gain their input into and ownership of the process. Stakeholder objectives should be understood to enable their involvement to be planned and their views considered in establishing risk criteria.

Establish the context

The process of risk management begins with the organisation defining what it wants to achieve and any external and internal factors that may influence success in achieving these objectives. This step is an essential precursor to risk identification and develops the scope and parameters for determining the risk criteria for the organisation. The management of risk should consider the resources, responsibilities, and authorities required to carry out risk management. The external context represents the external stakeholders and environmental factors that impact on the organisation. The external criteria represent an organisation-wide context, with specific legal and regulatory requirements. The internal context is aligned to the organisation's culture, processes, structure, and strategy, which can influence the way in which the organisation will manage risk (Australian Government Comcover, 2010).

Risk assessment

Risk assessment comprises four steps: risk identification, risk analysis, risk treatment, and risk monitoring. Risk identification requires the application of a systematic process to understand the 'what', 'how', 'when', and 'why' of a situation. Following the identification process, analysis of risk occurs. Analysis develops the causes, sources, likelihood, and consequences of a situation through the development of a risk rating system. From here, comparison of the level of risk found during the analysis process can enable a rank to be determined in order to decide whether risks can be accepted. These risks should then be continuously monitored and categorically reviewed to ensure they remain acceptable.

Risk identification

Identification involves the facility discerning the various risks that could potentially cause loss to the facility. These can be primary factors which are those aspects which are directly attributable to the daily operations of the facility, such as where a security staff member forcibly removes an intoxicated spectator, or an athlete injures themselves, slipping when entering the arena. They can also be secondary factors which represent those events that again affect the facility but not during the actual event or directly involving athletes, spectators, or staff during the competition. The components of weather, event or activity type, patron demographics, and facility location are types of secondary factors that prevail.

Risk analysis

Having identified possible risks to the facility or event, there needs to be analysis into which risk factors have potentially the greatest effect. These risk factors should therefore receive priority. The level of risk is analysed through combining estimates on the basis of two criteria, namely the severity of the loss and the likelihood of occurrence. Understanding each component enables the establishment of a risk rating to occur. A matrix of frequency (likelihood) to consequence (magnitude) of loss should be set up. Figure 7.2 displays a matrix for determining the level and consequence of risk.

The risk assessment matrix displayed in Figure 7.2 is a 5×5 version. Alternatives include a matrix in 3x3, 4x4, or even 7x7 formats. The crucial elements are to determine the likelihood/frequency of loss against the consequence of these losses and then apply the outcomes to potential risks from the identification phase. There is a strong overlap between risk evaluation and risk treatment. This is because each risk treatment option is tested until the preferred outcome acceptable to the organisation can be identified, usually one that presents the greatest benefit for the

Likelihood/ frequency Consequence	A: Almost certain	B: Likely/ frequent	C: Moderate	D: Unlikely/ infrequent	E: Rare
1. Catastrophic	Avoid	Avoid	Shift	Shift	Shift
2. Major	Avoid	Avoid	Shift	Shift	Shift
3. Moderate	Shift	Shift	Shift	Shift	Keep & decrease
4. Minor	Keep & decrease	Keep & decrease	Keep & decrease	Keep & decrease	Keep & decrease
5. Insignificant	Keep & decrease	Keep & decrease	Keep & decrease	Keep & decrease	Keep & decrease

Descriptors	
Likelihood/frequency:	**Consequence:**
A. Event is expected to occur	1. Death, huge financial loss, catastrophic impact on operations
B. Event will probably occur	2. Extensive injuries, major financial loss, major impact on operations
C. Event should occur at some time	3. Medical treatment required, financial loss, significant impact on operations
D. Event could occur at some time	4. First aid treatment, some financial loss, minimal impact on operations
E. Event not expected to occur	5. No injuries, low financial loss, no effect on operations

Figure 7.2 Risk assessment matrix: likelihood/frequency vs. consequence

least cost. The case study for this chapter presents a framework for applying this particular type of risk matrix.

Following the identification and analysis of risk, it is important to compare the level of risk found during the analysis process with previously established risk criteria and then decide whether risks can be accepted. If the risks fall into the low or acceptable categories, they may be accepted with minimal further treatment. These risks should be monitored and categorically reviewed to ensure they remain acceptable. If, however, the risks do not fall into the category of being acceptable, they should be treated using one or more of the possible treatment options.

Risk treatment

The treatment stage takes the matrix from the assessment stage and involves evaluation and selection from options, including analysis of costs and benefits, as well as new risks that might arise from each option. These risks are prioritised and treatment options are selected based on a planned process used to develop strategies for avoidance, transfer of risk, or internal procedures for managing the risk. These risk treatment views reflect on whether to avoid the risk completely or keep the risk and attempt to reduce its impact.

Avoid the risk

The event or facility manager makes a conscious decision not to proceed with the activity at all. Risks should be avoided when they cause a high degree of loss and occur often. The facility should consider the possibility of not hosting the event at all if there is the possibility of large negative consequence or monetary loss.

Accept the risk with support financing

The risk is accepted within the organisation itself and the organisation diverts some funds to cover for expected risk-related occurrences.

Reduce the likelihood of occurrence

Taking proactive actions to minimise risk occurrence can ensure a lower risk environment. For example, ensuring that the facility is designed to be a slip-free zone for spectators given any climatic conditions will reduce the likelihood of falls and potential lawsuits.

Reduce the consequences of the occurrence

This is again a proactive measure, in which the facility or event management reduces the impact or severity of injury through their actions. For example, removing wire fences at football grounds in the United Kingdom meant that people could gain access to the field but were less likely to be crushed against a barrier.

Transfer the risk

Transferring risk involves another party bearing or sharing some part of the risk. The combination of severity and frequency (likelihood) may not be large enough to warrant avoiding the risk. It may, however, be large enough to cause substantial monetary damage to the facility or event. The solution is to transfer the risk to an organisation that is willing to take the risk. This may occur through the drawing up of special conditions within contracts or taking out insurance. Many facilities now require the event owner to provide sufficient legal liability coverage for injury to spectators, thereby sharing some of the costs associated with risk.

Retain the risk

The facility manager can keep the risk and attempt to decrease the amount of loss or risk that could occur. In the matrix, risks that are kept and decreased are usually those that have a very low potential for loss. The facility manager should ensure that proper precautions are taken to decrease the occurrence and monetary losses associated with the risk. This can be accomplished through the use of documentation and implementation of standard operating procedures (SOP).

Risk monitoring

Risk monitoring involves the ongoing assessment and continual evaluation of possible risks and attention to new emergent risks that may affect operations. Few risks remain static, and factors and circumstances will change regularly. The sport facility and event manager must be aware of ongoing changes and reassess each risk accordingly (and regularly). A process of environmental scanning should occur regularly, taking on new information and learning lessons from previous successes and failures.

Risk monitoring should include the development of relevant manuals and standard operating procedures for risk. Information concerning treatment and decisions emerging from all risk situations should be documented in order to achieve the best possible approach and outcomes. Relevant information relating to key areas includes:

- development of maintenance charts,
- ongoing assessment of the level of care,
- regular staff training and planning,
- regular practising of emergency drills,
- introduction and monitoring of reporting systems.

Ideally, a risk management or emergency procedures (disaster plan) manual should be established that identifies crucial areas of concern. The manual should extend to incorporating methods of dealing with the media in times of crisis. The monitoring process should be reviewed on a regular basis in order to ensure that risks are adequately covered and regularly evaluated for frequency and loss outcomes.

SUMMARY

This chapter has introduced the complexities associated with a facility moving into event mode. The requirements associated with hosting events can be complicated and diverse. It is not a case of simply building the facility and waiting for events to come and take care of themselves. The facility manager must present the facility to the event owners and schedule events to maximise usage and minimise wastage, while ensuring that facility operations are not compromised. Furthermore, managing events in the facility requires the integration and implementation of contracts with a variety of service providers as well as the event owner, which represents a contract partner in its own right. There is also a key management requirement to ensure that risks be identified and managed. All of these elements place the facility and event manager in a position to maximise their operational efficiency and achieve success.

CASE STUDY

Assessing risk for an East Asian futsal tournament

The task of identifying and categorising risks associated with a major event is an extremely important function both facility and event managers must undertake. Understanding the risks associated with an event, then analysing, assessing, and treating those risks can result in the event being trouble free or troublesome.

Consider the following event:

> A six nation East Asian Futsal tournament to be held in Melbourne, Australia in a 10,000-seat capacity indoor stadium. The event is scheduled to take place from June 5–10, 2020. The invited teams include Australia, China, Chinese Taipei, Japan, South Korea, and Russia.

Given the East Asian futsal tournament description above, the development of a risk assessment matrix (5x5) should occur. Figure 7.3 presents a 5×5 matrix pro-forma that can be applied to considerations of risk surrounding this event.

Likelihood/ frequency Consequence	A: Almost certain	B: Likely/ frequent	C: Moderate	D: Unlikely/ infrequent	E: Rare
1. Catastrophic					
2. Major		Political/ diplomatic			
3. Moderate		Spectator safety	Athlete protection		
4. Minor				Athlete transportation	
5. Insignificant					

Figure 7.3 Risk assessment matrix: likelihood/frequency vs. consequence

All relevant events that can be foreseen, related to both event and facility circumstances, should be identified and analysed in terms of severity to the facility and event managers.

The list of possible risk areas is broadly reflected by:

- sport participation itself
- spectators
- legal issues (legal liability, contracts, insurance)
- athlete protection
- loss prevention
- storage
- accreditation
- facilities/equipment/property
- hiring
- training
- transportation
- safety/security
- environmental factors (natural events)
- economic circumstances
- political circumstances
- management activities and controls
- human behaviour
- terrorism.

Question

You are tasked with the preparation for the six-nation East Asian futsal tournament. You need to identify potential factors that need to be considered with respect to risk management in order to plan for this tournament. Once identified, these factors should then be prioritised according to severity.

To get you started, four possibilities of potential risk factors and severity associated with the risk are already included in Figure 7.3 above, and noted below:

- political/diplomatic environment (B2-4)
- athlete protection (C3)
- athlete transportation (D3-4)
- spectator safety (B2-3).

Note: You may wish to refer back to Figure 7.2 for a framework upon which the assessment of whether to avoid, shift, or accept these risks should be made.

REFERENCES

Australian Government Comcover (2010, August). AS/NZS *ISO 31000:2009: Risk management: Principles and guidelines (factsheet 01)*. Retrieved from http://www.finance.gov.au/sites/default/files/COV_216905_Risk_Management_Fact_Sheet_FA3_23082010_0.pdf

Graham, S., Goldblatt, J.J., & Delpy, L. (1995). *The ultimate guide to sport event management and marketing*. Burr Ridge, IL: Irwin.

Iversen, E.B., & Cuskelly, G. (2015). Effects of different policy approaches on sport facility utilization strategies. *Sport Management Review, 18*(4), 529–541.

Watts, E.W. (1999). *The elimination of waste through effective capacity management: Identifying techniques to improve venue management*. Proceedings of the 7th Congress of the European Association for Sport Management, Thessonaliki. pp. 339–340.

CHAPTER **8**

ATTRACTING CUSTOMERS: MARKETING SPORT FACILITIES AND EVENTS

CHAPTER FOCUS

1 Introduction to sport facility and major event management
2 Key success factors of operating sport facilities and running sport events
3 Feasibility analysis and market research for planning new sport facilities and events
4 New sport facility development: planning, design, and construction
5 New sport facility development: preparing the facility management infrastructure
6 New sport facility operations: attracting events
7 New sport facility operations: planning the event management infrastructure
8 **Attracting customers: marketing sport facilities and events**
9 Running the sport event: event operations
10 Destination marketing, image, and branding through major sport events
11 Performance management: evaluating operations
12 Performance management: legacy and measuring impact

CHAPTER OBJECTIVES

In this chapter we will:

■ Identify a variety of sport facility and event customers by way of a typology.
■ Stress the importance of identifying and understanding the different needs and wants of various customers.

- Discuss the facility and event product within a services marketing framework.
- Describe facility and event marketing strategy in terms of market segmentation, targeting, and positioning.
- Define the role a quality marketing information system plays in sport facility and major event marketing.
- Explain the internal and external factors inherent in consumer behaviour.
- Evaluate tools that assist with maximising service quality and customer satisfaction to facilitate customer retention.
- Explore the challenges of resource commitment and coordination associated with multiple marketing stakeholders.

INTRODUCTION

The previous three chapters have focused on preparing the facility management infrastructure, attracting events, and preparing the event management infrastructure. However none of this is relevant or feasible, in most cases, without one very important factor – customers. If you do not attract customers to use facilities or attend events, the efforts are most often a failure.

So who are the customers of sport facilities and major events? Well, they could be anyone, but we cannot market to everyone – and we certainly cannot and do not want to attract everyone. So how do we attract the right customers to utilise facilities and attend events?

Prior to addressing how to attract customers, facility and event professionals must understand the basic concepts of marketing. Over time there has been a major misconception that facility and event managers should not get involved with the marketing side of the business because their main job was related strictly to operational and managerial roles. This could not be further from the truth. In actuality, they need to have a solid foundation and understanding of the application of marketing related to all aspects of facilities and events. This includes everything from the development of marketing plans and the implementation of logistics, to understanding the sport consumers who use facilities and events, and effective promotional activities to attract those customers.

This chapter will provide a synopsis of the connection marketing has with managing sport facilities and major events, with a specific focus on attracting customers. This will include understanding customer needs and wants, the role the facility and event product plays in meeting those needs and wants, and the marketing strategies that must be activated as part of an integrated marketing management plan. This will lead to identifying what attracts customers, how to retain customers over the short terms, the building of relationships over long terms, and challenges inherent to addressing multiple stakeholders with different needs in a coordinated manner.

MEETING CUSTOMER NEEDS AND WANTS

To start, we look at the definitions of marketing and consumers. According to Armstrong et al. (2015), marketing is defined as 'a social and managerial process by which individuals and groups obtain what they need and want through creating and exchanging products and value with others' (p. 8). Schwarz, Hunter, and LaFleur (2013) define a consumer as 'an individual or organisation that purchases or obtains goods and services for direct use or ownership' (p. 5). Central to these definitions are 'needs' and 'wants'. The needs and wants of facility and event organisations are in general quite limited, with one of the more obvious being revenue generation. However, the needs and wants of customers span several different types, and their identification can be a complex task.

Before we turn our attention to uncovering these needs and wants, it is critical that we identify exactly who the customers for sport facilities and major event are. Armstrong et al. (2014, p. 75) list five types of customer markets:

- **Consumer markets:** individuals and households that buy goods and services for personal or household consumption.
- **Business markets:** organisations that buy goods and services for further processing or for use in their production process.
- **Reseller markets:** organisations that buy goods and services in order to resell them at a profit.
- **Government markets:** government agencies that buy goods and services in order to produce public services or transfer these goods and services to others who need them.
- **International markets:** overseas buyers including consumers, producers, resellers, and governments.

Consumer and business markets, in both the domestic and international sense, are the markets of greatest relevance in the context of facility and event management. It is also important to include international buyers as an important customer group, as many facilities such as Wembley Stadium in London, Staples Center in Los Angeles, and the Melbourne Cricket Ground in Australia host international events and have international consumers and international business partners.

Consumer market customers can be divided into two broad categories, namely spectators and participants. The spectator category includes people who place their 'bums on seats' in venues all over the world to watch an event unfold, and those individuals who, whether by choice or necessity, spectate 'at a distance' in front of the television, via the Internet, on their mobile device, or by radio. In contrast to remote spectators, participants are (normally) present at the facility to consume the participation product. For example, tennis players must get on the court to serve and volley; golfers need to get out on the links to drive, chip, and putt; cricket players must get themselves onto the field to bowl, catch, and bat; and swimmers need to be in the pool in order to swim.

Business market customers include (a) event owners and promoters that hire out a facility, (b) television or radio networks that broadcast the event, (c) Internet and digital media companies that deliver the product online, (d) sponsors that seek an association with a facility or event for the purpose of promoting their own organisation and its products, and (e) corporate box/suite holders, who may or may not also be sponsors.

The way in which a facility or event should be marketed depends on the customer market of interest (i.e. consumer or business), the smaller segments within these two broad domains (e.g. spectator or participant), and the even smaller segments within these categories (e.g. live-at-venue or television or digital). Therefore marketers must use different strategies to attract and retain the various customer groups depicted by the facility and event customer markets, as different types of customers often have very different needs and wants.

THE FACILITY AND EVENT PRODUCT AS A SERVICE

Thinking about sport facilities and events as products that offer multiple benefits can be conceptualised as services rendered. Schwarz, Hunter, and LaFleur (2013) distinguish between the service product and the manufactured product in distinct ways. Manufactured products are 'usually tangible products and are referred to as "goods", while intangible products are called "services" or the "experience"' (Schwarz, Hunter, & LaFleur, 2013, p. 138). The service product involves 'the process of providing quality, value and satisfaction to the sport consumer ... [including] providing a quality standard work or duties generally expected by the sport consumer ... and [is] provided to enhance the experience' (Schwarz, Hunter, & LaFleur, 2013). The major product type that a facility produces is an intangible service product (i.e. the event experience), whilst secondary product categories can include tangible manufactured product categories (i.e. merchandise, food, and beverages).

Services marketing is a particular type of marketing that emerged in the 1980s in recognition of the fact that services are very different from goods, and as such the marketing of services needs to be approached differently. The differences between services and goods are typically explained with reference to four unique characteristics shared by all service products – intangibility, perishability, inseparability, and variability (Shilbury et al., 2014).

Intangibility

Intangibility is the key distinguishing characteristic between services and goods. Moreover, it is from the service product's intangibility that the other three characteristics emerge. Intangibility refers to the product's inability to be touched and seen in the same way that other products can be (e.g. a tennis racquet, golf balls). As a deed, effort, or performance, a service is also an 'experience'. A key problem for facility and event marketers resulting from the intangible nature of services is the inability to store them – that is ...

Perishability

Perishability refers to the fact that services cannot be stored (i.e. inventoried). Services cease to exist if they are not sold when they become available. An inability to store the service product inevitably results in the problem of matching supply and demand. For example, a baseball stadium with a capacity of 40,000 might achieve an average occupancy of only 70 per cent throughout the season, but be sold out during the playoffs or finals (a very common problem). Unfortunately, the facility or event marketer does not have the ability to store the unused seats from earlier games during the season and sell them later in the season when demand is high.

Inseparability

Inseparability of production and consumption refers to services being produced and consumed simultaneously, or in 'real time', as opposed to being produced first and then consumed at a later date, as is the case with manufactured goods. With services, the customer and the service provider(s) are present when the service is experienced. In addition, there also may be influences from other customers that are present. The key marketing implication associated with service inseparability is that each of the parties present (the customer, service providers, other customers) can either enhance or detract from the service experience.

Variability

Variability refers to the changes in consistency from one service to the next. This inconsistency is largely due to the fact of not only inseparability, but also the three parties who directly influence the service experience – the primary customer, the service provider(s), and other customers. Thus a key marketing implication associated with service variability relates to quality in terms of ensuring that customers receive consistent levels of quality from one service experience to the next. Unfortunately, many times when something goes wrong with the facility or event service, the quality cannot be remedied before it reaches the customer. For example, when a long-term corporate customer of an event and their accompanying guests are provided with the wrong tickets, they are effectively 'locked out' of the stadium until a supervisor arrives to fix the mistake. Because this mistake occurs in real time, there is nothing that can be done to stop the impact it has on the customer. Instead, considerable effort needs to go into 'making it up' to the customer.

MARKETING STRATEGY

The implications of the four unique characteristics of services (intangibility, perishability, inseparability, and variability) need to be acknowledged by facility and event marketers and accommodated by using a services marketing framework when marketing their facility or event products. But beyond the products and services of sport facilities and events, there is also a need to develop a marketing strategy that seeks to move the organisation forward towards a vision. Inherent to this strategy are the pricing strategies developed, the distribution channels utilised, and the communication with potential customers through promotions. These four elements – product, price, place (distribution), and promotion – are known as the '4 Ps' of marketing, or the marketing mix.

The development of a market strategy is central to the strategic sport marketing planning process. A strategic plan is a complete and integrated plan for moving a sport organisation towards its forecasted projections as a business. For a sport facility or event, this could range from growth in the number of users/spectators to the continuous operation of the business – but most certainly all strategic plans have a vision for profitability and growth over time. Through the strategic planning process, internal strengths and weaknesses are measured and evaluated, external opportunities and threats are assessed and addressed, objectives and strategies are developed, organisational structures are refined, action plans are implemented, and key result areas are benchmarked and measured for performance.

From the viewpoint of attracting customers as part of marketing strategy, there is a need to determine who the customers of sport facilities and major events are. Consumers are as vastly different as the enormous population and various cultures of the globe. However, there are methods for reaching these consumers – perhaps not all of them, but at least those who are most relevant to your specific sport facility or event. This is where the central concepts of marketing strategy become valuable: market segmentation, target marketing, and product positioning. These concepts enable an organisation to better meet customer needs and wants, and thus simultaneously achieve its own objectives.

Market segmentation

The concept of segmentation involves dividing a large, diverse population with different characteristics into smaller groups with specific attributes. Usually these segmented groups have similar needs and wants, and it is expected that they can be marketed to in a comparable way. Segmentation is the most basic concept of marketing because the ultimate goal is the initial effort of identifying a specific market from a larger population.

Market segmentation starts by identifying the bases for segmenting, or breaking down the total market. Numerous types of segmentation criteria exist (e.g. demographics, psychographics, geographic, behaviours), with marketers often using them in combination (e.g. age and lifestyle). Managers of sport facilities and major events tend to utilise some combination of the four bases of segmentation to start identifying their clients. These include the consumer's state of being, the consumer's state of mind, product usage by consumers, and product benefits as perceived by consumers. For example, some of the more specific variables that multi-purpose facilities such as an aquatics centre might use to segment their consumer participant market include: type of user group (e.g. individual, family, school), preferred services (e.g. lap pool, leisure pool, fitness centre), and benefits sought (e.g. relaxation, fitness, rehabilitation). As a result, the choice of segmentation variables can vary greatly from one organisation to the next. What is important, though, is for the variables, and thus the resulting segments, to be meaningful.

Once the market is segmented, profiles of resulting segments are developed so they can be studied and understood. This requires the facility or event marketer to develop a profile of each segment in order to get to know, or develop an understanding of, the potential customers contained in that segment. For example, having identified three business market segments of potential sponsors, an event organisation such as NASCAR will seek additional information on each segment (e.g. values, objectives, expectations, product range). In combination with the next steps in market segmentation (i.e. targeting and positioning processes), an enhanced understanding of market segments enables a facility or event organisation to select the right markets. A compatibility of organisational values, for example, can be very important when it comes to targeting sponsors.

Market targeting

The concept of market targeting is to determine the best way to get the image of the sport facility and event products or services into the minds of the consumers who are most likely to be interested in those products or services. This is completed through a research and planning process that centres on the development of measures of segment attractiveness, and selecting the target segments.

After the facility or event marketer has identified and profiled a variety of market segments, they must identify which segment(s) to pursue. This is because it generally makes sense for an organisation to strive to meet the needs and wants of some rather than all potential customers. Therefore, the first step involved in target marketing is to measure the attractiveness of each segment, or determining those customers that offer the best potential for current and long-term profit for the sport facility or major event. For example, you are trying to determine who is most likely to take out a membership in a fitness facility or purchase tickets to a hockey game.

As part of this process, each segment is ranked according to its degree of attractiveness, based on such factors as size and growth potential, competitors (i.e. both current and potential), and the objectives and resources of the facility or event. Ultimately, these factors point to the profitability of a target market, which is a popular means of segmenting the market into targets.

Once the ranking process described above is complete, the facility or event marketer can select the most attractive target(s). The marketer may choose just one target market or several. As previously noted, facilities and events have a range of customers, and indeed product offerings, and will thus select several market segments.

Market positioning

Following the identification and selection of the preferred target market(s), the facility or event marketer needs to determine the position his or her organisation and its products and services should occupy in those target markets. Positioning focuses on how a sport organisation can best influence the attitudes, behaviours, motivations, and perceptions of current and potential customers regarding the image of their sport products and services. In the case of sport facilities and events, the goal is to get the targeted individuals to react in a positive manner to the messages being sent by the marketer because it will be easier then to entice them to purchase the products and services on offer.

Creating and maintaining a desired position is a critical marketing function, as the position a product occupies in consumers' minds affects their buying behaviour. This is accomplished by employing a variety of positioning strategies for each target segment. The choice of positioning strategy is normally based on competitive advantage, which focuses on the things customers believe the organisation does better than competitors. When contemplating competitive advantage, it is important to consider who the competitors of a sport facility or event competitors are. For instance, spectator sport is part of the entertainment industry, and consequently sport facilities and events are in competition not only with each other but with non-sport-themed facilities (e.g. concert halls and exhibition centres) and their respective events. Moreover, major facilities and events often find that their competitors are hundreds – if not thousands – of kilometres away and perhaps even in a different country. A facility or event can be positioned based on its product attributes (e.g. covered seating in a venue), the benefits it offers (e.g. the ability to go on the field after the game to score goals), and the class of user (e.g. corporate season ticket holder benefits such as meet-and-greet with coaches or special events).

A facility or event can also be positioned directly against, or even away from, competitors. The Commonwealth Games and the Olympic Games are both major international and elite multi-sport events, but the Commonwealth Games are positioned as the 'friendly games', whereas the Olympics' position is more in line with being the 'best of the best', which is consistent with its motto of 'faster, higher, stronger'. Instead of employing single positioning strategies, facility and event marketers may choose to use a combination of them.

Different positioning strategies will be more appropriate for certain organisations and certain products. As such, it can be difficult to think of one strategy as being superior to another. However, according to Armstrong et al. (2011), some of the prime positions to occupy are best quality (e.g. premium seating), best service (e.g. corporate hospitality), lowest price (e.g. tickets), best value (e.g. season tickets), and most technologically advanced (e.g. in-seat game analysis, food ordering, and communication tools).

Irrespective of the strategy chosen, what is important is that marketers determine the position they want their organisation and products to occupy rather than letting the market decide it for them. Consumers will position a known product in their minds even without any prompting or manipulation on behalf of the facility or event marketer. However, as positioning affects customer choice and hence organisational success, it cannot be left to chance but must be managed instead.

Lovelock, Patterson, and Wirtz (2014, p. 83) list four undesirable outcomes for those service organisations that fail to engage in positioning:

1   The organisation (or one of its products) is pushed into a position where it faces head-on competition from stronger competitors.
2   The organisation, represented by its offerings, is pushed into a position that nobody else wants because there is little customer demand there.
3   The organisation's service position is so fuzzy that nobody knows what its distinctive competence really is.
4   The service has no position at all in the marketplace because nobody has ever heard of it.

Develop marketing mix for each target segment

The development of the marketing mix for each target segment is the focal point of positioning products and services appropriately. As mentioned previously, the traditional marketing mix centred on the 4 Ps – product, price, place, and promotion. Over the past years as global sport business has evolved, especially in the services area, so too has the marketing mix to incorporate people, physical evidence, and process in marketing strategy. A brief summary of each element is provided below.

- **Product:** what type of good or service is offered to the target market, and what are its benefits.
- **Price:** how much money the product costs the customer.
- **Place:** also referred to in terms of distribution; the availability or accessibility of the product in terms of location and timing.

- **Promotion:** the communication of the benefits, or desirable characteristics, of the product to the target market via such means as advertising, sponsorships, public relations, personal contract, licensing, incentives, and atmospherics.
- **People:** the two groups of people that need to be considered, and thus managed, are those who provide the product (i.e. the employees of the selling organisation), as well as those who consume it (i.e. the customers).
- **Physical evidence:** the tangible component of the product; physical evidence in the context of facility and event marketing may include the facility itself, scoreboards, staff uniforms, tickets, and seating.
- **Process:** the series of steps by which the service is eventually delivered to the customer as a combination of 'backstage' (invisible to the customer) as well as 'front of stage' (visible to the customer) steps.

Each of the seven marketing mix elements must be consistent with the desired position of the products and services rendered through a sport facility or event. Therefore, each of the aforementioned elements must reflect this position. As well as being consistent with the positioning strategy, the marketing mix strategy must be consistent with the needs and wants, as well as characteristics of the customers that the facility or event manager is trying to attract. As such, strategies to attract and retain 'consumer market' customers need to be quite different from those needed to attract and retain 'business market' customers.

Marketing strategy constraints

Marketing strategy is constrained by many factors in addition to those pertaining to positioning and the needs, wants, and characteristics of customers. Figure 8.1 identifies many of these constraints, as well as a range of possible revenue sources flowing into the facility or event organisation and a variety of expenses flowing out. The items included in Figure 8.1 by no means form an exhaustive list; they may also vary somewhat between facilities and events, and over time (i.e. the duration of a particular event, a season, or several years).

Figure 8.1 shows that the extent to which revenue can be generated and money expended is very dependent on these marketing constraints. The design of the facility, for example, affects the amount of money the facility or event can generate in numerous ways. The larger the venue, the greater the number of tickets that can be sold; but also the higher the initial capital outlay on building the venue will be, as well as the ongoing costs of operational functions such as maintenance, cleaning, and utilities. Perhaps most important in terms of the relationship between revenue generation and both facility design and event production is whether the facility adequately caters to the media, as the media are necessary for promotion, sponsor attraction and satisfaction, and the production of a successfully broadcasted product.

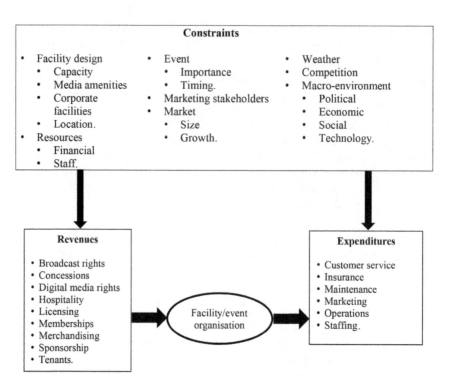

Constraints

- Facility design
  - Capacity
  - Media amenities
  - Corporate facilities
  - Location.
- Resources
  - Financial
  - Staff.

- Event
  - Importance
  - Timing.
- Marketing stakeholders
- Market
  - Size
  - Growth.

- Weather
- Competition
- Macro-environment
  - Political
  - Economic
  - Social
  - Technology.

Revenues

- Broadcast rights
- Concessions
- Digital media rights
- Hospitality
- Licensing
- Memberships
- Merchandising
- Sponsorship
- Tenants.

Facility/event organisation

Expenditures

- Customer service
- Insurance
- Maintenance
- Marketing
- Operations
- Staffing.

Figure 8.1 *Marketing strategy constraints*

MARKETING INFORMATION SYSTEMS

A key role for the marketer is to ensure that revenue generation exceeds expenditure. Exactly how this is achieved is a real challenge, and varies from event to event and between facilities. Compounding this challenge is the fact that that customer needs and expectations will continue to evolve. While events can quite easily be changed to accommodate the uniqueness of the market or venue, the marketer must work with a mostly inflexible 'bricks and mortar' facility structure that is difficult to modify in any significant way, and if it can be modified it is usually exceptionally expensive to do so.

As a result of these evolving needs and wants, a sport facility or major event needs to have a quality marketing information system in place. Such a system ensures that all aspects of the sport organisation understand they have the responsibility to collect, organise, review, evaluate, and articulate marketing information across the facility or event. The dissemination of information greatly assists with solving problems and making decisions related to ever-changing consumer needs and wants.

A marketing information system is made up of four components. First is market research, which focuses on designing data collection instruments and then gathering primary and secondary information in response to a specific marketing issue related to the facility or event. Once the data has been analysed and reported, the appropriate decision makers within the organisation will come up with a plan of action for solving a problem or implementing a new strategy.

The market intelligence system works beyond but in concert with the market research function in that the marketers of facilities and events collect primary and secondary intelligence via scanning the environment. In this second stage, primary intelligence is collected by the sport facility or event through their direct contact with customers through conversations and observations, as well as observing behaviours. Secondary intelligence is information obtained from reports and research published previously by other sources such as books, trade journals, and reliable sources online. The goal of collecting this data is to have a better understanding of the opportunity for, and threat to, the facility or event, and helps marketers and managers address issues in as proactive a manner as possible.

The third component involves the internal reports system. The internal report system does the same internally within the facility or event organisation as market research and intelligence does externally to the organisation. This examination of the internal operations of the sport facility or event involves being able to collect data from all relevant departments. For example, the facility operations department data could include the results of staff evaluations, internal assessment audits, benchmarking metrics, and evaluation results. From accounting and finance, it would include data mined from daily transactions, point-of-sales systems, and supply chain interactions. Ultimately, this data should be able to show the strengths and weaknesses of the organisation, and allow decision makers to implement positive change.

The final part of the marketing information system is the DSS, or decision support system. This system takes all of the information collected through market research, intelligence, and internal reports, and organises the data so that decision makers can make informed conclusions and implement solutions in a timely manner. The ultimate goal is to be able to make control, marketing, operational, and strategic decisions for sport facilities and major events that will lead to a higher level of customer satisfaction, which in turn will enhance brand image and maximise profits.

CONSUMER BEHAVIOUR

Beyond quality marketing information, sport facility and event marketers must also have a keen understanding of consumer behaviour. Consumers display all types of emotional behaviours related to the use of products and services in the sport industry. If we are to use the data collected through the marketing information systems combined with the strategic marketing plan strategies, there must also be a clear understanding of the range of emotions and behaviours customers may exhibit.

There are a number of factors that need to be considered. From the internal perspective of the customer, emotions and behaviours will be exhibited in the form of personality, attitudes, motivations, and perceptions. The most common external influences of consumer behaviour come from cultural influences, social interactions, and the environment. These all have a direct influence on the levels of commitment, involvement, and socialisation by spectators and participants via their interactions attending events or using facilities, and through the self-interpretation of the experiences during those interactions.

The main goal of understanding the various elements of consumer behaviour is to influence the customer to utilise a facility or attend an event, thereby meeting their needs and wants through the programming offered. This will hopefully also lead to customers making additional purchases of ancillaries (food, beverages, merchandise) or to return to the facility or event in the future as a returning customer.

ATTRACTING CUSTOMERS VERSUS RETAINING CUSTOMERS

More often than not, marketing strategy focuses on attracting customers rather than on retaining them. This is evident in consumer markets as well as business markets. However, keeping customers is just as important as attracting new customers, particularly when you consider customers in terms of lifetime value. Calculating a customer's or group of customers' lifetime value involves auditing the financial worth of retaining them over a certain period of time (not necessarily a lifetime), and therefore their importance to the facility or event organisation.

Customer lifetime value, as a function of the costs of serving a customer and the revenue received from the customer over the particular time period, is expressed as follows:

Time period × (Revenue − Costs) = Customer lifetime value

So, for example, the lifetime value of a golf club member over a 10-year period might be $50,000, whereby:

- time period = 10 years
- annual revenue = $6,000
- annual costs = $1,000.

Not only does a facility or event forfeit the money that lost customers would have spent on the core product (i.e. $5,000 annually in the golf club membership example), but it will miss out on the money spent on a range of peripheral products, such as food and beverages, merchandise, and peripheral activities such as use of the driving range or participation in tournaments. It is also possible that lost customers will cause

others to leave, making for an even greater loss in revenue. In our golf club member example, it is possible that two or three friends who regularly played with that member would follow him or her to utilise the services of a competing golf course.

The ramifications for other types of facilities can be much more serious when you consider how a decrease in live-at-venue customers for the spectator facility may also result in lost business customers. Many sponsors want large crowds at the events and facilities they sponsor because to them a large crowd is a sign of success, and sponsors wish to be associated with this success. Also, these crowds are often part of the sponsor's target market. Therefore, a smaller crowd represents a reduced opportunity for the sponsor to promote its products, and for some sponsors a reduced opportunity to sell products as well. This is accentuated when an event is covered by the media. Broadcasters also prefer large crowds at the events they televise, as a large and enthusiastic crowd contributes significantly to the atmosphere of the event and thus enhances the attractiveness of the sport as a television or digital product. In turn, it is the degree of attractiveness of the broadcasting product that drives advertising sales, which are the primary source of revenue for broadcasters.

In addition to the current customers they could lose, facility and event marketers should concern themselves with the loss of potential customers. Two of the most successful means of promoting services are through positive word-of-mouth and social media interactions. Those customers that are lost because they were unsatisfied with some aspect of the facility or event service provided are unlikely to recommend it to friends, colleagues, families, and other businesses. As a result, these lost customers may actually spread negative word-of-mouth and social media postings about a facility or event, actively deterring potential customers. Research shows that customers are much more likely to complain about products they find fault with, as well as the organisations that produce them, rather than to spread good news about those which satisfy them (Shi, Liu, & Zhang, 2011).

Although a convincing argument for retaining customers has been made, it is true that facility and event organisations often have the financial capacity to weather the loss of several and even hundreds of consumer customers. For example, any large facility such as the Millennium Stadium in Cardiff would not suffer too much if it attracted 69,000 spectators instead of its anticipated 70,000. This is not the case for business customers, as these customers are significantly fewer in number but contribute tens and hundreds of thousands (and sometimes millions) of dollars to the revenue stream of a sport facility or event. Retaining sponsors and broadcast partners are both critical, given that these customers generate more revenue for facilities and events than do spectators.

Strategies for retaining customers

We have highlighted the importance of retaining customers, and that the easiest way to retain customers is to satisfy them. But what is it that makes a customer's facility or event experience a satisfying one? Essentially, customers will be satisfied

Figure 8.2 The relationship between quality, satisfaction, and retention

when they get what they want, and all customers want quality! The relationship between quality, satisfaction, and retention is depicted in Figure 8.2.

As an example, Murray and Howat (2002) explained that sport and leisure centre participants' perceptions of service quality on a range of factors (e.g. staff, programme, parking, child minding) influenced their satisfaction and in turn their repeat purchase intentions. While the importance of retaining customers has already been stressed, customers spending more time at facilities and hence at sporting events are also an important factor. Essentially, the more time customers spend at an event, or in a facility, the more likely they are to spend large sums of money. This relationship also holds true also for business markets (i.e. event owners and promoters, sponsors, and broadcasters). Moreover, the ability to serve, satisfy, and retain one particular type of customer is related to the successful retention of another. If a quality facility or event produces satisfied spectators or participants who keep coming back for more, they contribute to the satisfaction and retention of event owner and promoter, as well as that of sponsors and broadcasters.

Sport Servuction Model

A useful tool for all facility and event marketers interested in maximising the quality of their services and hence customer satisfaction and repeat purchasing is Shilbury et al.'s (2014) sport-specific adaptation of the servuction model (Langeard et al., 1981), shown in Figure 8.3. The Sport Servuction Model depicts the different elements that constitute the facility and event service experience as well as how the service experience is created.

The Sport Servuction Model can be divided into two parts: that which is visible to the customer (i.e. customer A), and that which is not. The visible part of the model comprises three components: (1) facility, design, and physical evidence; (2) contact people including staff and service providers; and (3) and other customers (i.e. customer B). The invisible part of the model, which should play a 'support' role for the rest of the model, comprises just one component. Although Langeard et al. (1981) referred to this component as the invisible organisation and system, in a facility and event management context it is more aligned with the traditional marketing department role, whereby event owners/promoters work together with facility owners/managers to plan and organise the event. The services (i.e. bundle of benefits) experienced by the customers come from each of the model components as well as the way in which they are synchronised, or coordinated.

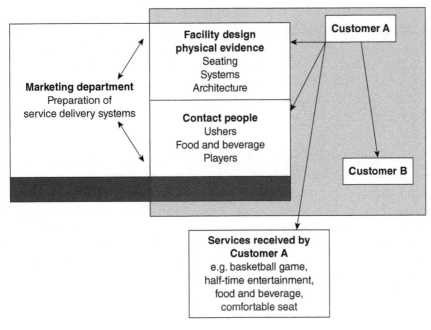

Figure 8.3 The Sport Servuction Model

Source: Shilbury et al. (2014)

The association the Sport Servuction Model has with the relationship between quality, satisfaction, and retention discussed previously in Figure 8.2 is that its visible and invisible components have the potential to positively, as well as negatively, influence a customer's service experience, and thus affect the benefits he or she receives. Together with a brief description of each component, examples of the ways in which each component may positively influence a facility or event customer's experience are outlined in the next sections.

Facility design and physical evidence

The non-living features that are present during the service encounter constitute what Langeard et al. (1981) referred to as the inanimate environment. In a facility and event management context, this means the facility itself, incorporating non-physical elements like music, lighting, and odours, as well as physical elements such as scoreboards and staff uniforms. A centrally positioned and air-conditioned corporate suite complete with digital television, Wi-Fi access, a top-of-the-range fit-out, quality food, and well-stocked bar is an example of how the facility design and physical evidence can positively influence the experience of the corporate customer.

203

Contact people

The contact that customers have with facility and event staff involves direct and indirect interactions. Direct interactions include spectators handing their tickets to ushers, or buying beer from food and beverage staff. Indirect interactions are remote in nature, such as spectators watching players participate in the game experience, or the official signalling a time out.

Customer B

Whereas customer A is the recipient of the bundle of service benefits, customer B refers to all other customers present during customer A's experience. Sport facility and event products are nearly always publicly consumed, whether it is watching a Formula 1 race in Shanghai, competing in the London Marathon, or networking in one of the Masters Golf tournament corporate marquees. Getting involved in fan interaction activities, laughing, talking, and cheering with fellow fans, and the atmosphere created by a full house, are all examples of how other customers can positively influence the spectator's experience.

Marketing department

This particular component of the sport servuction model relates closely to management philosophy and incorporates various rules, policies, and procedures, including the what, where, when, why, and how of service production. A plethora of considerations, including membership eligibility criteria, dress codes, the number of ushers, turnstile attendants, and security employed at any one event, all need to be addressed by the marketing department. In addition, a policy ensuring a streamlined and well-organised accreditation process, whereby the broadcaster's production crew and other VIPs are couriered their passes in a timely fashion, is an example of how the marketing department can positively influence the experience of those constituencies.

Sportscape Model

Another model modified for use from the services industry is the Sportscape Model, The framework for this model was derived from Bitner's Servicescape Model, which identified '(1) ambient conditions; (2) spatial layout and functionality, and (3) signs, symbols, and artefacts' as the primary dimensions of service (Bitner, 1992). It was with this framework that Wakefield, Blodgett, and Sloan (1996) postulated that the physical environment in sport facilities, and by connection the associated events taking place in those facilities, have a direct effect on the perceptions spectators have about the experience, and help in their decision-making process whether to stay longer at an event, or return to the facility for future events.

 In their initial model, Wakefield, Blodgett, and Sloan (1996) identified stadium access, facility aesthetics, and scoreboard quality as pleasurable factors that would

Attracting customers

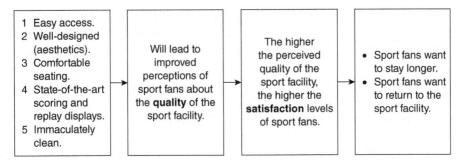

Figure 8.4 *The Sportscape Model*

Source: Shilbury et al. (2014) (originally adapted from Wakefield & Blodgett, 1996).

potentially influence spectators to stay at an event and repeat their patronage in the future. They also identified seating comfort and facility accessibility, both from the perspectives of space allocation and signage, as potential negative influences in terms of perceived crowding, which would detract from the desire to stay or return to the facility.

Over the years the Sportscape Model has been adapted and modified. One such modification is articulated in Figure 8.4.

This interpretation articulates that to improve the perceptions of facility and event users, customers want good access to the facility, need the design to be aesthetically pleasing, want comfortable seating, need the most current technology to be available for their use or viewing, and desire a clean and secure atmosphere (Shilbury et al., 2014). As such, if the facility or event user perceives that each of these areas is of the highest quality, they will be more satisfied with their experience, and hence will stay longer at events – and more importantly return to the facility or event as a return customer.

RELATIONSHIP AND EXPERIENCE MARKETING

Service quality, customer satisfaction, and customer retention are central to relationship marketing. As seen in the models from the previous section, this area of marketing evolved during the early 1990s, and then quickly accelerated to a place of great significance within the marketing discipline by the turn of the century. Relationship marketing is concerned with building, maintaining, and enhancing long-term customer relationships to the benefit of both customer and organisation.

Relationship marketing evolved due to the realisation that in a highly competitive market, it is often not enough to merely conduct transactions with customers. It had become increasingly necessary to retain customers that will purchase from the organisation on multiple occasions. Thus, underpinning relationship marketing is a repeat purchasing or customer retention philosophy, as well as a method for evaluating customer satisfaction. Further underpinning relationship marketing is a 'win–win' philosophy whereby the objectives of both the customer and the service provider are met.

Relationship marketing in sport facilities and major events initially involves creating quality customer service and face-to-face interactions. However, as there has been a significant shift towards a service-based economy, in addition to the continued evolution of wireless and digital technologies, relationship marketing has grown to include non-face-to-face interactions through social media and other asynchronous communication methods.

Beyond relationship marketing is the evolution of experience marketing. With the decrease in discretionary time and customers' desire to get more value for their money, sport facilities and events have needed to find additional ways for customers to receive additional personal interaction opportunities. These may include a pre-game concert outside the arena, activities in the lobby and rotunda for children to play, or even being allowed out on the field after the game to run bases or score goals. Through experience marketing, the goal is to offer more value and hopefully entice customers to want to come back because of their positive experience at the facilities attending an event.

No facility or event organisation should blindly engage in relationship or experience marketing activities with all customer groups, but should make an effort to reach as many as possible. Hence facility and event marketers need to carefully consider which customers are most worthy of the resource expenditure associated with relationship or experience building and maintenance. Also important to note is that not only are some customers better suited to relationship or experience marketing efforts than others, so too are some organisations. However, given the business customers that facilities and events typically have, as well as the fact that many facilities' customers are also members, most facility and event marketers should be engaging in at least some relationship and experience marketing activities.

MULTIPLE MARKETING STAKEHOLDERS: THE CHALLENGES OF RESOURCE COMMITMENT AND COORDINATION

A fundamental question still to be answered, especially in the context of business customers, is 'Who is responsible for marketing the facility or event?' The answer to this seemingly straightforward question is largely dependent on whether the organisation that owns the event also owns the facility in which it is run, and whether it will run and promote the event itself. However, with the exception of small and typically participation events, as well as some professional sport events (more often than not in the USA and the UK), most events are not owned, run, promoted, and housed by the one organisation. Instead, several different parties may be involved, each of which can play a marketing role.

As a result of the multiplicity of parties involved in running an event, and hence the larger pool of marketing resources and knowledge, it is surprising that this does not always result in more successful marketing campaigns. Instead, and particularly

in a professional sport context, it can be a challenge to get the various stakeholders (i.e. league, facility, club) to make a reasonable marketing contribution in terms of resource commitment. Likewise, it can be a challenge to coordinate the marketing efforts of the various parties, with efforts being duplicated in places and absent in others. These two challenges can easily result in a marketing campaign that does not reach its full potential, namely one that does not produce as many customers as possible and consequently puts fewer dollars in all parties' pockets.

When parties in addition to a league, facility, and club (as in the professional sport context) are factored into facility and event marketing strategy, the coordination challenge noted previously becomes even more complex. For example, major sport events such as the Rugby World Cup require multiple facilities (typically managed by separate entities), and often employ the outsourced marketing services of firms such as Octagon or the International Management Group (IMG) in addition to their own. Furthermore, and at least in an Australian context, when major facilities are seeking to attract events, they are often assisted by the marketing might of government-backed events corporations such as the Victoria Major Events Corporation, whose purpose is to attract national and international events to their respective states. Finally, there are also the promotional efforts of sponsors and broadcasters, with sponsors assisting promotional efforts by way of logo exposure, and broadcasters delivering the promotional message of the sport facility or major event to a mass audience. As a result, the question of who is responsible for marketing the facility or event is not necessarily a simple one.

SUMMARY

The emphasis of this chapter has been on the marketing of facilities and their events. Consistent with the definition of marketing presented at the beginning of the chapter, we stress the importance of facility and event marketers identifying, understanding, and meeting the needs of a variety of customer markets, including individual consumers as well as businesses. The facility and event product is described in terms of four unique characteristics of services: intangibility, perishability, inseparability, and variability. These characteristics, as well as their considerable implications, necessitate that facility and event marketers adopt a services marketing approach.

A particular focus of this chapter, including the case study, has been on marketing strategy, notably the steps of market segmentation, targeting, and positioning. In addition to describing this strategy process, we have introduced several strategy constraints specific to the marketing of facilities and events. We have also emphasised the importance of creating a quality marketing information system including sub-systems focused on market research, internal reports, intelligence, and decision support; as well as understanding the multiple internal and external factors that shape consumer behaviour.

The final part of the chapter emphasised the importance of retaining customers, noting the relationships between service quality, customer satisfaction, and customer retention. Two models to guide retention – the Sport Servuction Model and the Sportscape Model – were also presented. With this customer retention focus, we also discussed the evolution and importance of both relationship and experience marketing.

CASE STUDY

Attracting customers to the Singapore Sports Hub

The Singapore Sports Hub has become one of the crown jewels of sport complexes in Asia since its opening in 2014. The state-of-the-art sports, entertainment, and lifestyle facilities are integrated into a 35-hectare hub in Kallang that offers the opportunity for people to participate in and watch a variety of events.

The Singapore Sports Hub includes the following facilities:

- a 55,000-seat retractable roof National Stadium,
- a 13,000 seat indoor stadium,
- a 6,000 seat aquatics centre,
- a 3,000 seat multi-purpose arena,
- a water sports centre, which includes programming for canoeing and kayaking,
- the Kallang Wave Mall – a 41,000 square metre retail and dining area,
- a sports information and resource centre with an exhibition centre, library, and sport museum,
- a water park for children,
- numerous open spaces for community, sport, and recreational activities.

The Singapore Sports Hub is a public–private partnership between Sport Singapore and SportsHub, and is a central part of the sports master plan articulated in the Singapore Government's Vision 2030, the main goal of which was to create a major sport, recreation, and leisure district that can be used by all – from novice to elite.

While such a sport complex has several advantageous infrastructure and amenity assets, there also needs to be a significant plan to attract customers ranging from everyday users to world-class sport and entertainment events. For the Singapore Sports Hub, this includes a dedicated sales team that focuses on a multitude of traditional and personal marketing to encourage event owners to bring their products to one of the facilities. In addition, this team conducts regular market research to determine what the needs of customers are – including those attending the events as spectators, those participating in events as athletes, and recreational users – investing in the events as partners or sponsors, and operating events as clients of the Singapore Sports Hub.

The marketing and sales team also realised that they cannot do all the work by themselves to attract customers. They work cooperatively with the National Sport Association, the Singapore Sport Council, the Singapore Tourism Office, and other public and private agencies to determine the needs of clients and consumers alike, as well as to attract events to the complex.

Some of the efforts they have implemented include:

- Communicating directly with international sport organisations around the world to attract major events in a multitude of sports – with a special focus on athletics, cricket, football, and rugby.
- Submitting bids for sport tournaments at all levels – youth to professional.
- Submitting bids for international competitions and championships.
- Promoting the Singapore Sports Hub at international sport and entertainment conferences and conventions to get in front of potential clients.
- Educating international promoters about the vast offerings of the complex, as well as offering opportunities for co-promotion of events.
- Advertising through international trade publications, and pitching advertorial articles to build brand awareness.
- Using digital and social media to promote current events, and showing how they have the ability to hold multiple events at the same time, thereby creating an interactive experience across multiple audiences.

In their first full year of operation, it seems the marketing team at the Singapore Sports Hub has done well. According to their website (www.sportshub.com.sg), they had over 3.5 million visitors in 2015, which included 1.4 million guests across 124 sport and entertainment events, nearly 550,000 users of recreational and leisure facilities and programmes, and over 1.6 million attendees to festivals and carnivals.

Questions

1   Singapore is a city-state island off the coast of Malaysia with a population of around 5.5 million people. In 2015, approximately 10 per cent of the population (550,000) potentially used the recreation and leisure facilities. What would you do to market these facilities to attract more customers?

2   In facility management, there is always a 'honeymoon' period for a new complex where people want to go to the facilities during the first 2–5 years because they are new and want to experience them. Once 2020 comes and the 'honeymoon' period is over, what would you need to do as a facility marketer to ensure people keep coming back?

3   Singapore is a major international location that many people transit through to go to other parts of Australasia when travelling from North America and Europe. How would you go about marketing the Singapore Sports Hub to entice these travellers to stay in Singapore on a layover and attend events at the complex?

REFERENCES

Armstrong, G., Adam, S., Denize, S.M., & Kotler, P. (2015). *Principles of marketing*. 6th edition. Frenchs Forest: NSW Pearson.

Bitner, M.J. (1992). Servicescapes: The impact of physical surroundings on customers and employees. *Journal of Marketing, 56*, 57–71.

Langeard, E., Bateson, J., Lovelock, C., & Eiglier, P. (1981). *Marketing of Services: New Insights from Consumers and Managers, report no. 81–104*. Cambridge, MA: Marketing Sciences Institute.

Lovelock, C., Patterson, P., & Wirtz, J. (2014). *Services marketing: An Asia-Pacific and Australian perspective*. 6th edition. Frenchs Forest, NSW: Pearson Education Australia.

Murray, D., & Howat, G. (2002). The relationships among service quality, value, satisfaction, and future intentions of customers at an Australian sports and leisure center. *Sport Management Review, 5*(1), 25–43.

Schwarz, E.C., Hunter, J.D., & LaFleur, A. (2013). *Advanced theory and practice in sport marketing*. 2nd edition. Oxford, UK: Routledge.

Shi, W-H., Liu, J-Y, & Zhang, Y. (2011). The effect of service failure attribution on consumer complaint behavior: The mediating role of negative emotion. *The Journal of China Universities of Posts and Telecommunications, 18*(2), 169–173.

Shilbury, D., Westerbeek, H., Quick, S., Funk, D. C., & Karg, A. (2014). *Strategic sport marketing*. 4th edition. Sydney: Allen and Unwin.

Wakefield, K.L., & Blodgett, J.G. (1996). The effect of the servicescape on customers' behavioral intentions in leisure service settings, *Journal of Services Marketing, 10*(6), 45–61.

Wakefield, K.L., Blodgett, J.G., & Sloan, H.J. (1996). Measurement and management of the Sportscape. *Journal of Sport Management, 10*(1), 15–31.

CHAPTER 9

RUNNING THE SPORT EVENT: EVENT OPERATIONS

CHAPTER OBJECTIVES

In this chapter we will:

■ Consider the breadth and depth of management activities involved in the implementation and event phases of hosting an event.

■ Determine some of the value adding and value destructive moments of memorable customer experiences.

- Identify the key elements of logistics management and outline the practical on-site logistical tools, techniques, and coordination methods to effectively stage an event.
- Discuss the important communication, command, and coordination requirements of sport event incident management.
- Highlight the needs of different stakeholders through discussion of the practical arrangements required to specifically manage spectator, volunteer, and on-site media service needs.

INTRODUCTION

Lights ... Camera ... Action! Well, this is it! The moment of truth has at last arrived. All the hours, days, months, and in some cases years of event preparation are about to be put to the test. Time has run out, the adrenaline and anticipation levels are at an all-time high, and the focus of attention is entirely centred on producing a memorable, quality experience that exceeds stakeholder expectations at the same time as optimising resource utilisation.

To this end, we plan to provide a practical insight into the management activities demanded primarily of the implementation and event phases of the event lifecycle (see Chapter 2, Figure 2.3). Having determined some of the value added and value destructive moments of spectator experiences, we draw your attention to the key elements of logistics management. This will include introducing some of the on-site practical tools and coordination methods that help management to create effective and efficient people, information, and other resource flows around the sport(s) event venue(s).

To provide a greater depth of understanding and analysis of the operational aspects of a major sport event, the remainder of this chapter focuses on some of the practical arrangements in specifically managing event security, incidents, and emergencies, as well as spectator, volunteer, and media needs. These elements have been purposely selected on the basis of their transferability and functional importance to many other sport event scenarios. They also demonstrate the previously established principles of comprehending different stakeholder needs, and highlight the integrated and complex nature of managing sport events holistically, across the project lifecycle.

MEMORABLE CUSTOMER EXPERIENCES

As identified in Chapter 1, features including going beyond safety, necessity and usefulness, indulgence, and entertainment have become the cornerstones of modern day event consumption (Killian, 2009). To fulfil the hedonistic needs of affective gratification, spectators search out and are prepared to pay premium prices to engage with extraordinary moments and memorable customer experiences (Lindgreen, Vanhamme, & Beverland, 2009). However, effective management of hedonistic needs presupposes knowledge of what constitute the moments that ensure a highly satisfying and memorable customer experience.

Using the moments of truth of a mega-sport event spectator experience, Emery, Kerr, and Crabtree (2016) used a multi-method approach to appraise the critical incidents, the emotions, and the value added and destructive moments of a spectator's holistic experience. In summary, they identified five common moments that spectators expect of a memorable customer experience, namely to build the moment, watch the moment, be 'in the moment' (ideally an intense wow moment), capture the moment, and share the moment. The effect of some of these value drivers is evident in Figure 9.1, via the heart rate graph of one spectator attending the 2012 Olympic torch relay event. Triangulating heart monitoring, self-reported questionnaire, and interview data, an in-depth contextual understanding of this 50-minute segment of a 3-hour tracked spectator experience was ascertained. Elaborating further, Figure 9.1 reveals an average heart rate of 98 beats per minute (bpm), and reported a single high excitement memorable moment (point A), namely the 20 seconds of torch viewing. Heart rate increases are evident in the build-up phase, (point B – constituting approximately 23 minutes; 83 bpm to 120 bpm), being in the moment phase (approximately 3 minutes; highest recorded pulse rate was 123 bpm and occurred as the torch went past), and post-event sharing the moment phase (point C) over a coffee (between 35 and 50 minutes). Just talking about the experience highlighted a 91% of maximum heart rate recording of 112 bpm.

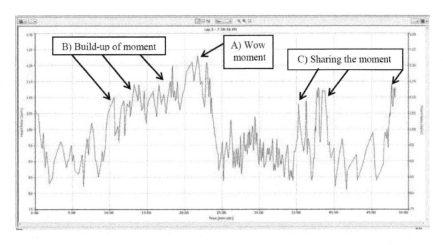

Figure 9.1 Heart rate graph of a torch relay (single-moment) non-ticketed event spectator experience

Similar data was triangulated with ticketed multi-moment sport event experiences and verified the self-reported occurrences of both positive and negative peaks of arousal emotions. Emery et al. (2016) found that these moments were found not necessarily to exist in isolation or to occur as a linear sequence. In essence, the holistic nature of the experience was considered to be a series of highly interactive single or multi-moments which collectively formed a very personal hedonistic experience.

Learning exactly when and where spectators experience value added and value destructive critical incidents and emotions provides useful insights into how to improve physical and social-servicescape management for maximum effect. For example, Emery et al. (2016) added:

> Managers can eradicate the frustrating hurdles of negative service encounters, such as time spent queuing, dysfunctional crowd movements, and by responding immediately to service recovery breakdowns. Similarly, detailed and fully tested 'last mile' traffic flow plans and staff training to recognise early signals of customer stress, can be implemented before pre-event rage occurs. To facilitate the occurrence of positive emotion encounters, more creative opportunities should be developed that stimulate the senses and valued added moments of the live experience.

Such findings demonstrate, however, an interesting paradox for sport event managers to address. While on the one hand spectators want to control their own individual experience space and expect authentic, spontaneous surprises, event managers are highly accountable and must provide safe experiences for all stakeholders. This requires detailed planning and a big brother approach to monitoring and controlling multifarious needs. As expressed by one event organiser:

> Meticulous planning and staging are crucial when trying to create a spontaneous and vibrant atmosphere. This can be understood in terms of 'staging' because things like lighting, space and noise and furniture are tools of 'mood' to be manipulated. Stage managing their environment can often ensure that the guests do not have to be 'ferried' around and will 'naturally' go home at the right time! It is interesting that the most tightly staged environment will often inspire guests to feel a natural part of a very exciting party.
>
> (Bowdin et al., 2012, pp. 493–4)

Due to the sheer complexity of activities, information, and people that memorable customer experiences are likely to involve, it is logistics management that provides the means to stage a successful event.

LOGISTICS MANAGEMENT

Effective coordination and communication at the event implementation and event phases require a clear understanding of the project goals, the different stakeholder needs, and an ability to manage practical logistics within the physical constraints of the venue(s). Logistics, defined as 'the time-related positioning of resources to meet user requirements' (cited in Bowdin et al., 2012, p. 524), is practically about making sure the right people, equipment, and services are available in the right place at the right time.

In the event management scenario, this means establishing coordinated systems, which ideally permit effective and efficient flows of people, information, and other resources around the event venue(s). As highlighted in Figure 9.2, the essential elements of establishing an overall event logistics system consider the supply of customers, products, and facilities to the event and around the event, and then determine the event shutdown arrangements.

Providing a linking function of procurement, supply, and movement, event logistics are particularly important where events involve large numbers of international participants, are multi-sport and multi-venue oriented, and include one-off hosting. For example, Glasgow 2014 Commonwealth Games had to process more than 70,000 accreditations and prepare more than two million meals for its stakeholders (100 tonnes of fruit and vegetables, 10,000 loaves of bread, 25,000 litres of milk)

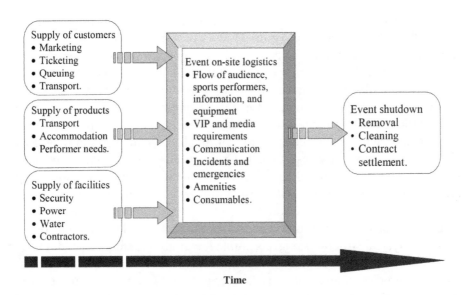

Figure 9.2 Elements of the logistics system

Source: Adapted from Bowdin et al. (2012, p. 525)

(Glasgow 2014, p. 27). While the Rio 2016 Olympic Games logistics team managed the complex arrival and accommodation of 800 boats and 315 horses for its sailing and equestrian events (Rio 2016, 2016), London 2012 (2011), created a logistics function focusing purely on materials and equipment movement and storage. Handling an estimated 30 million items, their logistics role specifically included materials management, warehouse operations, distribution, customs and freight forwarding, courier services, and venue and village logistics.

In considering the supply element of the logistics system, transport management is a potential major cost and risk to the success of most events. In the case of London 2012, as well as detailed arrangements for athletes, technical officials, media, and VIPs, a second edition of the Transport Plan for spectators and public transport users of more than 230 pages was published at least a year before the event commenced (Olympic Delivery Agency, 2011).

Before the event begins, clearly all stakeholders (including contractors) need to be aware of when, how, and where they can gain access to the venue immediately before, during, and after the sporting contest. Similarly, for an event to run smoothly, the timely supply of products and technical facilities (including power supplies) must be of an appropriate standard and be arranged according to the event owner's as well as national legislative requirements.

ON-SITE LOGISTICS AT THE EVENT

The on-site logistics, the main emphasis of this chapter, given its operational focus, mean that regardless of the event venue(s), the flows of materials, people, and information around the site (including sport and non-sporting venues such as hotels and airports) become critical elements in exceeding stakeholder satisfaction levels. The ultimate aim must always be to create a safe secure environment, which unfortunately has not historically always been the case. The secondary aim, and probably the main purpose of the organising committee's work, is to create an enjoyable and positively memorable experience for all concerned. Although these may sound like basic ideals, they are not necessarily easy to achieve due to the complex nature of the event management environment (as introduced in Chapter 2). For example, sport events are usually dependent on working with large numbers of volunteers (whose reliability and competence are largely untested) as well as many different organisations, each with their own agenda and assumed expectations of the local organising committee. Temporary physical structures (e.g. corporate hospitality marquees, media facilities, participant/spectator toilets, performer stages, spectator seating areas) and other service utilities are also often needed, each demanding its own 'bump-in'/'set-up' and 'bump-out'/'break-down' arrangements, which again have largely been untested.

Furthermore and as previously mentioned, time is the limiting factor for all concerned. As the event draws near, the tempo accelerates and everything becomes classified as urgent. Long working hours, confrontations, and a distinct lack of sleep are common occurrences at many sport events. On the one hand, the working environment is likely to become a highly energised and rewarding experience; on the other, it has the potential to be very stressful, where the smallest incident can create annoyance, conflict, and a crisis. Obviously, the easiest solution is to try to manage these uncertainties by preparing rationally for potential contingencies.

Given that safety must always be considered the first priority of event operations, let us initially introduce security, incident, and emergency management processes, before focusing our attention on managing some of the prime stakeholders' needs, and illustrating the use of tools commonly used in the operations of event management.

EVENT SECURITY, INCIDENT, AND EMERGENCY MANAGEMENT

Every organisation should be committed to establishing high standards of health and safety for the continuing quality reputation and image of the event, the venue(s), as well as all of the people associated with it. The bottom line is that event organisers must ensure the safety of all of the event's participants and comply with appropriate legislation by taking all reasonable and practicable steps to prevent, control, and guard against risks that directly affect the event.

In light of the terrorist acts of 11th September 2001 in the United States, high-profile sport events, attended by world-famous celebrities and receiving intense global media coverage, are particularly vulnerable to all types of risks and extreme activities. This means that every event manager must now be prepared to confront a wide variety of security issues and risks that need to be professionally managed.

In managing these risks, comprehensive communication, command, and coordination policies and procedures are required which are usually arranged around the following key areas of a sports facility:

- **Front of house (FOH):** general circulation and seated/stand areas where services are provided for the spectators (e.g. toilets, catering, merchandising outlets, seats).
- **Back of house (BOH):** the operational and management areas, which are rarely seen by the public (e.g. storage areas, meeting rooms, corridors, and the essential event control centre/s).
- **Field of play (FOP):** includes the sport performance and preparation areas.

As operational plans are usually determined in the first instance by the physical entrance (ingress) and exit (egress) parameters of each facility, it probably comes as no surprise to learn that the security systems of major events typically involve trained staff being strategically located at these points to check access rights at both the venue perimeter and the internally restricted zones. For spectators, entrance to the FOH activities generally means ticket inspection at the main entrance, followed by a progression through airport-style metal detectors and accompanying baggage being checked by X-ray machines. Given the popularity of some events and the likely queues that would result from these and other related security procedures, it is not uncommon for spectators to be advised to arrive at least two hours before the start of the event.

For other stakeholders (e.g. the athletes, officials, media, sponsors, VIPs, and event staff) who need to access the BOH and FOP activities of different venues, alternative entrances and exits are used. Similar procedures to those for spectators are usually implemented at the main perimeter entrance but, rather than using a ticket, entrance normally takes place through some form of official identification, commonly referred to as accreditation. The accreditation system is a stakeholder-focused access control system, and is considered a fundamental element of the operational security programme since it confirms identification and provides appropriate access rights to a particular venue and designated areas within a venue. For example, it keeps unauthorised people out of secure competition zones, and ensures elite athletes arrive in a safe, timely, and orderly manner in which to compete.

Accreditation passes typically take the format of a sealed laminated identity card that includes at least the name, position and photograph of the wearer, as well as details of the particular zones of access. Yet such is the increased concern for people's safety at sport mega-events that advanced computer security packages are now being developed to apply cutting-edge, non-intrusive biometric techniques to the accreditation process, such as iris/fingerprint scanning and voice/face-recognition systems to considerably improve the validity of the identification and verification processes. To illustrate this increase, the first Olympic Games to be held after the 9/11 terrorist attacks in New York City were held in 2002 in Salt Lake City, Utah (Winter Olympics) and had a price tag of US$400 million. In contrast, a decade later in 2012, the London Summer Olympics has a budget of over £1.1 billion (US$1.7 billion).

Whereas accreditation may be less significant in smaller events and merely involve face recognition or fluorescent bracelets as the means of access, in the case of major sport events the process of issuing passes to each client group needs to be carefully thought through. Key deadlines need to be established and the method(s) of accreditation pass distribution communicated to all relevant parties in a timely manner. This is to ensure that vital police checks and other security approvals can be achieved on time. In the case of the written and photographic press accreditation for an Olympic Games, accreditation requests are often submitted 16 months before the event, and collected in person just one month before use.

Normally there is at least one accreditation centre for issuing accreditation passes, which is set up close to, yet outside, the main sporting venue. This centre is supported by appropriate IT hardware and software that collects and securely stores the necessary graphical data, which are then used for security purposes. At the same time and location, staff are usually allocated their official event uniform. Common sense suggests that this uniform should be ordered to size to optimise resource utilisation, and staff collection times staggered to avoid the inevitable volunteer queues.

However, as London 2012 (2011, p.31) explains, even when coherent accreditation systems are established and operated:

> history and experience have proven that many persons will seek or expect accreditation with greater access privileges than what is actually needed for their roles. It is important to be aware of this and the likelihood of abuse. But, it should also be recognised that despite the best of efforts and intentions, there will also be many legitimate cases in which an individual's badge does not have the proper access privilege to do their job.

To avoid embarrassing and often heated conflicts at the moment of venue entry, additional 'what-if scenarios' should always be planned. For example, what happens if people lose or forget their accreditation passes, or cannot pick them up at the designated time? Or what happens if individuals need to access an area urgently to fulfil a task that they do not have accreditation approval for? Flexibility may be permitted in certain circumstances, but never at the expense of reducing event security.

The impact of a security breach or an incident occurring at a large sport event should never be underestimated. The 1989 Hillsborough Stadium football disaster (in Sheffield, England) reminds us of how a relatively minor incident, of late fans arriving, quickly escalated into panic and a major crisis, where 95 fans died. As a result of such event tragedies occurring around the globe, it has now become common practice for national legislation to insist that event and venue managers produce a workable incident, emergency, and crisis management plan before any major sport event can take place.

It is the local organising committee in consultation with the key multi-agencies of the police and other emergency services that initiate the incident, emergency, and crisis management plan and draw on the management process of scenario development. Derived primarily from the risk management process, this plan needs to address the many incidents requiring emergency action, such as fire, overcrowding, loss of electrical power, a bomb or bomb threat, and other acts of violence or terrorism. On the other hand, event incidents and emergencies by their very nature are often unpredictable, so it is important from the outset to realise that no emergency action plan will ever cover detailed procedures for every potential scenario. Flexible arrangements must always exist, but key principles relating to the formalisation of specific responsibilities, the establishment of synchronous communication mediums, and clear procedures for reporting and monitoring incidents are essential if stakeholder safety is to be paramount in the manager's mind.

Communication, command, and coordination are the three pillars to effective event operational decision making. To illustrate how these pillars create an integrated operational framework, let us draw on the incident, emergency, and crisis management arrangements for the International Association of Athletics Federations (IAAF) World Indoor Championships in Athletics (WICA) – a one sport and one competition venue event scenario.

From Figure 9.3, which largely focuses on the emergency incidents occurring at the WICA sport venue itself (other arrangements are made for alternative venues), it is evident that a clear hierarchical line of communication and control exists. This needs to be communicated and understood by all staff, whether internal or external, and whether working in a paid or voluntary capacity. Indeed volunteers are often the very first persons to identify incidents and they, like everyone else, need to be made aware of their role and the behaviour expected of them in case an incident does occur. Unfortunately, in the event industry today, management often adopt 'it'll be alright on the night' and/or 'it'll never happen to me' philosophies, which means many volunteers do not even know who their line managers are or the emergency procedures to implement if urgent action becomes necessary.

Communication is the lifeblood of an integrated operational response to an incident using the incident, emergency, and crisis management plan. However, understanding who needs to know what and when are fundamental additional requirements for establishing an effective incident system that permits clear information flows and escalation processes. Command escalation or transfer to emergency services in crisis situations are dictated by routine versus exceptional protocols. For example, Figure 9.4 illustrates WICA's reporting and escalation process, the operational procedure for informing the key decision makers of an incident/issue.

This process endorses the general principle that, where possible, a routine incident may be solved immediately and at the lowest appropriate level. However, if a volunteer identified an incident that was not considered to be routine, at WICA they were expected to verbally communicate the nature of it to the line manager. The line manager then determined whether or not to escalate it to the attention of the venue manager by radio or telephone. Using closed-circuit television cameras and radio or telephone communications to source and allocate additional resources to the incident location if necessary, meant that the incident could still be resolved at the local venue level. However, if this were not possible, the venue manager would contact the event communications centre, which in turn would inform the incident management centre and, in the ultimate case, involve contact with the police control room (Figure 9.3). Obviously, the nature of the incident would dictate both the urgency and primary means of the communication as well as the direct line of communication. For example, the identification of a serious fire or violent

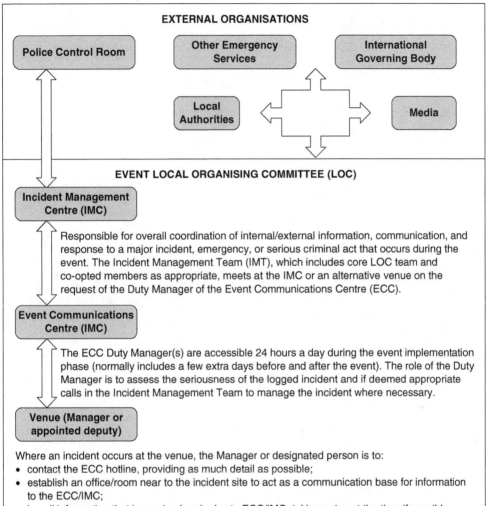

EXTERNAL ORGANISATIONS

Police Control Room

Other Emergency Services

International Governing Body

Local Authorities

Media

EVENT LOCAL ORGANISING COMMITTEE (LOC)

Incident Management Centre (IMC)

Responsible for overall coordination of internal/external information, communication, and response to a major incident, emergency, or serious criminal act that occurs during the event. The Incident Management Team (IMT), which includes core LOC team and co-opted members as appropriate, meets at the IMC or an alternative venue on the request of the Duty Manager of the Event Communications Centre (ECC).

Event Communications Centre (IMC)

The ECC Duty Manager(s) are accessible 24 hours a day during the event implementation phase (normally includes a few extra days before and after the event). The role of the Duty Manager is to assess the seriousness of the logged incident and if deemed appropriate calls in the Incident Management Team to manage the incident where necessary.

Venue (Manager or appointed deputy)

Where an incident occurs at the venue, the Manager or designated person is to:
- contact the ECC hotline, providing as much detail as possible;
- establish an office/room near to the incident site to act as a communication base for information to the ECC/IMC;
- log all information that is received and relay to ECC/IMC, taking notes at the time if possible;
- liaise with Police and Civic Authority Incident Officers representing IMT;
- establish details of those who may have been injured/involved. Forward a list to Police to request information or assistance;
- continue to liaise with police and IMC monitoring developments and issuing progress reports until relieved by an IMT-nominated person.

Figure 9.3 World Indoor Athletics Championship's incident communications

Source: Adapted from World Indoor Championships in Athletics (2003a)

incident between sports fans would probably involve direct communication with the respective emergency services, via a spectator, participant, staff member, or the representative of the emergency service member(s) actually present at the event. In

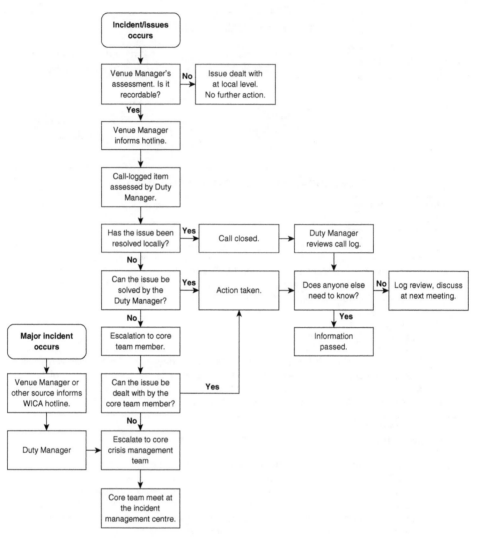

Figure 9.4 World Indoor Athletics Championship's reporting and escalation process

Source: Adapted from World Indoor Championships in Athletics (2003a)

such a situation, simultaneous communications are likely to exist. This is why the venue control centre usually contains the senior multi-agency staff of the event – so that they can collectively manage the incident through information gained from their own (e.g. police site incident officer) and other staff, as well as through the most advanced information technology on site. Emergency procedures should have been discussed and rehearsed in advance to determine the most appropriate implementation actions. This normally includes pre-scripted announcements to the general public as well as pre-typed forms that permit transfer of responsibility, for example from the event organiser to the police, through just two signatures.

Exceptional incident management, in the WICA scenario, therefore meant reporting deviance from the plan:

> For example, something that is deemed minor such as a delay to the opening of the training centre by five minutes. It is still a deviation from what is planned and has to be recorded. It may be something far more serious and which will require escalation to the core IMT [incident management team]. Once a recordable incident is logged at the ECC [event communications centre] it will be assessed by the Duty Manager ... available at all times. Where a log has been closed without escalation it will be for the Duty Manager to decide whether anyone needs to be informed urgently. If not, it can wait for the next update meeting. If required, the IMT will be contacted and will meet at the IMC to manage the major incident.
> (World Indoor Championships in Athletics, 2003a, p. 6)

Similar communication, command, and coordination processes underpin all sport event incident and emergency management procedures; however mega-events demonstrate a greater level of complexity and clarity due to their multi-venue and high-risk nature. For example, to control venue operations communications across the Olympic Games period, London 2012 (2011) used an event control room suite comprising the following:

- **Event control room:** at each competition venue that contained the emergency services forward command post. This was the central hub from which venue operations were directed and the safety of all persons on-site was monitored.
- **Venue security command centre**: the security operation communication hub that monitored the security perimeter and protected the event's assets.
- **Venue communications centre:** the area where all radio channels were monitored.
- **Venue operations centre:** the office space for the venue management team and all other functional areas to file their reports and manage their paperwork.

In addition, this venue suite reported to and communicated with the primary hub of Games-wide information, namely the 24-hour off-site management operations centre (MOC). Containing the representatives of key functional areas, external liaison officers of six other coordination centres, and the Director of the Games, the MOC provides the true coordinated integration of all resources and decisions affecting incidents and crisis management. A combination of responsive and proactive communication mediums, such as morning and evening briefings, reports, shift handover, communications, and forward look meetings, enables effective communication during large-scale events such as the Olympics. London's 2012 MOC, for example, used a dynamic web-based system (iTrack) to log and track all Games occurring issues (exceptional incidents). This meant that for each issue, MOC staff were expected to input sufficient detail to include what happened when, where, why, and involving whom; establish the issue's ongoing severity level; and track the issue over time as either being at the opening, monitoring, escalating, or closing stage.

In other words, the system of event incident reporting needs to be coherent, logical, and efficient. This also requires decisions and communication flow processes and actions to be well documented. Only then will safety, incident, and risk management be synonymous with professional management.

MANAGING KEY STAKEHOLDERS

Up to this point, we have largely focused attention on the incident and crisis management processes of the event delivery phase. However, successful on-site logistics management usually demands a greater level of stakeholder understanding and venue appreciation than currently presented. In this section, we will provide a more detailed and specific focus on managing some of the prime stakeholders, since there are important implications that are transferable to nearly all sport events.

Managing *spectators within the last mile*

The first and last impressions of an event are critical to the memorable nature of the spectator experience, so arrival and departure times are important to get right. While the chapter opened with the identification of the value-added moments of what constitutes a memorable customer experience, it also made reference to the value destructive incidents and particularly those pre-event spectator encounters that occurred within the 'last mile'. With Emery et al. (2016) reporting that 80 per cent of the Olympic Games spectator anxiety emotions occurred outside the venue and before the event took place (20% after), the last mile is a vitally important part of the spectator experience to be managed. Defined as 'the designated route from transport hubs such as tube stations to competition venues ... an area for the safe, enjoyable passage of ticketed spectators' (London 2012, 2011, p. 13), the last mile frequently encounters heavy crowd densities where considerable spectator uncertainty exists. As a shared area of management that involves local authorities, transport providers, emergency services, and local property owners, roles and responsibilities are often vague, resulting in incidents of anger and violence, particularly at football events.

Managing spectators travelling to and from the venue initially involves understanding both the nature of the event and the likely composition of its key stakeholders. For example, with more athletes than the Olympics, the World Masters Games, a mixed-ability multi-sport aged 35-plus participant event, would possess very different spectator management practices than a highly competitive professional football derby with passionate fan groupings.

With spectator events that are considered high profile and high risk, such as the Olympic Games, the area of responsibility outside each venue is effectively managed by the establishment of three concentric security rings. The first and innermost ring constitutes the purpose-built venue boundary. This includes 'hard' security measures of permanent barriers, security screening technology, and trained staff performing ticketing and accreditation checks at a limited number of access points. The second security ring is considered a traffic management checkpoint to sort spectators from the general public. Here, temporary physical elements are established, such as barriers, cones, and security personnel, who will turn away non-ticketed spectators. The third and outer ring, by comparison, largely focuses on 'soft' measures of security and primarily focuses on information sharing. For instance, this is often the first area that spectators come across staff and signage that provide traffic management information and assist with the pedestrian flow to and from the transport hubs and the sports venue(s). Throughout these three concentric circles, the aim is to keep spectators constantly moving so as to avoid the creation of any dangerous bottlenecks from which anxiety and anger can quickly escalate.

The more important the spectator group to the successful operation of the event, the greater the depth of logistical analysis and planning of this last mile. In practice, it was particularly challenging to manage last mile logistics at the 2012 Opening Ceremony (Olympic Park Precinct) due to the presence of the Westfield Shopping Mall (adjacent to the venue) and because there were only two VIP drop-off points (Mann, 2012).

Defined on a venue-by-venue basis, dynamic pedestrian flows and crowd management operations outside the venue clearly impact onsite logistics inside the venue. Important questions to consider include, what is the spectator arrival time, how many spectators are anticipated in total, and are they likely to arrive via public or private transport, all at once (known as a 'dump') or as a 'trickle' (across a longer time frame)? What car parking requirements are there? Similarly, how many of these spectators are likely to require special needs assistance?

In most developed countries around the world, organisations are rightly being pressured to remove physical and social access barriers that have existed for many years and disadvantaged many groups of the population. In the United Kingdom, for instance, the Equality Act 2010, broader than and replacing the previous Disability Discrimination Act, directly affects all event and facility providers, who are now expected to address historical physical access issues by installing ramps and lifts, improving signage for the visually impaired, installing induction loops for those with impaired hearing, and providing special needs car parking spaces.

Furthermore, to improve socially inclusive practices, it is not uncommon to involve special needs groups in the planning processes of an event. As well as establishing important marketing networks, long-term relationships, and key employees for the event, such meetings accompanied by site visits can provide vital information for the event organisers that enhance the experience of all spectators. From such knowledge, spectator expectation and the demand for particular services can be more effectively planned and promotional activity more specifically targeted to spectator needs. For example, Commonwealth Games spectators buying tickets were initially asked whether they would like wheelchair positions, companion seats, easy-access seats, and access to an induction loop or verbal commentary. Additional information explaining 'what you can expect' (e.g. wheelchair-accessible venues with appropriate parking, ramps/lifts, signage and toilets; escort service for spectators with a visual impairment; an induction loop system that could be linked to hearing aids) and similarly 'what you cannot expect' (e.g. short-term loan of mobility equipment; assistance with medication, feeding, or personal hygiene) proved highly valuable to both service provider and consumer. London 2012 similarly ensured that they addressed accessibility issues for 'people with disabilities, the elderly, very young and/or infirm' (London 2012, 2011, p. 38) in venue design, operations planning, and volunteer training, and offered consumers a Games Mobility Service that provided assistance with spectator movement through competition venues and public areas.

Spectator entry and exit gates are particularly important crowd management areas to control due to their potential for bottleneck capacity, because of their hard security measures and a limited number of pedestrian flow access points. At the venue threshold, queuing lanes aided by clear signage, pre-recorded announcements, way-finding staff – some with megaphones and high position umpire chairs – will all help to create orderly and safe spectator flow. Entering and exiting crowds may additionally require separating and involve flexible arrangements depending on the spectator type (e.g. aggressive loyal fan history), volume, and spectator flow. Where multiple sessions occur at a venue, tight turnaround times may exist that often require 'holding areas' and in the case of emergencies 'blow out' gates being available both for spectator and vehicle access.

Clearly all spectator and stakeholder movements within and external to the venue need to be carefully planned, tracked, and monitored by real-time communications. This involves pre-event spectator guides/information, cooperative management, dynamic contingency plans, and detailed executive handovers, particularly within the last mile of venue operations.

Managing volunteers

As mentioned in Chapter 2, volunteers are also one of the key stakeholder groups to be effectively managed. Indeed their contribution cannot be understated since they can determine whether the quality outputs of the event will be met. Globally, they are the backbone of sport, and many suggest that without them the majority of sport events would cease to exist (Doherty, 2009). As suggested by Flávia Fontes (2014), head of the Rio 2016 Volunteers Program:

> The volunteers are indispensable to the success of the Games, they are the soul of the event ... A person in the city could go through the Games without seeing an athlete with their own eyes, but it would be impossible not to meet a volunteer. They play a part in everything, helping and providing information to spectators, assisting heads of state and providing operational support at the ceremonies.

To demonstrate the initial desire to volunteer at mega-events, Rio 2016, for example, received 240,000 applications for 70,000 positions (IOC, 2016) spanning nine areas of involvement – operational support, customer service, sports, press and communication, protocol and languages, health care services, ceremony production, transportation, and technology. For a minimum 10 days of working up to 10 hours a day, promoted volunteer benefits were cited as 'exclusive training including an English course, meals on work days, transport within the metropolitan region of Rio de Janeiro, and a complete uniform' (Rio 2016, 2016).

However, it must be remembered that sport event volunteer involvement is not founded on the basis of receipt of an income, but on the satisfying of unique and often undeclared motivations. In this sense volunteers are both a human resource strength as well as a weakness in the event delivery phase. On the one hand, they have chosen to give their own free time and are therefore personally committed to the event, possessing expectations to be fulfilled. On the other hand, if their expectations are not met they can and will walk away at any time, potentially creating high risk management scenarios and the non-achievement of event goals. To avoid this disastrous and worst-case scenario, volunteers must be fully briefed, listened to, and sincerely valued at every opportunity.

From the very first contact made with them, volunteers are expecting to work with an organised, knowledgeable, and professional team of staff who are driven by a clear sense of purpose and unity. Minimally, this is communicated to volunteers through a pre-event training programme to induct them into the event and their designated role requirements, as well as provide them with timely access details to the event accreditation and uniform collection processes.

More specifically, referring to the practical implementation phase of managing volunteers at sport events, Allen and Bartle (2014) suggest that volunteer engagement is significantly enhanced by a management practice that offers volunteers choice, encourages self-initiation, listens to and acknowledges the volunteer perspective, minimises pressures and controls, and provides informational feedback. This is not to suggest that volunteers dictate their needs, but rather that they should be listened to and where possible their requests incorporated into highly account-able management activities. For example, each volunteer must be fully briefed as to the expectation of their role and be provided with details of their shift roster before the event begins. Assuming that staff cover is available, such shifts may be flex-ibly established to accommodate personal circumstances, such as transportation or prior commitment issues. Standard operating practices, however, should not be compromised, such as the commonly established staff check-in arrangements. This is where volunteer attendance is recorded, meal vouchers are distributed, and up-to-date information is provided, often in the form of a daily event newspaper or central noticeboard. Once checked in, the volunteer needs to report directly to the team leader, who confirms their specific role for the day as well as convenient rest and meal breaks for the shift. In this way, the appropriate team leader or substitute line manager is formally identified, and both parties become aware of each other's general location should any unforeseen incident or emergency occur.

It is important to realise that effective volunteer management also entails consid-erably more than just a polite introduction of names and faces in the event delivery phase. From a volunteer perspective, Walker (2001) suggests that there are com-monly five main incentives for becoming a volunteer, namely achievement, power, affiliation, recognition, and altruism. All volunteers are likely to have their own expectations, and management needs to recognise and reward these, applying the basic motivating principle of equity within their particular resource constraints. For many volunteers the tangible reward of receiving branded clothing or other memo-rabilia will be sufficient to satisfy their needs, particularly as these provide external social symbols that last well beyond the duration of the event. On the other hand, if volunteers are expected to provide the enthusiastic professional customer care service demanded of an event, they additionally need to encounter a similar work-ing environment of friendliness, openness, trust, and respect. As many volunteer training programmes suggest, 'a friendly smile supported by warm body language are internationally contagious'. Line managers must therefore lead by example and take every opportunity to listen, involve, and inspire volunteers both as individu-als and collectively as a team. In many cases, volunteers just enjoy the feeling of being of use (purposive objectives), and hence that their ideas and actions might have helped in some small way to achieve the event/department goals. External and internal praise must be constantly given to reinforce the very important 'valuing of volunteer efforts'. This might be in the form of daily verbal (de)briefing(s), writ-ten comments in the event newsletter, or even rewarding excellence through job enrichment or enlargement opportunities, volunteer merit schemes, or by creating spontaneous and unique photographic opportunities and thereby providing even more enduring memories of the event.

To further thank volunteers, it is customary practice to organise a social party directly after the event. This provides another opportunity to sincerely demonstrate appreciation of volunteer effort but also helps to meet affiliation objectives. For many volunteers, the sole purpose for becoming involved is to meet and make new friends. Through team building, social activities, and onsite areas to relax and have a break, very strong bonds can be developed that offer additional opportunities for developing friendship and employment networks. As a win-win scenario, well planned and managed volunteer programmes can spread the 'happy volunteer camaraderie' experiences and establish improved levels of satisfaction, and thereby create further volunteer/employment opportunities for staff and managers in the future.

Managing media services

Another increasingly significant stakeholder to be carefully managed at events is the media. Without a doubt, in this global and technological world, the media possess considerable power as they can convey positive and negative messages/images that can make or break an event. Given the media's power and influence, as well as the fact that at mega-sport events there are nearly as many media personnel as competing athletes to service, let us conclude this stakeholder focus of event operations by describing how the media expect to be managed at the event.

This is probably easiest to achieve by understanding who the media are and what they need at the live event. The collective entity known as the media is a diverse group of organisations and individuals that include journalists, accredited photographers, rights-holding television and radio representatives, and agents to other media sources. Put simply, they continuously require timely event information via verbal, electronic, and paper means so that they can communicate their contemporary and creative messages to their respective organisations and the public. Print deadlines are usually very tight, and the experience of broadcasting sports activities live means that there is often only one opportunity for them to get it right. A missed photograph opportunity or late report will not please the publisher. So media personnel normally operate in a very hectic, pressurised, and stressful environment, and require the very latest technological and human means to support their work. From a management perspective, this means establishing clear, effective, and efficient internal and external communication systems, fully tested and supported hardware and software, appropriate physical locations, accreditation, and extensive subsistence arrangements, as well as highly reliable and helpful staff who can problem solve under considerable pressure.

The types of media services provided by management are obviously matched to the demands of the sport, the nature of the event, and the specific requirements of the governing body(s). For example, the nature of an athletic competition is such that the event provides ongoing winners throughout the duration of the event, unlike that of a team sports event, where there is only one winner which usually signifies the end of the spectator venue experience. As the sport of athletics is one that creates perhaps the most complex demands of media services, this will form the main focus of sport event examples utilised for this client group.

Most major athletic championships, such as the 2015 International Paralympic Committee (IPC) Athletics World Championships in Doha, entail the establishment of physical structures that host the local organising committee media office and the international governing body (IPC) press office. Overseen by the head or director of media services, the following interconnected locations are then specifically organised and usually coordinated via a manager, an assistant, and a team of volunteers to carry out their respective servicing functions.

Media centre

This is the main central in-situ working and information area, where all accredited media staff can gain access to competition and general information, as well as be provided with the technical means to communicate globally (e.g. the Internet and pay phones). It usually contains a staffed media help desk, which is the coordination point that is verbally and physically connected to other media sites (via technical infrastructure, i.e. telecommunications, and human infrastructure, i.e. runners). As the main registration point, it provides media guides, pigeonholes for up-to-date event information, a message board, locker access, refreshments, and many other support services such as photocopying or useful contacts to arrange transport, accommodation, and/or tickets.

Audio/visual centre

This is similar in nature to the media centre, but it specifically focuses on the needs of the photographic press. Services again include a help desk; seated desks with Internet connections for digital photography needs; a camera loan and repair service, along with a film processing and dispatch desk; a hospitality area for refreshments; lockers; and the inevitable pigeonholes containing the news, start lists, results, and qualification lists.

Media box (in venue)

This is the working area set aside for the media that overlooks the field of play. In the case of athletics, these are the tabled and non-tabled seats located in the stadia at the finish line. As most of the media in the venue are providing live commentary, Internet connections and power cables need to be carefully taped down and be accessible to every tabled seat. While online services and electronic data are the primary source of information flow, volunteers, commonly referred to as 'runners', assist the media by quickly distributing start lists, results, and athlete quotes by hand and in a non-intrusive manner; this is particularly useful should there be a power failure. In practice, this is one of the most physically demanding volunteer positions, as it requires fit and agile volunteers to negotiate narrow rows and stair-ways as they constantly run to and from photocopying facilities and the media staff.

Mixed zone

Located just off the track, this is the secured exit that provides the accredited media with the first opportunity to ask the athletes questions on the competitive outcome. Immediately after the sporting competition has finished, athletes are obliged to walk through the entire mixed zone, which logistically takes them to the anti-doping test-ing centre before the medal ceremonies and then, where appropriate, to the press conference room. As well as external media there is usually an internal news agency team present in the mixed zone. It is their job to obtain 'info or flash quotes' from the athletes, and to distribute this information along with daily previews, reviews, and press conference summaries and other miscellaneous news items through the media centre.

Press conference

This is where the official press conferences take place with the event medalists; it also includes special news bulletin items, such as announcements of drug test results. The room is typically laid out in a conference style, and communication with interviewees (e.g. athletes, event organisers) is managed through a chairperson and the use of remote microphones.

It is apparent that media service needs at a sport event can be very specific and quite diverse. In this sense, it might be more appropriate to classify the management activities of media service requirements into four strands, namely:

- informational
- opportunity
- technological
- support service needs.

While informational and support service needs may be common to all media person-nel, specialist provision of opportunity- and technology-based activities/equipment needs to be very carefully planned and tested in consultation with both the event owner and category of stakeholder. For example, photographic media needs and procedures are likely to be very different from the needs of radio broadcasters and written journalists, and could specifically include:

- the expectation of a raised platform on the outfield for 100-metre head-on shots and medal ceremonies;
- a system to manage the maximum number of photographers permitted on the infield at any one time;

- cloud-based data storage facilities and high-bandwidth Internet connections to send and edit large media files;
- on-site digital enhancement hardware and software, along with a camera rental and a repair service.

Such focus and attention to detail, including media access to specialist equipment and facilities 24 hours a day and seven days a week, is, like all stakeholder management, a necessary condition in the event phase if the event is to be regarded as a success.

LOGISTIC MANAGEMENT TOOLS AND TECHNIQUES

To achieve such detail that can be shared, tested, and improved daily in the implementation and event phases of operation, Bowdin et al. (2012) suggest using the following logistic tools:

- **Venue site plan:** often includes details of the entrances/exits, fixtures, access and flow arrangements, car parking, electrics, accreditation zones, and the location of support services.
- **Contact list and communication system details:** for example the lines and means of communication, radio channel usage, incident and emergency procedures.
- **Production schedule:** a chronological master document with activities, timings, locations, and responsibilities.
- **Run sheets:** for specific jobs, e.g. VIP speeches and other announcements.
- **Cue sheets:** for prompting, if things do not go according to plan.

In briefly elaborating on each tool, the venue site plan usually refers to the sport(s) event venue(s) (although major sport events are also likely to include a venue plan of some of the non-sporting venues such as the athletes' village). Typically, venue plans are presented in a diagrammatic form and are customised to the needs of each client group. For example, Figure 9.6 summarises the important location details of the media facilities of the IAAF World Indoor Athletic Championships. Such a venue plan was further supported by a written guide, in the language(s) of the event owner, which details many of the operational aspects that directly influence the quality of service provision. In this instance the event media guide, for example, included the competition timetable; access, accreditation, and transport arrangements; the nature of the electrical and information technology provision; and details of the support services, other social events, and the vitally important contact and communication arrangements should further information be required. Site plans should provide clarity and become particularly useful aids to identify traffic flows and to establish contingency as well as emergency plans.

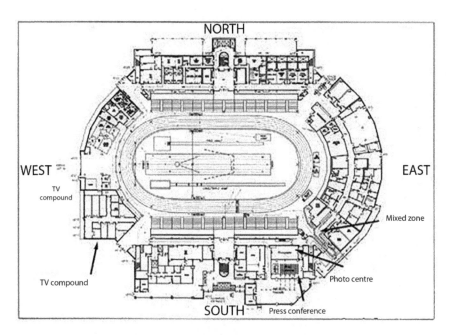

Figure 9.5 Media facilities within the National Indoor Arena, World Indoor Athletics Championships

Source: Reproduced with permission from World Indoor Championships in Athletics (2003b, p. 10)

To reduce the likelihood of emergencies and to efficiently operate crisis management plans should they occur, the contact list and communication systems for the whole event need to be recorded in some detail. For each stakeholder, key contact arrangements must be accurately and concisely thought through and shared with appropriate staff. For training purposes, communication decisions are often presented in flow diagrams (see Figure 9.4). However, given their importance in event operations, communication contact responsibilities and actions are usually printed and shared via an Emergency Procedures Sheet (see Table 9.1), with contact numbers/channels additionally included on the back of all accreditation passes. Since event communications are largely coordinated through an on-site control centre, and additionally an off-site control centre at larger events, lines of communication and radio channel usage must be carefully planned, tested, and reviewed to avoid congested channel traffic and inappropriate behaviour in the delivery phase of the event.

In essence, a variety of on-site logistics techniques underpins the venue site plan and communication arrangements. These include the logistical technique of

Table 9.1 International Sailing Federation (ISAF) Sailing World Cup (2015) on-water emergency plan procedures operations sheet

Level	Conditions	Action	Control and communication
1	■ Light winds ■ Slight sea ■ Well within competitor capability.	**Patrol/Rescue** ■ Rescue craft to patrol designated areas. ■ Rescued yachts to be towed to start-finish vessels or spectator crafts. ■ Rescue boats not to leave course without clearance from Course Race Officer.	■ Course Race Officer using monitor course radio channel.
2	■ Moderate winds ■ Moderate sea ■ Testing but manageable conditions.	**Elevated Patrol/Rescue** ■ Coach, jury, and media boats may enter course area and assist if requested by the Course Race Officer who will display code flag 'V' and make a radio announcement.	■ Course Race Officer using monitor course radio channel.
3	■ Heavy winds ■ Big sea ■ Beyond competitor capability for most.	**Abandon race. Rescue of personnel.** ■ All available boats including jury, coaches, to assist yachts in trouble as directed or as otherwise required at their own discretion based on their experience. ■ Rescue boats to either tow yachts to available craft or abandon yachts after tagging with (crew safe) tape.	■ Course Race Officer using tower to assist. ■ Liaise with Beach Marshall – head count/boats ashore. ■ Rescue Coordinator to assist.
4	■ Very strong winds ■ Big seas ■ Well beyond competitor capability.	**Outside assistance required** ■ Decision to call Water Police.	■ Rescue Coordinator ■ Liaise with Beach Marshall – head count/boats ashore.

Wind warning definitions from Bureau of Meteorology:

■ **Strong wind warning: 25 - 44 knots**
■ **Gale warning: 34 - 47 knots**
■ **Storm warning: 48 - 63 knots**

Source: Adapted from ISAF (2015) Sailing World Cup – Royal Melbourne Yacht Squadron

'just in time' delivery, where the back of house transport and chaperoning arrangements ensure punctual athlete arrival at training, competition, and social venues. The techniques of 'demand smoothing' (manipulating peaks and troughs to ensure a more balanced flow) and creating 'on-site marketing places' (temporary storage of consumables) are also used to ensure appropriate food, toilet supply and maintenance, venue cleaning, and waste removal are achieved. Furthermore, to avoid irrational decision-making under pressure, 'what if' scenarios and contingency planning are prepared, even if it is just to address the basic questions of what will happen if X (person/equipment) does not arrive on time or what will happen if there is inclement weather.

The complexity of managing so many arrangements (due to the diversity of stakeholders and numbers at major events) means that project management techniques (see Chapter 4) are no longer being used purely for the pre-event stage but also in many cases for the event stage of the lifecycle. Such detailed operational planning is then summarised in the form of a production schedule(s) as well as run and cue sheets.

For example, in considering the arrangements of the London 2012 opening ceremony, Bill Morris (2012), Director of Ceremonies, elaborated:

> Probably the greatest logistical challenge of the whole games is faced on the very first day with the Opening Ceremony. It sets the standard for everything else to follow ... with creative, operational and logistic risks involved, there must be military precision and operational controls to manage this on time.

Indeed some of the London 2012 Opening Ceremony logistic and operational planning details are illustrated in Table 9.2, where it is evident that each scene of the ceremony was scripted to the second.

Pushed by the project driver of time, with an estimated global broadcast audience in excess of 4 billion, this 3-hour opening ceremony had to finish at midnight. Murton Mann (2012), the Program Manager of Ceremonies, similarly noted the strict process of managing and controlling time at the event:

> I was running a time check from four key points in the ceremony ... We know if we are running late at any moment in time. We know exactly what the time sheet reads and how far you are behind with time ... you also need to know where and how you can pick up lost time ... We identified very early on the controllable and the uncontrollable and then manipulated them as best we can ... Such controls start pre-event where we drive people to arrive early so that no operational and visual challenges exist for the global broadcast.

In this case, everyone had to be in their seats at least 90 minutes before the ceremony started, where a one-hour pre-show was used to entertain and practise routines

Table 9.2 London 2012 Olympic Opening Ceremony schedule and logistic examples

Sequence	Scene title	Duration (hour:minute:seconds)	Logistics examples
2	Green and pleasant land	00:04:24	To reflect the English countryside real flowers (included a daily watering schedule) and farm animals were used (40 sheep, 12 horses, 3 cows, 2 goats, 10 chickens, 10 ducks, 9 geese and 3 sheep dogs – 34 animal handlers)
…			
5	Second to the right, and straight on till morning	00:11:26	600 dancers all of whom are National Health Service staff, and 320 beds
…			
9	Welcome	01:29:00	10,490 athletes will compete but not all of them will participate in the Athletes' Parade; 7 billion pieces of paper dropped (one for each person on the planet); music played at 120 beats per minute to ensure athletes walk faster
10	Bike a.m.	00:03:01	70 volunteers … but on the night cut due to a lack of time!

Source: Adapted from London 2012 (2012c) Opening Ceremony Media Guide

such as handling 100ft-long blue silks or using the seat technologies at the appropriate moment in the live ceremony.

Whereas production schedules provide the chronological list of control activities against time, run and cue sheets tend to provide more detail on the quality driver, such as the scripted content of key speeches and announcements. Operating checklists, templates, and pre-scripted and pre-recorded announcements are used for event arrival, departure, and emergency arrangements. However, the stadium announcer also plays a critical role in the live performance and control process of all project drivers. As Mann (2012) further explains:

> The stadium announcer is the key to maintaining flow, momentum and adding to the creative visual. There is so much going on in the stadia, you get mesmerised so the announcer assists your understanding by explaining where to look and when.

In comparison, the two areas that are uncontrollable during the ceremony, where the organisers knew that they could lose time, were the Parade of Athletes and the crowd applause. Mann (2012) reveals:

> Whilst we can influence the Parade (for example, use a fast drum beat to quicken up the athlete walking speed and line up the athletes and putting them into pens 1 hour beforehand) we cannot script which athletes attend and when they want to take a picture, wave, or depart. We cannot predict when/where euphoria takes over. Some walk straight into the stadia and then straight out. The crowd applause is also very spontaneous and reactive to the ceremony components ... You do not want to rush things through or to interrupt the crowd establishing their own atmosphere. But the announcer must try to get back to the planned and timed script.

Where time is lost and the finish time is finite, the event organiser always knows that certain elements can be cut, such as the 3-minute and 1-second 'Bike a.m.' scene that was removed from the London 2012 ceremony. Furthermore, such was the level of detail in the transport planning that traffic light manipulation was even used to manage Heads of States' punctual arrivals and departures to and from the Olympic Opening Ceremony.

Ideally in the event phase, at any particular moment in time, everything will be perfectly controlled, coordinated, and in its rightful place if the event quality targets are to be fully realised. Additionally, event on-site logistics need to continually flow into the event shutdown logistics, where equipment removal, venue cleaning, and contract settlement provide project closure. This entails all subcontractors knowing when and how they can remove their equipment before extensive venue clean-up is undertaken in preparation for the next venue occupant. In essence, the inevitable search for excellence to exceed stakeholder expectations while optimally managing the golden triangle of project quality, cost, and time is the ultimate challenge that lies ahead of every sport event manager. But no one said that the sport event management role was an easy one!

SUMMARY

To provide a memorable and high-quality event experience is clearly not an easy task, particularly within the unique and complex environment encountered at most major sport events. However, successful event management is possible and personally very rewarding, provided it is founded on the basics of competent planning, organisation, implementation, and control. Whereas many of the generic management functions and tools of planning and organisation have been introduced in previous chapters, this chapter has extended their application, additionally highlighting the breadth and depth of management activities required for effective event delivery.

While the process of logistics management can provide a general understanding of the likely multi-agency flows of people, information, and other resources typically experienced at the event, the on-site logistical tools of a venue site plan, contact list and communication systems, production schedule, and run and cue sheets, are all used to implement and coordinate the detailed action and contingency plans of the event.

To further highlight the depth of integrated management activity normally experienced at an event, we have discussed the practicalities of managing security, incidents, and emergencies, and managing key stakeholder needs, namely the spectator in the last mile, volunteers, and the increasingly important media services. Selected on the basis of their transferability and functional importance to other sports events, these activities demonstrate the importance of really understanding the diverse needs and support services of different stakeholders and place heavy emphasis on the establishment of effective and efficient communication systems in the implementation phase of an event.

Through applied examples throughout this chapter, we have sought to build on previous event and facility management knowledge and to reinforce the notion of managing organisational synergy across a breadth of interrelated activities and client groups, as well as across the duration of the event lifecycle.

CASE STUDY

Hong Kong International Races Day: accreditation

Hong Kong is where the 'Sport of Kings' (i.e. thoroughbred racing) is definitely the 'King of Sports'! Thoroughbred racing is Hong Kong's number one sport, with more money being bet per race there than anywhere else in the world.

Held annually during the second weekend of December, the Hong Kong International Races Day is the country's premier race day. One of the most exciting and prestigious events on the international racing calendar, the race meet attracts the world's best horses, best jockeys, and biggest gamblers. It comprises four feature races: the Hong Kong Cup, the Hong Kong Mile, the Hong Kong Vase, and the Hong Kong Sprint. These races carry total prize money of approximately $US7 million.

Sha Tin, one of Hong Kong's two race tracks, was opened in 1978 and, with ongoing redevelopment, has become one of the most modern race-courses in the world. Sha Tin has an impressive grandstand that holds up to 85,000 people, and on International Races Day it is filled to capacity. The races can also be viewed from other areas of the racecourse, including the public lawn, corporate marquees, bars, lounges, private boxes, and dining rooms.

As with most race days, International Races Day spectators fall into several different categories, namely general admission, members (and guests of members), sponsors, corporate guests, and VIPs. International tourists are particularly well looked after at Sha Tin: on showing their passports they have access to the members' stand rather than being restricted to the general public areas. Members, sponsors, and corporate guests have the privilege of superior dining options, including the right to purchase fine-dining hospitality packages. These spectator groups also have access to the racecourse's best views and betting facilities.

The Hong Kong Jockey Club (HKJC) manages almost all aspects of Hong Kong's thoroughbred racing industry, including International Races Day. The HKJC's key source of revenue is betting. Essentially, the more people that bet, the more revenue the club makes. It is thus in the club's best interests to ensure that betting facilities, particularly at major race meetings like International Races Day, are of the highest possible standard. Furthermore, it is critical that a sufficient number of betting facilities be available. When on-course, bettors can place their bets with the totalisator (i.e. the 'tote'), electronically through betting machines, or via their phone accounts.

The ability of the HKJC to maximise gambling revenue from International Races Day not only depends on the quality and quantity of betting facilities – it also rests on the sport being 'clean'. That is, people will not bet if they believe that a race is rigged (except, of course, those people involved in the rigging). Fortunately, the HKJC is known internationally for its commitment to clean racing. It protects the integrity of racing via several methods, including:

a   employing hundreds of thoroughly trained computer and security staff;
b   conducting extensive security checks on everyone who works in the stable area;
c   installing surveillance cameras in the barns and tote rooms;
d   strictly monitoring jockeys for interference during racing;
e   conducting drug testing on the horses both pre- and post-race;
f   utilising one of the most modern drug-testing laboratories in the world.

All the horses competing on International Races Day are stabled at Sha Tin in two- and three-level barns, with ramps leading to each level. Prior to racing, just like any athlete, the horses need to be warmed up. Strappers walk the horses around briskly. The horses are then led out to the mounting yard to their jockeys. The horses canter towards the barriers, where stewards (the 'officials' of thoroughbred racing) are located to help the jockeys get their horses into the barriers. When the barrier gates open and racing commences, the race caller 'comes to life' and takes centre stage with the horses and the jockeys. With the crowd's attention focused on the race, hardly anyone notices the ambulance that circles the inside of the track behind the horses and their jockeys.

After racing, the jockeys dismount and stewards accompany them back to the jockeys' room. It is here that the jockeys are weighed in after every race (nobody is even allowed to touch them before this). While the jockeys are being weighed, and again in the presence of stewards, the strappers take the horses on another walk to cool down and then back to their stables. It is in the stables that the horses are tested for illegal substances.

For the people who go to watch the horses (i.e. the spectators) and the athletes themselves (i.e. the horses and their jockeys), a day at the Hong Kong International Races offers much more than just the racing. Akin to other famous race meetings, such as the Melbourne Cup, the Kentucky Derby, and the Dubai World Cup, International Races Day at Sha Tin is as much about socialising, fun, fashion, entertainment, hospitality, and networking as it is about racing and betting. One particular breed of racegoers (i.e. the 'partygoers') may not even watch a race, let alone bet on one, given that there are so many other things to do.

To support the tens of thousands of people who attend International Races Day, there are hundreds of staff working in the areas of ticketing, gate entry, catering, hospitality, security, cleaning, gardening, maintenance, administration, and wagering. Then there is the staff more directly concerned with the actual racing, including the stewards, strappers, stable hands, veterinarians, and laboratory attendants. In addition to the staff employed by the racecourse and the HKJC are other people who need access to the racecourse, such as emergency services, various contractors (e.g. electricians and carpenters), and the media, not to mention the horse owners and trainers.

Although spectators access Sha Tin racecourse only during opening hours, most staff have to get there earlier. Likewise, for the stages, marquees, and corporate hospitality venues to be set up, contractors need to arrive much earlier to 'bump the event in', as do the people responsible for delivering hundreds of tonnes of food and thousands of litres of beverages.

Question

Develop an accreditation plan for Hong Kong International Races Day. You will need to consider all parties who require access to the racecourse, not only during the actual day but those who need to access it prior to race day in order to bump the event in, as well as those people who need to bump the event out. (Tip: Do not forget the horses!) Your plan should include the following:

- identification of the various accreditation zones;
- identification of those with access to the various accreditation zones;
- justification of access to the various accreditation zones;
- overview of the accreditation process, including:

  - how accreditation passes are applied for or are awarded;
  - when the accreditation process begins;
  - when and where accreditation passes are received or picked up;

- a policy on lost, forgotten, or stolen accreditation passes (i.e. the processes you would recommend that the HKJC follow if a spectator, staff member, or contractor arrived at the course without accreditation);
- a policy on emergency access to an unaccredited area (i.e. the processes you would recommend that the HKJC follow if an emergency necessitated spectators, staff members, or contractors accessing an area they were not accredited to enter).

REFERENCES

Allen, J.B., & Bartle, M. (2014). Sport event volunteers' engagement: management matters, *Managing Leisure, 19*(1), 36–50.

Bowdin, G.A.J., Allen, J., Harris, R., McDonnell, I., & O'Toole, W. (2012). Events *management*. 3rd edition. Hoboken: Taylor and Francis.

Doherty, A. (2009). The volunteer legacy of a major sport event. *Journal of Policy Research in Tourism, Leisure and Events, 1*(3), 185–207.

Emery, P.R., Kerr, A.K., & Crabtree, R.M. (2016). Critical incidents, emotions and value added moments: The London 2012 spectator experience. *Event Management, 20*(3).

Fontes, F. (2014). *Rio 2016 launches volunteer programme.* Retrieved from http://www.olympic.org/news/rio-2016-launches-volunteer-programme/237186

Glasgow 2014 (2014). *XX Commonwealth Games post-Games report.* Retrieved from https://www.thecgf.com/games/2014/G2014-Official-Post-Games-Report.pdf

ISAF (2015). *ISAF Sailing World Cup – Melbourne and invited classes regatta: On-water emergency plan.* Unpublished Royal Melbourne Yacht Squadron working documentation.

IOC (2016). *Over 240,000 volunteer applications for Rio 2016.* Retrieved from http://www.olympic.org/news/over-240-000-volunteer-applications-for-rio-2016/242294

Killian, K. (2009). Experiential marketing and brand experiences: A conceptual framework. In A. Lindgreen, J. Vanhamme, & M.B. Beverland (Eds.), *Memorable customer experiences: A research anthology.* Farnham: Gower. pp. 25–44.

Lindgreen, A., Vanhamme, J., & Beverland, M.B. (2009). *Memorable customer experiences: A research anthology.* Farnham: Gower.

London 2012 (2011). *LOCOG concept of operations v2.0.* Unpublished LOCOG working documentation.

Mann, M. (2012). Research interview with Programme Manager of Ceremonies, 9th November 2012.

Morris, B. (2012). Research interview with Director of Ceremonies, 4th December 2012.

Olympic Delivery Authority (2011). *Move. Transport plan for the London 2012 Olympic and Paralympic Games.* 2nd edition. London: ODA.

Rio 2016 (2016). *Rio 2016 homepage.* Retrieved from http://www.rio2016.com/en

Walker, D. (2001). Motivating *yourself ... and your volunteers. L-829.* Leadership and Development.

World Indoor Championships in Athletics (2003a). *Operational manual.* Birmingham: WICA.

World Indoor Championships in Athletics (2003b). *Media guide: 9th IAAF World Indoor Championships in Athletics.* Birmingham: WICA.

CHAPTER 10

DESTINATION MARKETING, IMAGE, AND BRANDING THROUGH MAJOR SPORT EVENTS

CHAPTER OBJECTIVES

In this chapter we will:

■ Distinguish between the concepts of destination marketing, destination image, and destination branding.

- Explain the contextual relationship between marketing of a destination and the hosting of major sport events.
- Analyse the theoretical foundations of the influence of major sport events on destination image.
- Assess the challenges and potential risks involved in marketing major sport events and a destination.
- Evaluate strategies for implementing measures related to the influence of major events on destination image and brand.

INTRODUCTION

Traditionally, mega-sporting events have been measured by their economic impact on the host destination. However, there are questions regarding the validity and reliability of economic impact as a measure of success for these events, and in fact some studies have surmised that mega-events add little to nothing to the local economy (Hall & Page, 2008). There is a growing practice to go beyond economic impact to look at other benefits of major sport events. For example, Sportcal (www.sportcal.com), a world-leading sports market intelligence company based in London, developed the 'Global Sport Index' of sporting events and their hosting cities and nations. The purpose of the index is to establish a comprehensive and consistent model to assess the influence of social, environmental, media, brand, and sport development factors across events of different sizes and over time. As a result, benefits such as increased community visibility and enhanced community image may in the long run be greater than the immediate economic impact generated by the spending of visitors to these events (Liu, 2015). From a practical standpoint, the measurement of these additional impacts shows that major sport events have also increasingly been used for destination marketing purposes as they can draw large audiences from home and abroad and generate worldwide television exposure (Chalip, 2004; Liu & Gratton, 2010).

The focus of this chapter is to provide a contextual relationship between the hosting of major sport events and the marketing of a destination. This will lead to further analysis regarding the theoretical foundations of the influence of major sport events on destination image. This will be addressed by investigating the challenges and potential risks involved in marketing events and the destination. Strategies for succeeding in these efforts will be provided with recommendations for implementing measures to evaluate the true influence of major events on destination image and brand.

DESTINATION MARKETING

In looking at the four lenses of tourism – transportation, accommodations, food and beverages, and attractions, sport events provide a significant influence. Sport events are one of the major attractions that influence tourists to visit a destination, which in turn often has a positive impact on the other factors. Inherent relationships between tourism and sport events in turn provide increased awareness and an enhanced image for the host destination.

With the globalisation of the world's economy, the accelerating pace of technological changes, as well as the greater propensity for long-distance leisure travel, cities across the world are under growing pressure to compete with each other for tourist dollars. As a result destination marketing has become a significant part of hosting events by expanding beyond traditional production-based activities to an expanded emphasis and dependency upon services in areas such as tourism, hospitality, and recreation.

The first definition of destination marketing (Pike & Page, 2014) focused on:

> The management process through which the National Tourist Organisations and/or tourist enterprises identify their selected tourists, actual and potential, communicate with them to ascertain and influence their wishes, needs, motivations, likes and dislikes, on local, regional, national and international levels, and to formulate and adapt their tourist products accordingly in view of achieving optimal tourist satisfaction thereby fulfilling their objectives.
> (Wahab, Crampon, & Rothfield, 1976, p. 24)

Today, destination marketing is a practice implemented by local authorities to improve the market position of their municipality in order to appeal to important stakeholders, including inward investors, companies, tourists, and local residents. Since it makes sense that a destination can be promoted and marketed in a similar way to any other product or service in order to attract customers, the process of building the image of a place has become a key factor influencing the destination choice process for major events owners (Chi & Qu, 2008).

Destination image is defined as 'any visual, oral or written representation of a tourism location that is recorded and can also be transmitted to others' (Hose & Wickens, 2004). It is also generally referred to as the overall impression that a place creates in the minds of various target groups, including its functional and symbolic elements, and it encompasses the physical attributes, services, attractions, name, logo, and reputation, and the benefits that those provide to the target groups by the destination (Walmsley & Young, 1998). The image of a destination can be enhanced or changed. The deliberate use of various strategies to form, enhance, or change the image of destination by marketers is often called destination branding.

A brand is 'a name, term, design, symbol, or feature that identified one product or service as being different from another' (Schwarz, Hunter, & LaFleur, 2013). Consequently, destination branding can be thought of as 'the purposeful symbolic embodiment of all information connected to a city in order to create associations and expectations around it'. Destination branding is conceptualised in three major domains: (1) branding related to the production, creation, and management of a brand – including organising and governing the branding process; (2) branding focused using and consuming the brand – including the understanding and interpretation of the branding process; and (3) branding as a positive or negative factor on the major economic, social, and environmental impacts (Lucarelli & Berg, 2011).

When looking at meeting the needs and wants of sport event spectators and participants through destination marketing, while also creating a positive destination image, there are five main areas to consider (Upadhyaya, 2012):

- **Accessibility** in terms of affordability, accommodations, facilities, local infrastructure (hotels, transportation, dining options, leisure activities);
- **Attraction** of architecture, geography, history, and activities;
- **Atmosphere** such as scenery, climate, culture, and safety;
- **Friendliness** including hospitality and receptiveness;
- **Relaxation and Enjoyment** beyond the core activities.

In recent years, major sport events such as the Olympic Games, FIFA World Cup, and Formula 1 Grand Prix have increasingly been employed by cities as an imaging tool as they can draw large audiences from home and abroad and generate worldwide television exposure (Liu & Gratton, 2010). For example, according to the market research firm Nielsen, the 2008 Beijing Olympics attracted a record number of television viewers from home and abroad. It is said that about 94 per cent of the Chinese audience watched the Games, and in total it attracted about 4.7 billion television viewers worldwide, surpassing the 3.9 billion who watched the 2004 Athens Games. Nielsen estimated that the dazzling opening ceremony alone on 8th August, led by film director Zhang Yimou, attracted almost one-third of the world's population, or about 2 billion television viewers (China Daily 2008 September).

CHALLENGES FOR MAJOR EVENTS IN CREATING A POSITIVE DESTINATION IMAGE

Cluttered sponsorship environment

There are many challenges major events face in producing a positive image for a destination. One such challenge is making an impact on the viewer of the event. There is a widely held misconception that if an event is hosted by a destination, the positive image associations of the destination will actualise automatically, and people will attend the event or watch it through any number of broadcast mediums. In reality, it is not that simple. Research has shown that while many sport events broadcasters and event owners (logically) focus on covering the event rather than promoting the destination, whether at the actual event or watching via a broadcast, there are a limited number of mentions or images promoting the host destination during the event itself (and when mentioned or shown were brief in nature and often difficult for the viewer to perceive) (Green, Costa, & Fitzgerald, 2003). Therefore, while destinations often justify the use of sport events as a component of their marketing mix on the basis of their power to generate media exposure and to build desirable destination brand image and awareness, it seems that event media may not be a particularly potent source of exposure. There is a correlation between the challenges of generating destination imagery and the recognition of sponsorships during sport events. The need to create content during a sport event that is eye-catching in terms of the cluttered surroundings, without negatively affecting the viewer, is a major challenge faced by sport marketers today in terms of sponsorship recognition (Breuer & Rumpf, 2015). Destination hosts face similar challenges to build awareness and image recognition during sport events that often have many sponsors, and in which their target market (the viewer) is focusing on the event itself (Breuer & Rumpf, 2015).

Stakeholder management

A second challenge is the breadth of stakeholders of a major sport event and the subsequent difficulty accommodating different, and in some cases conflicting, interests of a variety of stakeholder groups. Stakeholders of a major sport event refer to 'any group or individual who can affect or is affected by the achievement of the organisation's objectives' (Freeman, 1984, p. 46). Among other things, what makes major sports events stand out is the breadth and diversity of their stakeholders. A non-exhaustive list of event stakeholders has been summarised by Parent (2008) including the organising committees; paid staff and volunteers; the various levels of government; the residents, sponsors, businesses, schools, and community groups composing the community; the international, continental, national, and provincial sport organisations; the print, radio, television, and Internet media; and the athletes, coaches, VIPs, officials, and support staff composing the delegations. All these stakeholders may have differing interests and concerns. What further complicates the issue is the nature of the organising committee of the sport event being a temporary organisation with a fixed and predetermined lifespan (Parent 2008), making the coordination and management of stakeholders all the more difficult. Very often, the destination marketing department of a host is not very well represented in the organising committee of the major sport event. As a result, destination marketing through the event is just one of the many ever-changing concerns of a wide variety of stakeholder groups and may easily be ignored or forgotten by stakeholder groups. For instance, media personnel are not necessarily interested in promoting the destination, and television in particular might even resist incorporating the broadcast of destination imagery in order to maximise the time available for paid advertising. Consequently, a well-planned destination marketing strategy requires developing and implementing the principles of the marketing mix outlined in Chapter 7. Furthermore, realising that a complex stakeholder environment exists, local organising committees and local, state, and national tourism agencies should work closely together to provide opportunities for enhancing the image of the host destination.

Temporal nature of events

Another challenge facing destination marketers in using major sport events is that the image impact of a sport event is inherently limited due to the temporal nature of sport events in general, and one-off events in particular. It has been argued that a single event, even one with a high profile, has only a passing effect on the destination brand (Ritchie & Smith, 1991). In addition, most sport events, especially those single-sport events, would only appeal to a limited number of socio-demographic audiences, as 'events are short lived, which restricts the frequency of any associated destination marketing messages, and events typically have a narrow (though often avid) audience, which restricts the reach of its marketing communications' (Chalip, 2005, p. 167). It comes as no surprise that a single sport event may have minimal image impact on the host destination despite its stature and high volume of media exposure.

Media

There are also inherent challenges to working with the media to create positive destination imagery via various communication mediums. It is generally believed that the most important destination marketing impact of hosting a major sporting event comes from the possible media exposure and coverage of the host city brought by the event (Hudson, Getz, Miller, & Brown, 2002). However, the challenge from a destination marketing perspective is that media are independent, and not able to be controlled by either the organising committee or the government of the municipality regarding the content they produce and disseminate. On the one hand, the attention of the media during an event is understandably on the event itself or media sponsors, which usually means only negligible exposure for the destination (Green, Costa, & Fitzgerald, 2003). On the other hand, there exists the possibility of negative media publicity associated with hosting a major sporting event such as terrorist threats associated with the 2008 Paris, France–Dakar, Senegal Rally (which now is held in South America because of continued terrorism fears in Africa); terrorist bombings at the finish line of the 2013 Boston Marathon; or poor pre-event preparation in the case of the 2010 Commonwealth Games in Delhi, India, the 2014 Winter Olympic Games in Sochi, Russia, or the 2016 Summer Olympics in Rio de Janeiro, Brazil.

Image fit between event and destination

A final challenge is to create an image fit between the sport event and the destination. This is often accomplished through the process of co-branding, which is defined as

Destination marketing, image, and branding

'a form of cooperation between two or more brands with significant customer rec-ognition, in which all the participants' brand names are retained' (Blackett & Boad, 1999, p. 7). This suggests that by pairing the brand of the event with the destination brand, elements of the event brand will transfer to the destination brand through the event and place communication. The transferal of event-to-destination brand would prime consumers' attention to the destination, leading to image enhancement or change (Xing & Chalip, 2006). However, it is also important to recognise the fact that the brand of a sport event may also contain elements that are not necessarily compatible with the image of the destination. Negative transfer, as well as positive transfer, could occur as a result of hosting an event. For example, in an experimen-tal study, the race media (advertising and telecast) of the Gold Coast IndyCar race received negative feedback because there was an incompatibility between the Gold Coast's natural environment and the event's noisy and technological image (Chalip, Green & Hill, 2003). Image fit not only affects the image impact on the destination, but also may directly impact future visit intentions. Another study based on active tourists participating in sport events in Germany showed that image fit would serve as a predictor for future visits to the host destination (Hallmann & Breuer, 2010). As a result, it is essential to host events that would match the image of the destina-tion's brand, but then the difficulty of what constitutes a match-up is also widely acknowledged. Meanwhile, the breadth of customers a city seeks to appeal to can further complicate the challenge. While sport events may attract fans, they do not necessarily look appealing to other tourist segments the destination is looking to attract (Liu, 2013; Liu & Wilson, 2014). In general, more work needs to be done to further understand the determinants of image fit between sport events and destina-tions and how events can be better used in marketing the host destination.

In looking at the challenges created by the breadth of event viewers/spectators and stakeholders, the limitations due to the cluttered sponsorship environment, stakeholder management, temporal nature of events, working with media, and the image fit between events and a destination are substantial. The ability to implement destination marketing plans and increase the image of the destination has many road-blocks. However, for every challenge there are strategies that can be implemented to ensure success in destination marketing efforts and create a positive destination image through major sport events. Two of the most common are getting key major sport event stakeholders to work together towards the goal of improving the image of a destination, and the use of event portfolios to enhance destination image.

STRATEGIES FOR ENHANCING POSITIVE DESTINATION IMAGE USING MAJOR EVENTS

Sport events can be an effective agent of destination image change. However, it is important to recognise that sport event consumer (e.g. spectator, participant) behaviour is complex and multi-dimensional, including the way in which consumers construct and interpret what they view and how they experience the event and destination. There are also external factors that may positively or negatively influence this behaviour, ranging from weather to the media.

Stakeholder engagement and collaboration

One of the strategies that can be implemented to create a positive destination image from major sport events is to get the key stakeholders to work together to ensure the image impact of hosting sports events. These include event organisers, destination marketing organisations (DMOs), sport organisations, event sponsors, media, and the travel trade. While the sport event organiser is central to stakeholder interaction, it is believed that leadership and strategy should come from the destination marketing organisation, and event organisers and destination marketers should explicitly recognise their co-branding responsibilities and share in the required actions (Getz & Fairley, 2005, p. 136). For example, the Victorian Major Events Company (VMEC) utilises the Australian Open to enhance the destination image of Melbourne via printing the large word 'Melbourne' on the baseline courts during competition. Considering the length of exposure this increases the brand and image awareness of the city in an otherwise cluttered sponsorship space. The length of the Australian Open tournament (two weeks in January) and its annual occurrence increases the ability for VMEC to enhance the host destination's brand over a sustained period of time.

The host community is recognised as an important stakeholder. From a destination marketing point of view, the host community is important because a destination may not be able to enter the bid for a major sport event in the first place if the bid is not supported by the community. The hospitality of the local community is vital to the sustainability of event tourism industry, and sport events bidding and organising should accommodate host community needs. This is because residents are '(1) an integral part of the place brand through their characteristics and behaviour; (2) ambassadors for their place brand who grant credibility to any communicated message; and (3) citizens and voters who are vital for the political legitimisation of place branding' (Braun, Kavaratzis & Zenker, 2013).

Event portfolio and destination image

Marketers who seek to use events to build their destination brand should develop an event portfolio. An event portfolio is defined as 'a strategic tool rather than a random collection of miscellaneous events that are hosted in a community' (Ziakas, 2014, p. 329), and such an event portfolio approach has the benefit of enable creating and harnessing cross-leveraging opportunities among different events. The challenge with developing an event portfolio is how to select appropriate events

250

and build them into the portfolio. In terms of destination branding, it is suggested that a sport event can play the following different roles depending on the nature of its brand relative to the destination brand: (1) as a co-branding partner with the destination brand; (2) as an extension of the destination brand; (3) or as a feature of the destination brand (Chalip & Costa, 2005).

Chalip (2005, p. 172) further suggested that the following three criteria should be applied in addition to timing and target market when it comes to development an event portfolio to market the host city brand:

1   First, consumers' perceptions of the event's brand should include attributes and/or benefits that allow destination marketers to fashion a marketing message that affirms a logical link between the event and the destination.
2   Second, the event's brand should incorporate attributes or benefits that the destination marketer wants to reinforce in the destination's existing brand, or that the destination marketer seeks to import into the destination's brand.
3   Third, the event's brand should not include attributes or benefits that are likely to become linked to the destination's brand, but that are incompatible with the brand that the destination seeks to promote.

One example of the successful implementation of event portfolio would be the city of Melbourne, Australia, which has aggressively promoted itself as the major sport event capital of the world. Two organisations that are instrumental in making this a reality are Tourism Victoria and the Victorian Major Events Company. Tourism Victoria takes the lead as the official tourism agency for the State of Victoria, where Melbourne is the largest city. Their mission is to attract visitors to the city and the state through innovative marketing campaigns, implement State Government policies, support the development of tourism investment opportunities, and provide advice on best practices in tourism. The Victorian Major Events Company (VMEC) is a not-for-profit organisation that works closely with the government with an entrepreneurial vision to create and acquire sport, entertainment, and cultural events for Melbourne and Victoria.

Through the efforts of these organisations, Melbourne has attracted some of the world's major sporting events whose destinations change over time:

- 2011 President's Cup Golf
- 2012 UCI Track Cycling World Championships
- 2014 World Cup of Golf
- 2015 AFC Asian Cup
- 2015 ICC Cricket World Cup.

Or have negotiated long-term contracts to return to Melbourne annually:

- Australian Open
- Formula 1 Grand Prix
- The Melbourne Cup.

Melbourne has been ranked as the SportBusiness Ultimate Sport City three times (2006, 2008, 2010) and came in second twice (2012, 2014 – both years behind London who hosted the 2012 Olympics); is annually the top sport city in the Southern Hemisphere; and in 2016 was bestowed with the Anniversary Award as the top sport city of the past decade. In July 2016, the evolution of these efforts was the amalgamation of Tourism Victoria, the VMEC, and the Melbourne Convention Bureau under one umbrella organisation 'Visit Victoria'. Visit Victoria operates with, but at a distance from, the Government, as a company limited by guarantee to allow for a commercial focus to market Melbourne and Victoria, and to attract domestic and global visitors, as well as sporting cultural, and business events to drive growth in the competitive and dynamic global tourism marketplace.

The actions of Melbourne and Victoria affirm that the purpose of long-term event leveraging is to build an event portfolio that enhances the image and/or market position of a destination (Chalip, 2004). In practice, major sport events could be used to either create a new image or to reinforce positive images already established in the minds of the target audience. Sometimes, major sport events are also used to change a destination's negative image or connotation. As an example, one of the aims of India hosting the 2010 Commonwealth Games was to show the country in a positive image and hopefully entice future sporting events to consider India as host. The country was also attempting to showcase the destination image of India in a positive light for tourism, as well as overcome the perceptions of incomplete or inadequate infrastructure, government corruption, and safety concerns.

SUMMARY

Due to the huge sums of public money spent on the staging of major sporting events, public officials, event organisers, and international sport organisations are also under increasing pressure to justify these public subsidies by demonstrating that the benefits brought to the host destination by these events exceed the cost. As the validity of economic impact has been increasingly questioned, the destination marketing effect has been suggested as a very important rationale for justifying the hosting of major sport events subsidised with public money. However, it can be seen from previous sections in this chapter that the destination marketing impact may not be as effective as it first appears to be. Hosting a major sport event may not automatically bring about substantial media exposure to the host destination itself. And even if it does, there is no guarantee that the exposure will be positive and

Destination marketing, image, and branding

benign. As a result, a strategic leverage approach has been put forward to improve the potential for a destination to realise image benefits.

It is important to assess the existing destination marketing strategy carefully and determine whether sport events in general are suitable for the destination and could be built into the overall marketing strategy of the destination. Not all cities can afford to host major sport events, nor do all of them need sport events to enhance or change their image as destinations. Additionally, when it has been decided that a strategy of destination marketing through major sport events is to be used, it is still important to select the right event or a portfolio of events by assessing cost, feasibility, and compatibility between the event(s) and the destination. It is also necessary to take a holistic view by involving different stakeholders and coordinated effort and collaboration between destination marketers and event marketers in order to integrate the hosting of an event into the overall destination marketing initiative. Finally, media management, including media relationship building and professional media service, is essential to fully leverage the potential image benefits of hosting a major sporting event.

CASE STUDY

Evaluation of media impact of hosting major sport events: the World Snooker Championship

Introduction and context

Known as 'home of snooker', the city of Sheffield in the United Kingdom has been closely associated with the sport of snooker, not least because it is also the host to the World Snooker Academy, the birthplace for world-renowned elite snooker players. Since 1977, the Crucible Theatre in Sheffield has been the host venue for the World Snooker Championship, the leading professional snooker tournament in terms of prize money and prestige. Although from time to time, there have been talks and speculation of moving the World Snooker Championship to China or the Middle East, this showpiece event of snooker will remain in Sheffield at least until 2017, largely thanks to local support and intervention of the government – and to the relief of the host community (Howson, 2015). The value of the World Snooker Championship has been evaluated annually by the Sport Industry Research Centre (SIRC) at Sheffield Hallam University and commissioned by the Major Sports Events Unit of the Sheffield City Council since 2002. Apart from the economic value, the event is said to have generated a significant amount of media exposure and place marketing effect for the host city.

Media impact

The media impact of World Snooker Championship is evaluated based on an assessment of the public profile achieved via television coverage of the event on the BBC and Eurosport, and then a notional value of the exposure is obtained by converting the exposure into a cash equivalent. Specifically, within this coverage, the amount of time that the logos or messages of the sponsors are clearly visible or audible is measured (using specially trained staff and software) as follows:

- verbal mentions of 'Sheffield' or the 'Crucible Theatre',
- on-screen credit text (in seconds) of 'Sheffield' or the 'Crucible Theatre',
- 'EventSheffield.com' (and 'Welcome to Yorkshire'),
- other exposure of Sheffield and the Crucible from 'postcard' features of the event.

The volume of exposure obtained is then converted to the cash equivalent of how much that exposure would cost to buy in the form of a 30-second television advertisement.

All audience figures used in the evaluation were collated by TNSSPORT from official sources. In the United Kingdom, the figures are supplied by the Broadcasters Audience Research Board (BARB). Firstly, BARB confirms independently that the broadcasts actually took place. Secondly, indicators are deducted such as the viewing figures, market share, and other performance indicators that relate to the event in question.

Results

The television coverage and media value achieved by the event can be summarised as follows:

- Television coverage of the event was featured on 17 consecutive days from 18th April to 4th May inclusive, on a combination of BBC1 and BBC2 channels.
- 62 separate broadcasts totalled 126 hours and 10 minutes of coverage on BBC TV.
- The cumulative audience in the UK was 46.3m viewers and an estimated 5.1m different people watched at least some of the snooker coverage.
- The percentage market share varied from 3.6 per cent to 16.7 per cent, and the more important TVR from 0.1 per cent of the UK population for a highlights programme on day two of the championship to 5.4 per cent for

Destination marketing, image, and branding

the decisive last session of the final. Analysis of the TVR also revealed that viewer interest in the event increased as the event progressed.

- During the near 100 hours of coverage, 'The Crucible' and 'The Crucible Theatre' were mentioned 464 times and 'Sheffield' was mentioned 170 times.
- Combining the commercial cost of the exposure achieved by both the BBC and Eurosport coverage, the aggregate cost of such exposure would have been £3.12m. It can be seen that £1.6m of the value achieved was attributable to the 'Crucible', with £1.5m linked to 'Sheffield'-related exposure.

However, the report also adds a word of caution that although the verbal mentions would cost £2.7m to buy commercially, it does not necessarily follow that the value of this exposure was actually worth £2.7m. That is to say, there is no guarantee that exposure by association is necessarily effective. For instance, most of the verbal mentions of 'Sheffield' or the 'Crucible Theatre' are incidental, and thus it would be difficult to argue that such mentions contribute towards positive images such as Sheffield as a place in which to invest, relocate, or to take a holiday. As a result, the report suggests that there should be a clear distinction between the 'cost' of exposure and the 'worth' of such exposure, and indiscriminate use of such media evaluation data is not recommended. (Source: adapted from Shibli & Coleman, 2005.)

Questions

1   How has the World Snooker Championships enhanced the destination image and destination brand of Sheffield, England?
2   Describe what additional destination marketing effort you would implement for Sheffield to continue hosting the World Snooker Championships beyond 2017.
3   Research the Crucible, the host venue for the World Snooker Championships. How are they benefiting from the destination image and branding associated with the event to bring in more events to their facility?

REFERENCES

Blackett, T., & Boad, B. (1999). *Co-branding: The science of alliance.* London: Macmillan.
Braun, E., Kavaratzis, M., & Zenker, S. (2013). My city – my brand: The different roles of residents in place branding. *Journal of Place Management and Development, 6*(1), 18–28.
Breuer, C., & Rumpf, C. (2015). The impact of color and animation on sports viewers' attention to televised sponsorship signage. *Journal of Sport Management, 29*(2), 170–183.

Chalip, L. (2004). Beyond impact: A general model for host community event leverage. In B.W. Ritchie & D. Adair (Eds), *Sport tourism: Interrelationships, impacts and issues*. Clevedon, UK: Channel View Publications. pp. 227–252.

Chalip, L. (2005). Marketing media and place promotion. In J. Higham (Ed.), *Sport tourism destinations: Issues, opportunities, and analysis*. Oxford, UK: Butterworth Heinemann. pp. 162–176.

Chalip, L., & Costa, C. (2005). Sport event tourism and the destination brand: Towards a general theory. *Sport in Society, 8*(2), 218–237.

Chalip, L., Green, B. C., & Hill, B. (2003). Effects of sport event media on destination image and intention to visit. *Journal of Sport Management, 17*(3), 214–234.

Chi, C., & Qu, H. (2008). Examining the structural relationships of destination image, tourist satisfaction and destination loyalty: An integrated approach. *Tourism Management, 29*(4), 624–636.

China Daily (2008, 6 September) *Beijing Olympics attracts record 4.7 billion TV viewers*. Retrieved from http://www.chinadaily.com.cn/olympics/2008-09/06/content_7005208. htm

Freeman, R.E. (1984). *Strategic management: A stakeholder approach*. Boston: Pitman.

Getz, D., & Fairley, S. (2004). Media management at sport events for destination promotion. *Event Management, 8*(3), 127–139.

Green, B.C., Costa, C.A, & Fitzgerald, M.P. (2003). Marketing the host city: Analyzing exposure generated by a sport event. *International Journal of Sports Marketing & Sponsorship, 4*(4), 335–353.

Hall, C.M., & Page, S. (2008). Progress in tourism management: From the geography of tourism to geographies of tourism – a review. *Tourism Management, 30*(1), 3–16.

Hallmann, K., & Breuer, C. (2010). Image fit between sport events and their hosting destinations from an active sport tourist perspective and its impact on future behaviour. *Journal of Sport & Tourism, 15*(3), 215–238.

Hose, T.A., & Wickens, E. (2004). Typologies, tourism locations and images: Meeting the real needs of real tourists. In S. Weber & R. Tomljenović (Eds.), *Reinventing a tourism destination: Facing the challenge*. Zagreb: Institute for Tourism. pp. 103–114.

Howson, N. (2015). World Snooker Championship to remain at Sheffield's Crucible indefinitely after 2017. *IB Times*. Retrieved from http://www.ibtimes.co.uk/ world-snooker-championship-remain-sheffields-crucible-indefinitely-after-2017-1484136

Hudson, S., Getz, D., Miller, G. A., & Brown, G. (2002). The future role of sporting events: Evaluating the impacts on tourism. *Proceedings of the Leisure Futures Conference*, Innsbruck, Austria.

Liu, D. (2013). Major sports events, destination image and intention to revisit: A perspective of foreign tourists. *International Journal of Sports Marketing and Sponsorship, 14*(3), 178–189.

Liu, D. (2015). Image impact of mega-sporting events perceived by international students and behavior intentions. *International Journal of Sports Marketing and Sponsorship, 16*(2), 103–117.

Liu, D., & Gratton, C. (2010). The impact of mega sporting events on live spectators' images of a host city: A case study of the Shanghai F1 Grand Prix, *Tourism Economics, 16*(3), 629–645.

Liu, D., & Wilson, R. (2014). Negative impact of hosting mega-sporting events and intention to travel: A test of the crowding-out effect using the London Games as an example, *International Journal of Sports Marketing and Sponsorship, 15*(3), 161–175.

Lucarelli, A., & Berg, P.O. (2011). City branding: A state-of-the-art review of the research domain. *Journal of Place Management and Development, 4*(1), 9–27.

Parent, M. (2008). Evolution and issue patterns for major sport event organising committees and their stakeholders. *Journal of Sport Management, 22*(2), 135–164.

Pike, S., & Page, S.J. (2014). Destination marketing organizations and destination marketing: A narrative analysis of the literature. *Tourism Management, 41*, 202–227.

Ritchie, J.R.B., & Smith, B. (1991). The impact of a mega-event on host region awareness: A longitudinal study. *Journal of Travel Research, 30*(1), 3–10.

Schwarz, E. C., Hunter, J. D., & LaFleur, A. (2013). Advanced *theory and practice in sport marketing*. 2nd edition. Oxford, UK: Routledge.

Shibli, S., & Coleman, R. (2005). Economic impact and place marketing evaluation: A case study of the World Snooker Championship. *International Journal of Event Management Research, 1*(1), 13–29.

Upadhyaya, M. (2012). Influence of destination image and destination personality: An empirical analysis. *Journal of Marketing Communications, 7*(3), 40–47.

Walmsley, D.J., & Young, M. (1998). Evaluative images and tourism: The use of personal constructs to describe the structure of destination images. *Journal of Travel Research, 36*(3), 65–69.

Xing, X., & Chalip, L. (2006). Effects of hosting a sport event on destination brand: A test of co-branding and match-up models. *Sport Management Review, 9*(1), 49–78.

Ziakas, V. (2014). Planning and leveraging event portfolios: Towards a holistic theory. *Journal of Hospitality Marketing and Management, 23*(3), 327–356.

CHAPTER 11

PERFORMANCE MANAGEMENT: EVALUATING OPERATIONS

CHAPTER OBJECTIVES

In this chapter we will:

■   Highlight the need for performance measurement for sport facilities and events.
■   Introduce performance management approaches to measuring performance, highlighted by the balanced scorecard approach.

- Examine methods and key metrics for generating key sport facility and event performance measures.
- Discuss the effective use of performance measures for the strategic management of sport facilities and events.
- Present the concepts of data benchmarking and process benchmarking.

INTRODUCTION

Performance management takes on many definitions within a sport organisation. In some cases, it involves the tasks undertaken to make sure that the strategic objectives of an organisation are met in an efficient and effective manner. In other cases, it incorporates metrics created to measure the operation of the overall organisation, specific departments, individual employees, and the products and services offered. Performance management can also be defined as a process utilised to align the major parts of the organisation, including employees, resources, and operational systems as a part of the overall strategic management process. Ultimately, performance management is a continuous process utilised by management to communicate to employees and executives alike how the organisational structure is meeting the strategic objectives.

Performance management is an important aspect of sport facility and event management because when implemented appropriately it provides evidence of the successes and failures of the organisation, and facilitates making a positive change based on the information collected. Performance management allows managers to understand the drivers of performance and how to influence them, as well as a way to accurately document and report performance, with the ultimate result of engraining the practice of evaluation across the organisational culture as part of ongoing and continuous improvement programme.

However, measuring performance just does not happen. It is an intricate process of understanding performance management principles, examining various methods and benchmarking techniques, developing performance measures/metrics specific to sport facilities and major events, integrating these processes within the strategic management process and organisational culture, and articulating the impact quality performance has on and for stakeholders. But it all starts with one basic question ...

WHY MEASURE PERFORMANCE?

Some of the most common performance measures utilised in sports are wins, losses, and players' statistics. This information, along with a myriad of other data, often serves as the framework for measuring the performance of teams and athletes.

Athletes, coaches, and owners all use these records to measure their own progress or that of the organisation. These are considered performance measures and are used as benchmarks to measure changes in performance. Like coaches, trainers, and athletes, facility and event managers track performance and benchmark their own performance against competitors' and industry leaders' and even their own organisation's past performance. However, the performance of a facility or event organisation is rarely as straightforward a measure as winning or losing an athletic competition, and appropriate benchmarks are much more difficult to identify. Still, an organisation can make little progress towards its goals if it makes no attempt to track its progress.

Regardless of the industry, when talking about the concept of management, one of the most important tools is to have valid, accurate evidence to guide decisions. This is the core of this chapter – the collection, evaluation, and use of good performance evidence to help determine if strategies and objectives are being realised, ascertain financial changes that will guide financial decision making, validate customer behaviours towards products or services to guide marketing decisions, and determine the level of service quality being provided by employees to aid in making appropriate human resource decisions (Schwarz, Hall, & Shibli, 2015). It is also important to remember that an internal examination of one's own organisation is not enough – there also should be an external evaluation of competition and other providers of similar products and services to get a full perspective of performance across an industry and individual performance in comparison to the industry.

In Marshall Meyer's hallmark publication 'Rethinking Performance Management – Beyond the Balanced Scorecard', he specified seven distinctive purposes of performance measures: (1) to look ahead, (2) to look back, (3) to motivate, (4) to compensate, (5) to roll up, (6) to cascade down, and (7) to compare (Meyer, 2002). At the organisational level in particular, it is important to look back at past accomplishments in order to build on the successes (and learn from and redress the failures) of the past. Similarly, it is important to look ahead to understand the context in which the organisation will operate, and to set goals and objectives for the organisation. Performance measures that look ahead can keep employees focused on the activities that will meet the strategic objectives of the organisation. Further, performance measures can be effective tools to motivate and compensate employees at all levels of an organisation. Properly linked, performance measures can focus activities and attention on the strategic objectives of an organisational unit. Benchmarks can motivate individuals and teams to achieve goals, as performance-based compensation requires the use of performance measures to determine rewards. Lastly, performance measures can be used to compare output and outcomes across units and to provide specific, bi-directional feedback throughout the organisation.

The purpose of any particular performance measure predicts both the appropriateness of the type of measure chosen, and the way in which each measure can be used. This is articulated in Table 11.1.

Table 11.1 Summary of key staffing functions and performance measurement for sport facilities

Purpose	Question the measure can help to answer	Need to achieve purpose
Evaluate	How well is the facility/event performing?	Outcomes, combined with inputs and with the effects of external factors.
Control	How can I ensure that my employees are doing what they should?	Inputs that can be regulated and controlled.
Budget	On what programmes, employees, projects, or events should my organisation spend its money?	Efficiency measures (specifically, outcomes or outputs divided by inputs).
Motivate	How can I motivate staff, managers, stakeholders, and community members to do the things necessary to improve performance?	Almost real-time outputs compared with production targets or output measures.
Promote	How can I convince government, ministers, stakeholders, media, and the community that my organisation is doing a good job?	Easily understood aspects of performance that people really care about.
Celebrate	What accomplishments are worthy of the important organisational ritual of celebrating success?	Periodic and significant performance targets that, when achieved, provide people with a real sense of accomplishment.
Learn	Why are things working or not working?	Disaggregated data that can reveal differences from what is expected.
Improve	What exactly should we do differently to improve performance?	Inside-the-black-box relationships that connect changes in operations to changes in outputs and outcomes.

Source: Adapted from Behn (2003)

However, individual measures provide only a partial view of performance. Using a single measure is akin to measuring the performance of a football team solely by the number of points it scores. The measure cannot possibly be equated with competitive success (i.e. winning) without also measuring the number of points the opposition scored. A single measure can be a useful benchmark for improvement in one area, but it fails as a measure of overall performance. In addition, and more critically, organisations may then focus their efforts on improving that single dimension at the cost of others. More practice in scoring goals or touchdowns takes time away from practising defensive techniques. Thus, this effort could result in an even poorer overall performance on the field.

The previous example is fairly simplistic compared to the complexity of measuring the performance of a facility or an event. However, the same principle applies – what gets measured gets done! This poses a real danger to organisations whose performance measurement systems focus on a narrow range of measures, or on measures that are either irrelevant or misleading. The wrong performance measures can lead a company to divert scarce resources or to use them unproductively. The purpose of measuring performance is not necessarily to maximise performance on each measure: it is to determine progress in attaining organisational objectives.

Facility and event organisations each operate in a unique environment, structure themselves in a distinctive way, and set objectives that serve the individual purpose of their organisations. Consequently, every organisation will measure success in its own way. Performance measures must take into account the internal and external environment facing the facility or event, the inputs and processes that produce the products and services, and the outputs and outcomes desired by the organisation and its stakeholders. Each internal and external system influences the other.

As a result, an effective performance measurement system must integrate a collaborative approach towards evaluation between operational areas, resulting in an interrelationship between these collaborations and the technical approaches to evaluation (Chouinard, 2013). This is a systems theory approach to an integrated performance measurement system – in which performance measures have been traditionally used for evaluation and control (Robbins & DeCenzo, 2014). Historically, performance measures emerged from a financial accounting model directed at maintaining financial control. Accounting has often been termed the language of business, and many performance measures have focused on financial performance; however, while financial performance is necessary to the success of any business, it is not sufficient to predict business success (Chouinard, 2013). Financial indicators are insufficient to measure success for two reasons: timing and breadth.

Financial indicators and timing

With regard to timing, key performance indicators (KPIs) typically measure performance in terms of profitability, liquidity, activity, and leverage, much of which focuses on short-term financial performance. Long-term performance is much more difficult to measure, as many of the standard financial measures indicate past performance such as earnings from the past quarter or annum. These lagging indicators help managers to understand what has already happened.

In turn, information about past performance can certainly provide information relevant to future performance, but there is also a need for forward-looking, forecasting data such as leading indicators. Leading indicators reduce uncertainty about what will happen. They only provide up-to-date information about current performance and also can help managers look forward by measuring the drivers of future performance.

In terms of sport facility and events, a manager might measure participants' satisfaction with the local fixtures. Satisfaction level can then be utilised as an indicator of repeat participation. This principle also follows through in terms of enjoyment during the game experience – where satisfaction can be a measure of repeat purchase. In turn, an early indication of participant dissatisfaction can provide sport facility and event managers with the chance to make changes before losing customers.

Attention to and balance of these two types of indicators can help a manager to better plan and successfully implement strategies and tactics. Thus the timing issues associated with financial indicators highlight the need to go beyond the standard lagging indicators of financial performance.

Financial indicators and breadth

Breadth in terms of the outcome of financial performance measurement is limited due to the abstract ways of capturing the value of intangible and intellectual assets. These assets are particularly important to the success of service entities such as facility and event organisations. For example, customer service is critical to successful service organisations. Game experience, augmented services (concessions, entertainment), interactions with staff, social outcomes, and environmental factors (ambiance, design) are often stated as being among the most important factors of quality management (Ko et al., 2011), and significantly affect customer satisfaction, loyalty, and repurchase intentions (Athanassopoulos, 2000). However, intangible assets such as these are difficult to value. Consequently, they are rarely included in standard financial reports. Yet in today's business environment it is the intangibles (e.g. employee skills, customer loyalty, process capabilities) that are critical to success.

Many organisations do in fact measure some intangibles. However, this is often done in isolation. For instance, a health and fitness centre may systematically measure the quality of service provided to its members by surveying customers to obtain evaluations of the service provided. Service quality measures may be used to evaluate employee performance, to design employee training, to reward good customer service, or even as proxy indicators of customer satisfaction. Service quality measures are useful indicators of performance, but how does a measure of service quality link to the overall performance of the business? What effect does customer satisfaction have on the financial performance of the business? Or on the overall strategic thrust of the organisation? Customer evaluations of service quality need to be considered with reference to other information about the business and its performance.

The same organisation might track the number of people attending each of its cardiovascular exercise programmes, or the number and type of equipment breakdowns. Each of these measures is important to the overall performance of the company. However, the main consumers of the information provided by each indicator may be isolated from the others. Although staff responsible for facility maintenance might focus on data regarding equipment breakdown, marketing might focus on service quality information, and programmes on participant numbers.

If these indicators remain compartmentalised, it can become difficult for managers in each area to understand the way the performance of their own department relates to the overall performance of the organisation, and thus to its overall strategy.

Moving forward with performance measurement

It is important to recognise that what is measured, how it is measured, and how the information measured is used, are all integral parts of performance management. Measures can lead to quite erroneous conclusions if not considered with reference to overall operations and objectives. One example to illustrate this is in the case where maintenance might look excellent if there are few equipment breakdowns. However, if the lack of breakdowns is a consequence of low utilisation because the equipment is difficult to use or out of date, then the correct conclusion would not be that maintenance is effective or the equipment is reliable; it would be that the equipment needs to be modified or replaced. The point is that performance measures should be linked to the overall operational structure and the strategic goals of the organisation. Each component of the system can then understand its place in the performance of the business as a whole.

In summary, performance measurement has been hindered by three problems. First, no performance measure can be considered in isolation. Single indicators are not valid indicators of performance: a performance management system is required. Second, performance measures are often backward-looking: they report on past performance rather than providing lead indicators of impending performance issues. There needs to be a balance between lead and lag indicators of performance. Third, there is often a bias towards the exclusive use of financial performance measures. This prevents a company from focusing on underlying intangible assets and processes. In effect, a purely financial analysis fails to consider changes in human and process capabilities that could lead to improved performance. Nor does it promote ownership and commitment to the strategies and objectives of the organisation.

PERFORMANCE MANAGEMENT MODELS

Performance management involves a process of setting organisational objectives that are measurable, actionable, specific, time-bound, works towards an ends not a means, and are ranked (Schwarz, Hall, & Shibli, 2015). We measure performance in numerous ways using terms like financial performance, efficiency in performance, effectiveness of performance, equity in the delivery of performance, and customer satisfaction. Performance indicators are then used to evaluate performance in a variety of ways including relevance, cost effectiveness, comparability, ease of use, and timeliness – to name a few. To meet these levels of performance, targets are set for what will be achieved by when. However, all of these processes can be managed through a variety of performance management structures including the balanced scorecard, the European Foundation for Quality Management (EFQM) Excellence model, and the Towards an Excellent Service (TAES) model.

Balanced scorecard

Probably the best known and most used performance measurement model used across the world today is Kaplan and Norton's balanced scorecard. Developed in 1992, the initial goal of the model was to include strategic performance measures that were not financially focused, but still include financial measures, to provide a balanced view of overall performance, as seen in Figure 11.1.

The balanced scorecard has been advocated as a means by which to translate the strategic objectives of a facility or event into a set of cohesive performance measures and indicators organised along four dimensions: finance, customer, internal business processes, and learning and growth. In addition, the scorecard approach is able to communicate mission and strategy by measuring and articulating the

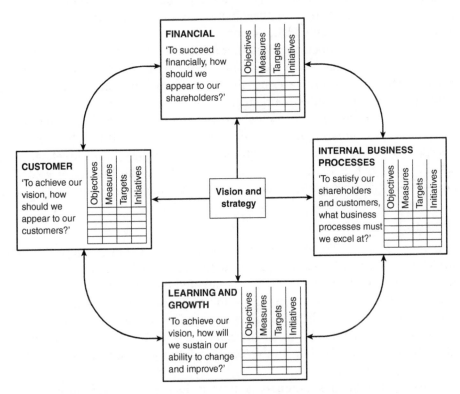

Figure 11.1 The balanced scorecard model

Source: Modified from Kaplan & Norton (1996); republished from Schwarz, Hall, & Shibli (2015)

outcomes desired by the organisation and the drivers of those outcomes. Unlike other performance management approaches, the balanced scorecard is not focused on compliance or control – rather it provides a framework within which to articulate and communicate strategy, as well as to align organisational, departmental, cross-departmental, and individual initiatives, resulting in the achievement of a common goal.

Finance perspective

The finance perspective takes a look at how an organisation appears to shareholders. Financial performance measures are the indicators that are traditionally used to determine whether the strategy and operations are contributing to the bottom line. Although the balanced scorecard considers financial measures to be insufficient indicators alone, financial measures are vital elements of the overall constellation of measures.

Traditionally, financial analysis has focused on such measures as return on investment, debt-to-equity ratio, and related ratios calculated from the organisation's financial statements (liquidity, activity, profitability, and leverage). Although these may still be important to management when using the balanced scorecard, there are several other financial indicators that contribute significant information when considered in conjunction with other measures used in a balanced scorecard.

Three types of indicators are recommended as part of the balanced scorecard approach. First is analysing revenue growth and mix, which are measures that indicate the degree to which the organisation is expanding its revenues, reaching new markets, or improving its market share. Second is assessing cost reduction and productivity improvement to increase efficiency and profitability. Third is measuring asset utilisation in terms of how efficiently the organisation's assets are being allocated. Each type of financial indicator is linked to the long-term goal of the organisation – to provide optimal returns for the capital invested in the business.

Customer perspective

The customer perspective seeks to understand how customers view the organisation. The customer perspective begins with the identification and selection of customers and market segments, since the targeted consumers will be responsible for delivering the revenues indicated by the financial perspective. Two types of performance indicators for the customer perspective address the organisation's performance in its selected market segments: core customer outcomes and performance drivers. The former are lagging indicators; the latter are leading indicators. Both types of measures are needed.

Core customer outcomes are fairly generic measures of interest to facility managers, event managers, and nearly every other service organisation. The core measures include market share, customer acquisition, customer retention, customer satisfaction and customer profitability. As lagging measures, these help the manager determine how the organisation has been doing. Customer value propositions drive customer outcomes. They represent the attributes of an organisation that create satisfaction and develop loyalty among targeted customer segments. In other words, these are the attributes by which customers determine the value of your product or service. The attributes are categorised along three dimensions: (1) good/service attributes, (2) customer relationships, and (3) image and reputation of the business.

In order to formulate performance drivers – or indicators – for the customer perspective, facility and event managers must first identify their targeted customer segments. Once that has been done, a set of core outcome measurements can be generated. However, customer outcome measures share with traditional financial indicators the limitation that they are lagging measures. Leading indicators are identified by determining what target markets value about your products and services. These become the basis for creating measures of product and service attributes, customer relationship, and image and reputation. The attributes dimensions can serve as an early warning system, alerting the organisation to areas of potential customer dissatisfaction.

Internal business process perspective

In the internal business process perspective, managers identify the critical internal processes that the organisation needs to excel at in order to meet its objectives. This perspective builds on both financial and customer perspectives. Internal business processes are those which deliver the value propositions that attract and retain targeted customers, which in turn affect the organisation's ability to meet its financial objectives. Consequently, internal business process measures focus on the processes that have the greatest impact on customer satisfaction and on achieving an organisation's financial objectives. Kaplan and Norton (1996) recommend examining internal business processes throughout the value chain (see Figure 11.2). Three principal business processes form the value chain that links customer need identification to customer satisfaction: (1) innovation processes, (2) operations processes, and (3) post-sale service processes. Operational excellence is often seen as the dominant factor in the value chain. It makes sense that a facility or event should focus on processes that deliver superior goods and services, so we will examine operational processes first.

Measures of service quality focus an organisation on improving the existing service delivery processes that are necessary to satisfy the needs of its customers. Seating comfort, facility cleanliness, knowledgeable and pleasant staff, and crowd handling are some of the many components of service quality for both facilities and events. Customer satisfaction within these aspects is often used as an indicator of service quality. However, customer satisfaction is an outcome variable.

By itself, customer satisfaction provides managers with little insight into how to go about improving the components of service quality. For that, one needs to

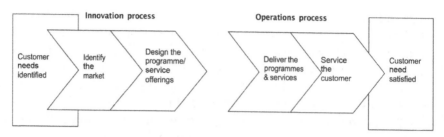

Figure 11.2 *Sport facility and event management value chain*

Source: Adapted from Kaplan & Norton (1996, p. 96)

examine the internal business processes that produce the service. What, for example, do we do operationally that can affect customers' perceptions of the cleanliness of our facility? The most obvious answer is that someone cleans the facility. But how does the cleaning process work? Who cleans the facility? Is it done in-house or outsourced? When is the facility cleaned? How often? Is cleaning linked to use patterns? What is the procedure for responding to customer complaints or alerts about cleanliness? Each of these questions corresponds to a business process that can be measured and monitored. Therefore, the facility manager might measure the frequency of cleaning, the duration of cleaning, or average response time to customer complaints.

Similarly, perceptions of crowding can negatively affect event patrons' experiences. Event managers might examine the internal processes that can affect perceptions of crowding. What type of queuing system is used? How many ticket booths are available? How much space is allotted to crowd movement? Is there adequate signage to ensure good crowd flow? Performance indicators might include measures of the average wait time to purchase a ticket, food and beverage, or souvenir; or the number of tickets sold per hour. A lead indicator for crowd flow could be a measure of the number of times patrons requested directions per time period.

Both facility and event managers would do well to attend to service recovery processes. By definition, services are produced and consumed simultaneously. Consequently, service providers such as sport facilities and events do not have many post-sales processes distinct from operations. Traditional post-sales processes for product-based companies have focused on warranties and repairs. Facility and event managers must be able to 'repair' service breakdowns as they occur. Service recovery processes, then, become part of the operations process, and the measures must be linked to the internal processes that produce customer outcomes.

This is also true of the first link in the value chain – the innovation process. Operations processes tend to emphasise short-term value creation; i.e. the operations provide value for the duration of the customer's visit to the facility or event. Long-term value creation can be enhanced through the innovation process. This is

Evaluating operations

the process of researching the emerging needs of customers and creating products and services that will meet those needs. Whereas the operations process focuses on improving operations and enhancing existing operations to enhance value, the innovation process focuses on creating new value. During the innovation process new customers and new markets are identified and nurtured, and then new products and services are designed to reach those customers. Thus, innovation processes are the research and development functions that consist of two types of processes, those which identify the market and those which create new product and service offerings.

Potential performance indicators for market identification processes would quantify market research processes aimed at understanding customer needs, and providing reliable and valid information on such factors as market size, market accessibility, and customer preferences. As such, the service creation process is a development aspect of a sport business. The inclusion of indicators of successful innovation processes allows management to emphasise research and development processes that may yield new products, services, and markets. Tracking measures help managers identify the success (or lack thereof) of an organisation's existing operational processes. Together, these processes create the value chain linking customer need identification to customer satisfaction. When combined with the customer perspective, the internal business process perspective identifies the factors most critical to current and future success. Maintaining superior performance in the facility and event industries requires an organisation to continually improve its capabilities and the capabilities of its employees.

Learning and growth perspective

The learning and growth perspective references the infrastructure necessary to long-term growth and improvement, resulting in continuous improvement and creating value. The objectives in this perspective are the drivers for achieving the objectives from each of the other three perspectives. The objectives and measures in the first three perspectives identify where the facility or event organisation must excel. The learning and growth perspective identifies the capabilities necessary to achieve the performance targets identified. In effect, performance in organisational learning and growth builds the capacity of the organisation to develop and implement the necessary business processes to meet customer and shareholder needs and expectations. Organisational learning and growth emerge from three principal sources within the organisation: (1) employee outcomes and capabilities, (2) information systems capabilities, and (3) organisational procedures and alignment. Organisational learning and growth are particularly important in the sport events industry. Rarely do any two sport events have the same requirements or target the same audience. As a result, event staff must constantly build their expertise, information systems must remain flexible, and procedures can never be set in stone. It is through capacity building that sport facility managers can expand their repertoire of events, and event managers can successfully bid on an increasing array of events.

Similar to the customer perspective, employee outcomes and capability measures of organisational learning and growth include a smattering of generic outcome measures, as well as some business-specific drivers that serve to enable the desired outcomes (see Figure 11.3).

Standard outcome measures include employee satisfaction, employee retention, and employee productivity. Employee satisfaction is seen to drive retention and productivity (Mondy & Mondy, 2014; Rosser, 2004). Unsatisfied employees are less productive and tend to leave the organisation. Satisfied employees are essential to providing quality service. Employee morale is particularly important for service providers such as sport facilities and events.

Employee retention is an important component of organisational learning. This is a particularly difficult objective to achieve for many sport event organisations. Due to the cyclical nature of event employment, a great deal of organisational knowledge is lost with the loss of employees after an event (Hanlon & Jago, 2001). This is true for paid staff as well as volunteers. Retaining volunteers from one event to the next

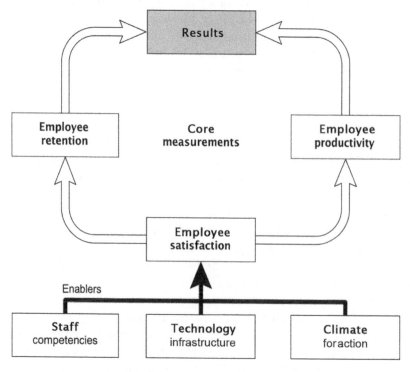

Figure 11.3 Employee outcomes and measures

270

can significantly reduce staff time spent training volunteers, and can cut the costs of recruiting new volunteers.

Employee productivity is a function of the impact of 'enhancing employee satisfaction, innovation, improving internal processes, and satisfying customers' (Kaplan & Norton 1996, p. 131). Productivity measures, then, should be a function of the number of employees and the amount produced by those employees.

In addition to the core employee indicators discussed above, each sport facility and event may have unique, situation-specific drivers of learning and growth. While the actual measures may be unique to the sport facility or event, they tend to be drawn from three critical enabling factors: (1) staff competencies, (2) technology infrastructure, and (3) a climate for action.

In order to achieve customer and internal business process objectives, employees may face new responsibilities. New responsibilities often necessitate changes in the skills required to carry out those responsibilities effectively. Staff competencies form part of the infrastructure necessary to meet the organisation's objectives. When responsibilities change, there may be a demand for reskilling employees to meet new objectives.

Systems performance is indicated by the availability of accurate, critical customer and internal process information to employees at the coalface. Measures of the technology infrastructure of an organisation should provide an indication of the degree to which your internal systems provide decision makers with the information necessary to take action. Employees may have the job skills necessary to achieve organisational objectives, but they need information about their customers, internal processes, and the financial consequences of their decisions. Front-line employees need information about all products and services offered.

The third enabler for learning and growth objectives is a climate for action. Having highly skilled employees with access to necessary information still may not lead to organisational success. Employees need to be motivated to contribute to the success of the sport facility or event. Further, they need to be empowered to make decisions and take action to ensure the success of the organisation. Therefore, employees need to feel that they have a voice and a stake in the success of the organisation. The ongoing participation of employees might be measured by the number of suggestions for improvement made per employee.

Using the balanced scorecard

Each scorecard measure must be linked to the strategy of the organisation. The strategy of the sport facility or event is illustrated by linking your outcome and performance driver measures through a series of cause-and-effect relationships. Ultimately, all causal paths from all the measures on the scorecard should be linked in some way to the financial objectives of the organisation.

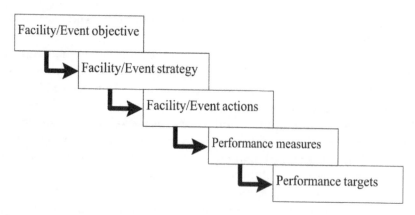

Figure 11.4 Cascading objectives for sport facility and event management

The balanced scorecard provides a means to measure business performance retrospectively and prospectively, and to do so in a manner that is consistent with the organisation's strategic plan. Beyond understanding what the elements of a balanced scorecard are, a sport facility or event manager must also consider how to create measures that are specific to their individual organisation. Measures of each type are created by cascading objectives as seen below in Figure 11.4.

The process begins by identifying an overall objective, usually a financial objective. For example, Mega Events, Inc., a major sport event company, might choose revenue growth as its top financial objective. The next step is to consider which strategies would help to achieve the objective. Mega Events Inc. might consider any of the following strategies: improve ticket sales, obtain more sponsors, or purchase more advertising. Each is a valid strategy, as are others not mentioned here. To keep the example simple, we will limit the strategy to one – improving ticket sales. The next step is to consider any actions that need to occur to ensure that the strategy is carried out. To improve ticket sales, Mega Events Inc. might provide sales training to all employees, hire more experienced salespeople, or lower the price of tickets. Typically, each objective will have more than one strategy, and each strategy will have multiple actions, with each action having more than one measure, and so on.

Step four of the process is to create measures to check progress in achieving the actions and strategies. Appropriate measures for Mega Events Inc. might include the percentage of staff with sales training, or sales staff turnover. Note that these measures are future predictors (i.e. lead indicators) of sales. The level of sales training today is a good indicator of the growth in sales tomorrow, assuming that Mega Events Inc.'s strategy is effective. Note also that the measure provides a clear link back to the actions taken as a result of the strategy selected. Further, it is all linked to the overall financial objective of revenue growth. It is easy for staff at all levels (e.g. salespeople, sales trainers, managers) to understand how their own actions affect Mega Events Inc.'s performance. Employees at all levels now contribute to the same goal. The targets provide both strategic feedback (does the strategy work?) and tactical feedback (did we implement the actions properly?). If Mega Events Inc. meets its targets of 85 per cent staff with sales training and less than 25 per cent turnover in sales staff, then it will show improved revenue growth.

In closing, the balanced scorecard ultimately is a strategic management system that if used properly can ensure that performance measures are fully integrated with an organisation's strategy. A balanced scorecard approach can help a sport facility or event management company to '(1) clarify and translate vision and strategy, (2) communicate and link strategic objectives and measures, (3) plan, set targets, and align strategic initiatives, and (4) enhance strategic feedback and learning' (Kaplan & Norton, 1996, p. 10).

EFQM Excellence model

Also called the Business Excellence model, the European Foundation for Quality Management (EFQM) introduced this performance management framework in 1992, which today is still one of the most widely used frameworks in Europe. The goal of the EFQM Excellence model is to be a practical tool to help organisations measure the steps on their strategic excellence continuum on an ongoing basis so managers can build on strengths, understand weaknesses in a timely manner, and ultimately improve performance by turning decisions and problem solutions into positive actions. As seen in Figure 11.5, the model is based on nine criteria, with five being enablers of organisational action, and four being results of organisational achievements. It also offers a feedback loop through innovation and learning to allow the results to drive positive change and improvement of the enablers.

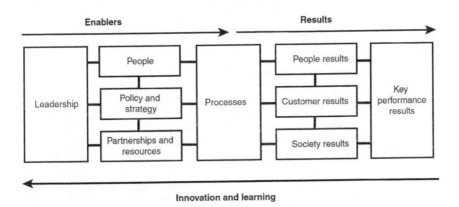

Figure 11.5 The EFQM Excellence model

Source: Modified from EFQM (2012); republished from Schwarz, Hall, & Shibli (2015)

The key to this model is self-assessment rather than external evaluation. This allows management to address change more quickly by assessing using the established criterion for quality performance, with measurements of performance including being: (1) results oriented, (2) customer focused, (3) consistent in purpose through quality leadership, (4) managed by processes and facts, (5) motivated by development and involvement of staff, and (6) engaged in a culture of continuous learning, innovation, improvement, and social responsibility.

The EFQM Excellence model serves as the framework for the quality accreditation system in the UK designed specifically for sport and leisure services called Quest (http://www.questnbs.org), which focuses on continuous improvement in the management of leisure facilities and development. It also serves as a quality framework used by the Improvement and Development Agency (IDeA) for local government in the United Kingdom in the creation of their TAES (Towards an Excellent Service) model. The TAES model, developed by a cohort of relevant government agencies (Department of Culture, Media, and Sport; the Audit Commission) and professional organisations (Institute for Sport, Parks, and Leisure; Institute of Sport and Sport Management; and the National Association for Sports Development), is a self-assessment and improvement planning tool that influences the quality of cultural services in terms of equality and access in eight key areas: (1) leadership, (2) policy and strategy, (3) community engagement, (4) partnership working, (5) use of resources, (6) people management, (7) standards of service, and (8) performance measurement and learning (UK Government Web Archives, 2007b; Schwarz, Hall, & Shibli, 2015).

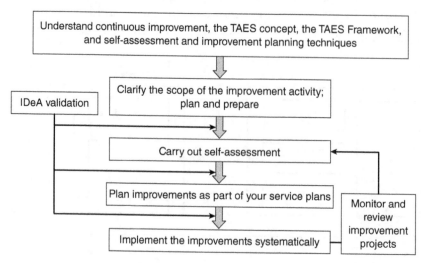

Figure 11.6 The TAES self-assessment and improvement model

Source: Modified from UK Government Web Archives (2007a); republished from Schwarz, Hall, & Shibli (2015)

The model, shown in Figure 11.6, documents the process where there is a prior-itisation of improvements; the plan for improvement is realistic, has resources, and shows clear accountability, and dates for completion of tasks are clearly stated; the measurement monitors both action and if the desired effect is occurring.

BENCHMARKING

As discussed earlier in the chapter, beyond taking a look at performance manage-ment from an internal evaluation standpoint, it is equally important to conduct comparisons with competitors and other related industry organisations. This is where the process of benchmarking comes into consideration. There are two major types of benchmarks – data benchmarking and process benchmarking. Data bench-marking comprises numerical standards for calculating performance indicators. This would include the use of analytics, second-party and third-party data, indica-tor data, and even in some cases big data. On the other hand, process benchmarking looks at the comparison in processes and procedures utilised by different organi-sations, and is aggregated with performance data to develop an understanding of methods that will improve performance.

Benchmarking is limitless, as there are always data to evaluate and processes to review. It is also a process that should be engaged in at all levels of the organisa-tional structure. Once only viewed as a management function, it has evolved into almost every area of sport facility and event management – from human resources to marketing to operations. The saying 'that which gets measured gets done' is especially true if performance as compared to the benchmarks set by competitors are not met.

SUMMARY

Consistent performance measurement allows sport facility and event managers to monitor and control the strategies, processes, and outcomes of the organisation and its employees. Further, it is a useful way to benchmark performance against industry standards and one's own competitors. Effective performance measurement requires an organisation to develop an array of measures that provide a complete picture of the processes and outcomes of the organisation's operations, and should be linked to its strategies and objectives.

This chapter presents various performance management methods, with the most common being the balanced scorecard approach developed by Kaplan and Norton (1996). Their model provides sport facility and event managers with a comprehensive manner by which to develop and implement an effective performance manage-ment system beginning with the strategic objectives of the sport facility or event. It then helps the manager to translate organisational objectives into a set of cohesive performance indicators organised along four dimensions: finance, customer, internal business processes, and learning and growth. Measures within these four dimensions provide a balance between process and outcome, and between leading and lagging indicators. Together, the indicators provide managers with a systematic performance measurement initiative that is fully integrated with the organisation's strategic management system.

Also presented was the EFQM Excellence model, which helps measure performance through five enablers of organisational action, four results of organisational achievements, and a feedback loop through innovation and learning to allow the results to drive positive change and improvement of the enablers. The TAES model evolved from the EFQM model and is a process where there is a prioritisation of improvements; the plan for improvement is realistic, has resources, and shows clear accountability, and dates for completion of tasks are clearly stated; the measurement monitors both action and if the desired effect is occurring.

The previous models are internal performance measurement evaluation processes, whereas benchmarking provides an external perspective to evaluating internal performance. Benchmarks usually fall into two main categories. Data benchmarks are numerical standards for calculating performance indicators, whereas process benchmarking compares processes and procedures and is aggregated with performance data. The use of benchmarks is crucial to providing an external perspective to evaluating internal performance.

CASE STUDY

Benchmarking for sport facilities and major events in Australia

The CERM Performance Indicators (PI) Project has been an integral tool utilised by a range sport and leisure services for over 25 years. Developed by the Centre for Environmental and Recreation Management (CERM) at the University of South Australia, the original model of facility management performance indicators was designed for use by public aquatic centres and leisure centres in collaboration with the managers of local government indoor sports and leisure centres in Australia and New Zealand. The CERM PIs provide benchmarks for a variety of services including subscription management, publication offerings, pricing, and customer service quality reviews. It also extends into many other areas, ranging from marketing to operational management to finance.

The CERM PI provides protocols for reliable data collection and indicators in the following three areas:

- Customer service quality (CSQ) through effectiveness indicators;
- Operational management (OM) including facilities and event services, but also including marketing, finance, human resources, and utilities;
- Community service obligations (CSO), with an additional focus on priority participant groups, using government statistics.

From a sport facilities and event perspective, the major research focus areas for the CERM PI are on sport and leisure centres, tennis facilities, and golf courses. The CERM PI is also used by botanical gardens and national parks to measure performance.

The CERM PI has been the primary performance measurement instrument used by the City of Melbourne, Australia for over a decade to evaluate its wide range of facilities and associated events. The performance indicators and demographic data are used to improve operational decision making, including regular internal and external benchmarking against similar operations. The City of Melbourne believes the CERM performance indicators are the most appropriate measuring stick available to compare like with like. The council uses CERM to measure its customer service for its main recreation facilities, swimming pools, golf courses, and the skate park.

In addition to the CERM measures, contracts between service providers and the City of Melbourne specify quality control requirements. The City of Melbourne's Parks and Recreation officers regularly assess each facility against a number of occupational health and safety (OH&S) measures. Each of these measures is used by the City of Melbourne to provide performance bonuses within the contractual arrangements with service providers.

The City of Melbourne's performance management strategies ensure the facility and event services are providing value for money, and also act as a mechanism for accountability to the council and ratepayers. Measuring the performance of the facilities and events within the City of Melbourne assures participants and stakeholders that they are being provided with high-quality sport and recreation services. As a result, performance management is an integral component of effective planning and management.

The University of South Australia keeps a database of recreation and indoor leisure facilities, and annually collects performance indicator data for measurement against other similar facilities across Australia. This data includes the performance of components within facilities, as well as performance indicators that are accessible to participants to aid in guiding their operational and strategic planning.

Questions

1 The case looks at CERM PI primarily from a facility perspective. However, this can be effectively used for major sport events as well. Select a major sport event and develop a set of five key performance indicators (KPIs) to evaluate performance.

2 Organise your recommended KPIs using the balanced scorecard approach, the EFQM Excellence model, and the TAES self-assessment and improvement model. Explain which model you feel provides the best organisation of your KPIs in order to identify strengths and weaknesses.

3 Using the model you deem best, identify and list the strengths and weaknesses related to the KPIs.

REFERENCES

Athanassopoulos, A.D. (2000). Customer satisfaction cues to support market segmentation and explain switching behavior. *Journal of Business Research, 47*(3), 191–207.

Behn, R.D. (2003). Why measure performance? Different purposes require different measures. *Public Administration Review, 63*(5), 586–606.

Chouinard, J.A. (2013). The case for participatory evaluation in an era of accountability. *American Journal of Evaluation, 34*(2), 237–253.

Hanlon, C., & Jago, J. (2001). Pulsating sporting events: An organizational structure to optimize performance. In *Events beyond 2000: Setting the agenda. Proceedings of conference on event evaluation, research and education.* University of Technology, Sydney.

Kaplan, R.S., & Norton, D.P. (1996). *The balanced scorecard.* Boston: Harvard Business School Press.

Ko, Y.J., Zhang, J., Cattani, K., & Pastore, D. (2011). Assessment of event quality in major spectator sports. *Managing Service Quality: An International Journal, 21*(3), 304–322.

Meyer, M.W. (2002). *Rethinking performance measurement: Beyond the balanced scorecard.* Cambridge University Press, Cambridge.

Mondy, R.W., & Mondy, J. B. (2014). *Human resource management.* 13th edition. Boston, Mass.: Pearson.

Robbins, S.P., DeCenzo, D., & Coulter, M. (2014). *Fundamentals of Management: Essential Concepts and Applications.* 9th edition. New York: Pearson Education.

Rosser, V. (2004). Faculty members' intentions to leave: A national study on their worklife and satisfaction. *Research in Higher Education, 45*(3), 285–310.

Schwarz, E.C., Hall, S.A., & Shibli, S. (2015). *Sport facility operations management: A global perspective.* 2nd edition. Oxford, UK: Routledge.

UK Government Web Archives. (2007a), *Parks and open spaces: Towards an excellent service, 1: Introduction.* Retrieved from http://webarchive.nationalarchives.gov.uk/20110118095356/http:/www.cabe.org.uk/files/TAES-01-Introduction.pdf

UK Government Web Archives. (2007b), *Parks and open spaces: Towards an excellent service, 2: The TAES framework.* Retrieved from http://webarchive.nationalarchives.gov.uk/20110118095356/http:/www.cabe.org.uk/files/TAES-02-TAES_Framework.pdf

CHAPTER 12

PERFORMANCE MANAGEMENT: LEGACY AND MEASURING IMPACT

CHAPTER FOCUS

1 Introduction to sport facility and major event management
2 Key success factors of operating sport facilities and running sport events
3 Feasibility analysis and market research for planning new sport facilities and events
4 New sport facility development: planning, design, and construction
5 New sport facility development: preparing the facility management infrastructure
6 New sport facility operations: attracting events
7 New sport facility operations: planning the event management infrastructure
8 Attracting customers: marketing sport facilities and events
9 Running the sport event: event operations
10 Destination marketing, image, and branding through major sport events
11 Performance management: evaluating operations
12 Performance management: legacy and measuring impact

CHAPTER OBJECTIVES

In this chapter we will:

■ Explain the role of legacy in bidding for major sport events, in infrastructure development, and to evaluate the long-term performance of implementation.
■ Identify examples of sport facility and major event legacies.
■ Compare and contrast the concepts of 'legacy' and 'impact'.

- Articulate the triple bottom line of short term performance related to sport facility and major events.
- Examine the economic, social, and environmental impacts of facility and event performance.
- Consider ways to measure and monitor the economic, social, and environmental impacts of facilities and events.

INTRODUCTION

The concept of legacy has been used with increasing frequency to describe the social and long-term impact of sport events and the facilities that host the events. The popularity of the word legacy is largely due to its association with the Olympic discourse, referring to the long-lasting impacts of the Olympic Movement and Olympic Games. Among the many so-called mega-sporting events, the modern Olympic Games easily stands out by its scale and influence, and is widely recognised as the largest multi-sport event of global significance. However, with the growing scale and cost, it has become increasingly controversial as to whether it is worthwhile for a city to host the Olympics. Despite a wide variety of benefits that have been suggested for Olympic host cities, competition to stage the Olympics in recent years is diminishing; 11 cities bid for the 2004 Summer Olympics whilst there were only five bidding cities for the 2020 Summer Olympics (Chappelet, 2013), and only four for the 2024 Games. The situation for the Winter Olympics is even worse, especially after Russia spent a record high of US$50 billion hosting the Sochi Games in 2014. With local communities and/or governments vetoing the decision to enter into a bid, only two willing candidates were left in the final stage in 2015 to compete for the 2022 Winter Games (Almaty, Kazakhstan and Beijing, China). Both IOC and Olympic host cities have been under growing pressure to justify the staging of the Olympics and the huge cost incurred subsidised by public spending. The concept of 'legacy', together with the concept of 'sustainable sport development', has become an essential part of the IOC and the Organizing Committee of the Olympic Games (OCOG) vocabulary (Girginov & Hills, 2008), and by extension to sport facilities and major events across the spectrum of recreation, leisure, and entertainment.

This chapter explains the concept of legacy in terms of the key elements that are used to measure benefits. In consideration of the difficulty of measuring the benefits of legacy, an analysis of the benefits of legacy versus that of impact will be covered through an examination of the triple-bottom line of impact – economic, social, and environmental.

LEGACY

The concept of legacy was first considered in an Olympic context during the 1990s and the planning of the 1996 Atlanta Games, when the organisers desired to 'leave a legacy'; however, the word itself is not well-defined and means different things to different people. For instance, Cashman (2005, p. 15) writes that

> when the term is used by organising committees, it is assumed to be entirely positive, with there being no such thing as negative legacy ... that legacy benefits flow to a community at the end of the Games as a matter of course ... and is often assumed to be self-evident, so that there is no need to define precisely what it is.

The definition of legacy then evolved to include being 'planned and unplanned, positive and negative, intangible and tangible structures created through a sport event and remain after the event' (Preuss, 2007). As the term has gained wider currency, the definition has evolved into 'a working definition of the concept: the legacy of a mega sporting event is all that remains and may be considered as consequences of the event in its environment' (Chappelet, 2012, p. 77).

Despite the lack of clarity of a clearly defined concept, there is wide use of the legacy concept by various parties including international sport organisations and host cities.

According to the International Olympic Committee (IOC) (2012), legacies can be tangible or intangible, and generally fall into one of five categories:

- economic
- environmental
- social
- sport development
- urban.

While the implications of creating a legacy through major sport events such as the Olympics are often focused on all the positive benefits they can bring about, the reality is that negative legacies are a possibility. For example, it has been argued that the emphasis on legacy by the IOC is aimed at justifying the use of public resources for both sport and non-sport infrastructure investment, as well as motivating other cities to bid for future events. Legacy may also be a tool for the IOC to avoid the public in the host nation blaming the IOC for the public debt left as a result of hosting the Olympics (Gratton & Preuss, 2008). While many cities believe the legacy of the Olympics and other major events in terms of advances in public infrastructure is worth the expense, other cities have ended their bids for the Olympics as a result of public referenda against incurring the costs (e. g. Oslo, Norway for their 2022 Winter Olympics bid; Hamburg, Germany for their 2024 Summer Olympics bid). Other notable negative legacies include construction debt, sport facilities that become 'white elephant' infrastructure, opportunity costs, negative publicity, increases in property prices, and displacement of residents (Karadakis & Kaplanidou, 2012; Liu, Broom, & Wilson, 2014). As a result, forming a strategic legacy from the start based on a holistic approach and including all relevant facility and event stakeholders is the key to leveraging the most potential positive legacies while minimising the negative ones.

LEGACY ... OR IMPACT

Different perspectives have been proposed regarding event legacy content and its measurement. For instance, in 2000 the Olympic Games Global Impact (OGGI) project was launched by the IOC to improve the evaluation of the overall impacts of the Olympic Games on the host city, its environment, and its citizens, as well as to propose a consistent methodology to capture the overall effects of hosting the games (Gratton and Preuss, 2008). The OGGI project covers an eleven-year period, starting with the bidding stage right through the hosting of the event itself, to two years after the event had been held, and the effects are measured along three dimensions: economic, social, and environmental (Furrer, 2002).

As a result of this and other studies, a major question emerged: are we measuring legacy or impact? Often articulated as overlapping terms, the reality is they are two very different concepts based on the dimension of time. Legacy is long term as a result of changes in the host cities' location factors (e.g. post-event tourism due to increased interest in the host city), whereas impact is caused by a short-term impulse (e.g. consumption by event visitors) (Preuss, 2007).

CHALLENGES TO MEASURING LEGACIES

Despite such increasing recognition of the importance of maximising the legacy of major sport events, there are few studies that attempt to measure systematically such long-term benefits (Gratton & Preuss, 2008). Studies of major sport events often measure the economic impact or those impacts that are related to economics. The studies that focus on social and other impacts lack hard evidence about legacies, as a majority are written prior to the event. Legacy is long-term and measurement will take 15–20 years to identify the true legacy of major events (Gratton & Preuss, 2008).

Without a true longitudinal analysis of legacy, it becomes nearly impossible to accurately measure whether there has been a positive or negative legacy from major sporting events. In reality, many of the reports on legacy of events are predictions and perceptions of what the legacy is could be in the future. In fact, many studies that claim they have measured legacy often actually are measuring impact because researchers are looking at the benefits and deficits within four, eight, or even 12 years after an event.

As such, appropriate measurements of major sport event legacies would be conducted at the time of this book's printing (2017) on events that took place pre-2002. Over the past two decades, several events have been studied to measure major event legacy both as a positive and as a negative. One example is the 1976 Montreal Summer Olympics, where there is general agreement about the negative legacy of financial mismanagement, unfulfilled expectations, and a 30-year tax bill on residents – earning it the nickname 'The Bankrupt Olympics' – while on the other hand it provided a positive legacy in terms of the social investment in making the province of Quebec one of the most progressive sport and physical activity regions in Canada (Kidd, 2013). Another example is the 1994 FIFA World Cup in the United States, which resulted in the legacy of creating a viable professional soccer league in the United States (Major League Soccer, or MLS) that still continues to grow and thrive today. Beyond the two examples above, a report published in 2010 by Deloitte (a global company that specialises in providing audit, consulting, financial advisory, risk management, tax, and related services) provides additional examples of major sport event legacies, which appear in Table 12.1.

Table 12.1 Major sport event legacies

Event	Positive/ Negative	Explanation
1972 Summer Olympics in Munich Germany	Positive	Subway system was built that still serves the city today
	Negative	Terrorism at the Olympics as 11 Israeli team members were kidnapped and killed by the Palestinian group Black September
1992 Summer Olympics in Barcelona, Spain	Positive	An improved global image for tourism and business appeal through large infrastructure projects including the redevelopment of neighbourhoods, transportation, and telecoms
1994 Winter Olympics in Lillehammer, Norway	Positive	The first "Green Games"
1995 Rugby World Cup in South Africa	Positive	Post-apartheid emergence from years of racial oppression and segregation, the event served as a catalyst for the country's re-emergence as a full member of the world's sports community, as well as the international political community

BENCHMARKING IMPACT: THE TRIPLE-BOTTOM LINE

Many of the studies over the past decade that explain the evaluation of legacies related to sport facilities and major events may therefore in fact be reporting on the benchmarking of impacts. As discussed in the previous chapter, the use of benchmarks is crucial to providing an external perspective to evaluating internal performance. However, it also plays an important role in measuring impact on and for stakeholders in terms of traditional factors including economic, environmental, and social impact. The construction and maintenance of sport facilities and the events they host represent substantial financial investments that have led to increasing interest in the economic impact of facilities and events on the wider communities that host them. In addition, social and environmental impacts have been recognised as necessary complements to economic impact when assessing the effects and value of investments, technology, and infrastructure. Taken together, economic impact, social impact, and environmental impact are known as 'the triple bottom line', all of which need to be assessed on their own merit, as well as their effects on both individual stakeholders and the stakeholder management process.

ECONOMIC IMPACT

Sport facilities and events are expected to provide the community at large with economic benefit. They are expected to induce spending in the local area, thus profiting local businesses. The induced spending spills over into tax collections in the form of sales taxes or goods and services taxes. Ultimately, more money circulating in the area stimulates a growth in earnings and employment (Coates & Humphreys 2003). Consequently, economic impact is an increasingly important measure of facility and event performance.

Assessing economic impact

Economic impact is assessed in terms of three components – direct, indirect, and induced impacts. Direct (or primary) economic impact is the change in economic activity during the first round of spending by visitors directly stimulated by a facility or sport event. It is important to note that this spending must be new to the economy. Examples of direct expenditures include the money spent by visitors (local, national, and international) on tickets, food, accommodation, entertainment, shopping, and transport. Other direct expenditures may be related to participants, organisers, and sponsors. The key determinant is that expenditures would not otherwise have occurred; they would have been spent somewhere else or not at all.

Indirect (or secondary) impact is the economic activity generated on other businesses as a result of the facility or event. This would include the change in economic activity, or second round of spending, by businesses and public authorities that are influenced by the facility or event. For example, when a major event such as the Super Bowl in the United States takes place, beyond the economic impact related directly to the event, additional business and jobs are created beyond the core sport activity to support the direct economic activities. In marketing terms, it is how the supply chain is affected by the sport facility or major event. So when a restaurant is expecting more customers than usual, they need to purchase additional food and beverages from vendors. The positive economic activity for these vendors is the indirect impact.

Then there are induced impacts – which are the expenditures by employees and businesses from earnings related to the sport facility or major event. When this additional money is spent in the economy, there are businesses with additional revenue – and employees with extra income either from overtime or taking on a temporary position. This additional economic power via spending of those earnings is the induced impact of the sport facility or major event.

Conducting an economic impact study

The first challenge in conducting an economic impact study is to estimate visitor numbers. At first glance, this may seem straightforward because events typically have readily available data regarding tickets sold, facilities should have data on the number of people using their facilities, and attendance and user numbers provide a good initial estimate of visitor numbers. But other visitor groups must also be estimated. For example, sport facilities and events may have vendors living outside the local area. Vendors are not usually considered attendees, yet they are often deemed to be visitors. Events often focus purely on spectator attendance and fail to consider the spending of players, officials, administrators, and/or corporate sponsors. Each of these groups may be accompanied by one or more others who may or may not attend the event. Consequently, when estimating visitor numbers, one should begin by identifying potential spending groups.

Once groups have been identified, the size of each group should be estimated. As economic impact is estimated by extrapolating data collected from a sample of visitors to the total number of visitors, an economic impact study is only as accurate as its estimate of visitor numbers (Crompton, Lee, & Shuster, 2001). Care should be taken to avoid double-counting visitors. This can be problematic for multi-day events in particular. Estimates can be obtained from the visitor survey itself by asking respondents to indicate which days they attended the event. When extrapolating to the entire visitor population, ratios can be calculated to estimate single-day attendees, two-day attendees, and so on. In the same way, the proportion of local versus out-of-town visitors can be determined.

Economic impact is clearly linked to out-of-town spending. Thus, it is important to determine the parameters for any economic impact study. Who will be considered local? How will that be determined? The area of impact can vary. Will events supported by a local council be interested only in the impact within the council or city limits? Postcodes are a simple way of defining the geographic limits of any impacts. Respondents listing postcodes within the local shire or county are considered locals. Those with other postcodes are considered non-locals. For state-supported events, locals are often defined as those residents whose primary residence is within the state. An event funded by the Victorian Major Events Company (an organisation specifically set up to attract events to Melbourne and Victoria in Australia), for example, would show very little impact on the state of Victoria if the majority of attendees at an event in Ballarat (a city in Victoria) came from Melbourne (the capital of Victoria). However, the economic impact of the event for Ballarat could be significant. Consequently, it is important to determine the boundaries of expected impacts early in the measurement process.

Once the area of impact has been determined and a procedure has been devised to measure visitor numbers, visitor surveys can be implemented. Remember, direct economic impact is a measure of stimulated spend. Standard economic impact studies use one of several tools to collect spending information. Visitors may be asked to keep a diary of their expenditures while visiting a city to attend an event or visit a facility. Alternatively, visitors may be asked to complete a brief questionnaire that requires them to estimate their spending while visiting. These are commonly completed as on-site exit interviews. Minimally, these questionnaires gather information about the size of the travelling party, the length of stay, spending in a variety of categories, and postcode.

All questionnaires should have a way to differentiate locals from out-of-town visitors. Locals do not provide any new spending. Local spending is spending that would have occurred in the local community anyway. A local resident's expenditure at a local restaurant, for example, does not represent a new source of funds for the local economy. Postcodes or location of residence are common items used to differentiate locals from non-locals. Similarly, a question addressing the number of days attended helps to differentiate repeat visitors from new visitors. In this way, no attendee is counted more than once. It also assists agencies in comparing the economic impact of events of various lengths.

Locals are not the only group that should be excluded. Time-switchers and casuals (Crompton, 1999) should also be excluded from the analysis. Time-switchers are visitors to the event destination, but they are visitors who were intending to visit anyway. These visitors merely changed the dates of their visit to coincide with the event. Thus, they would have spent money in the local economy anyway, just at a different time. Consequently, their spending was not a result of the event and cannot be included in the economic impact of the event. The same is true of casuals. Casuals are event attendees who were already at the destination and happened to go to the event during their stay. Expenditures by casuals would have occurred even

Legacy and measuring impact

without the event. Like expenditures by time-switchers, expenditures by casuals cannot be attributed to the event and should not be included in measures of the economic impact of the event. There is an exception – some time-switchers and casuals may stay longer at the destination because of the event. In this case, the additional spending can be included in the analysis. Screening questions can be embedded in the visitor survey to identify time-switchers and casuals. For example, a visitor survey for the 2014 Commonwealth Games held in Glasgow, Scotland might include the following questions to identify casuals and time-switchers:

- Would you have come to Glasgow (or Scotland) at this time even if this event had not been held?
- If yes, will you stay longer than you would have if this event had not been held?
- If yes, how much longer?
- Would you have come to Glasgow (or Scotland) in the next three months if you had not come at this time for this event?

Knowledge of group size is important in that it helps to prevent researchers from over- estimating spending. Visitors often travel with others and often are responsible for paying for others in their travel party. For example, a parent typically pays the bills for all family members on a family holiday. Thus, one person's spending estimates may include the spending of others. As most studies report per person expenditure, group size is an important variable in any economic impact analysis.

Respondents are asked to estimate the amount that was (or will be) spent by their travel group in a number of categories. Common categories include food and beverage; night clubs, lounges, and bars; other entertainment (e.g. theatres, museums, amusement parks, other tourist attractions); retail shopping; accommodation; transport during the stay; and any other expenses. It is often useful to have respondents estimate their spending within the area of interest (i.e. city, region, state, country) and their spending outside the area of interest (Crompton, Lee, & Shuster, 2001). This helps respondents to differentiate between spending on their trip (which may include spending on the way to and from the destination) and spending while at the event destination (the expenditure of interest). Total expenditures by non-locals can be calculated as follows:

$$\frac{\text{Total non-visitors}}{\text{Average group size}} - \text{Average expenditure per group}$$

Spending in each of the specified categories is aggregated to determine direct expenditures. However, spending in each category affects the economy in different ways. The ways in which revenues are spent and re-spent vary by industry and by locality. The circulation (and recirculation) of revenues within the economy provides additional, indirect benefits to the economy. Indirect benefits are estimated via the use of 'multipliers'. Multipliers are used to account for the ripple effect of money through the economy. Money that is spent and re-spent within the economy has a cumulative impact greater than the initial visitor expenditure. Multipliers are designed to account for the cumulative impact by estimating the indirect expenditures resulting from initial spending.

However, not all direct expenditures circulate entirely within the local economy. Expenditures leaving the local economy are referred to as 'leakage'. Figure 12.1 shows the direct, indirect, and induced impacts of $100 spent by a non-local at an event. The $100 spent at a local restaurant is considered a direct expenditure. Now let us consider the indirect effects of the $100 spent in the restaurant. The local restaurant spends this money again. It buys produce from a local grocer and pays its chef, who lives in the local community. Thus, $50 is recirculated in the local economy. The other $50 is leakage. It is used to pay bills outside the local area (e.g. insurance, out-of-town employees). The $50 that stays in the local economy is again re-spent. The grocer spends $10 on vegetables from a local farm, and sends $35 to its parent company in another state. These are indirect impacts. The chef spends $5 at the local grocery, and $5 outside the local community. Secondary spending in the community by employees of affected businesses is called induced impacts. Thus, the chef's purchase at the local grocery store is an example of induced impact. Direct, indirect, and induced impacts contribute to the total impact of building a facility or hosting an event. In this example, the recirculation of revenues results in an impact of $100 (direct) + $40 (indirect) + $10 (indirect) + $10 (indirect) + $5 (induced), or $165 total impact.

Rather than try to trace actual expenditures through the economy, multipliers are used to represent the indirect impact of the direct expenditures. Three types of multipliers are commonly reported in economic impact studies: (1) sales, (2) income, and (3) employment multipliers. A sales multiplier measures the direct, indirect, and induced effect of an extra unit of visitor spending on economic activity within the local area. If the example shown was indicative of spending patterns in the restaurant industry in a particular region, then a sales multiplier of 1.65 would be appropriate for the food and beverage category. Sales multipliers are substantially higher than income multipliers. But, as Crompton (1999, p. 21) notes, 'in an economic impact analysis sales multipliers are not useful ... [residents] have no interest in the value of sales per se because it has no impact on their standard of living'.

Economic impact studies can provide reasonable indications of the tangible impacts of sport facilities and sport events. However, these same studies often fail to measure the intangible impacts of a sport facility or event. Intangible impacts are more difficult to measure, however they are no less important. This may include the ability to enable sport or leisure to take place hence increasing the quality of

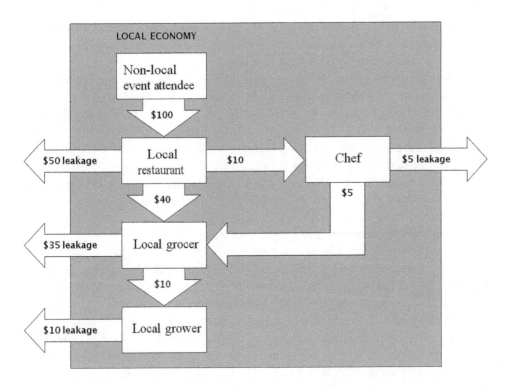

Figure 12.1 The multiplier effect: direct, indirect, and induced spending at an event

life, the psychic income a sport facility or major event brings to the community, and how the destination brand – and hence the tourism mix – is positively affected by the infrastructures. Another significant benefit of facilities and events can be the social capital that they engender (Jago et al., 2003). Event employees and volunteers can build new skills and enhance their social networks. A successful event may enhance residents' pride in their community. Each of these benefits can have economic value, although that value is difficult to quantify and is not normally included in estimates of event value. Nonetheless, the value of events for social capital may represent a significant benefit to the host community. It also has a direct effect on social impact.

SOCIAL IMPACT

The intended and unintended consequences of sport facilities and events are also measured and managed through social impact assessment. Social impact assessment can be used to evaluate the impact of sport facilities or events on the behaviour, attitudes, interests, health, or economic well-being of residents, organisations, social movements, and political systems. Social impact assessment examines the effects that sport facilities and events have on the objective and subjective quality of life for people and organisations in the community.

Sport facilities can affect the behaviours of people within their critical trading radius. It is easier for people who live or work near a sport facility to attend events at the facility or to participate in activities at the facility than it is for those who live or work further away. Thus, sport facilities can have a noticeable impact on the social lives of those who live or work nearby. Similarly, sport events can have a substantial impact on the lives of people in the host community. Crowding, traffic, pollution, and noise may all become more intense. On the other hand, there may be a party-like atmosphere or heightened community pride during the event. Consequently, events can also have a significant effect on the lives of people who reside in the host community (Fredline & Faulkner, 2002).

Although social impact assessment has not yet had the political impact enjoyed by economic impact analysis or the kinds of legislative mandates common to environmental impact assessment, the emergence of triple-bottom-line frameworks has heightened the appeal of social impact assessment to governments and community groups. Consequently, it is reasonable to expect that social impact assessments will be undertaken with increasing frequency and increasing rigour. The specific methods used in any particular social impact assessment (e.g. surveys, interviews, media analysis, behavioural observation) will vary as a function of the expected impacts and the context. However, the fundamental process will generally follow the following nine steps:

1   Establish the terms of reference for the study.
2   Identify alternative pathways that project development might take.
3   Determine the social condition, identify stakeholders, and ascertain what and who are likely to be affected.
4   Project what is likely to happen and who might be affected under the alternative pathway scenarios identified in step 2.
5   On the basis of steps 3 and 4, identify indicators to be examined and measures to be used, then determine the nature and magnitude of like impacts under alternative scenarios.
6   Evaluate net benefits for stakeholder groups, and determine who benefits, who loses, and whether the aggregate impact is acceptable.
7   Identify means to counteract unacceptable impacts.
8   Monitor ongoing impacts, and compare with predicted impacts.
9   Feed findings from step 8 into ongoing planning and implementation.

ENVIRONMENTAL IMPACT

Environmental impact focuses on three main areas. First is the ecological footprint in terms of visitors' consumption patterns at major events and their effect on the

global ecology – looking at a number of areas including transportation, food/drink consumption, waste generation, and the efficiency of associated facilities. Second is the analysis of environmental inputs and outputs, which involves a transactional analysis of the economy and the environment to determine the impact of visitors to events on the natural environment. The third area is environmental management, sustainability, and environmental practices to combat wastage and pollution threats such as recycling, renewal, regeneration, and transformation.

Sport facilities and the events they host often cram large numbers of people into a relatively concentrated space. The effect on the environment can be devastating: the environmental damage caused by the construction of sport facilities and the running of the 1992 Winter Olympic Games in Albertville, France, is a historical example that clearly demonstrates this problem. The effect was sufficiently intense to evoke widespread criticism from environmental groups, thereby bringing sport facilities and events under heightened environmental scrutiny. The International Olympic Committee (IOC) responded in 1994 by adopting the environment as the third pillar of the Olympic Movement (along with sport and culture), and followed with the creation of a Sport and the Environment Commission. The World Conference on Sport and the Environment in 2001, sponsored by the IOC in cooperation with the United Nations, called on all participants and enterprises associated with sport to continue and intensify their efforts in implementing environmental, economic, and social sustainability in all of their policies and activities. In fact, the resolution reflected pressure on sport organisations at all levels that was already causing them to consider environmental issues in all that they did.

In the years following the 1992 Winter Olympics in Albertville, a number of reports and guidelines were developed for sport facilities and sport events. The United Nations Environmental Program later sponsored a handbook for the environmental management of sport facilities and events (Chernushenko, van der Kamp, & Stubbs 2001). Every kind of facility – gymnasia, ice arenas, swimming pools, ski fields – raises its own set of environmental problems. Similarly, the specific environmental issues raised by different kinds of sport vary as a function of the environment and the sports' characteristics. For example, swimming events and golf events both make extensive use of chemicals. However, the chemicals are different – water treatment chemicals in the case of swimming, and herbicides and fertilisers in the case of golf. Thus, the specific management problems are different. Similarly, a mountain biking event raises fewer problems having to do with chemical management but serious issues having to do with the management of erosion and protection of the natural environment.

An environmental impact assessment (EIA) is most commonly undertaken prior to facility construction or event implementation. It is reported in an environmental impact statement (EIS). The EIS considers the justification for the sport facility or event, and includes a detailed specification of the potential environmental effects. It may also consider alternatives to the project. When completed, it is usually a public document subject to scrutiny and comment by interested persons or groups. However, at times, since it is often left to facility developers or event organisers to undertake the EIA, and the developer/organiser has a vested financial stake in the project, it is in their interests to produce a report that plays down the environmental risks and emphasises the benefits a project might provide.

When done well, the EIA is conducted by an independent consultant, as the content and focus of environmental impact assessments can vary as a function of the particular context and concerns being addressed, but the common objective is to ascertain how the environment will be changed by the proposed facility or event. An environmental impact assessment will forecast or measure the effect on such variables as terrestrial flora and fauna, marine biota, local geology and soils, and surface and subsurface waters. In practice, governments often require the completion of an environmental impact assessment prior to an event taking place or a facility being constructed. An assessment of environmental impacts may also be required periodically while the facility is in operation or after the event has ended.

By identifying areas of the environment that are most at risk as a result of a facility being built or event being hosted, as well as the particular operations that are most likely to cause environmental disruptions, it is possible to plan or redesign a sport facility or event in a manner that minimises environmental risks. This should include means to restore environmental damage.

SUMMARY

This chapter articulates the concept of legacy and impact in terms of the key elements that are used to measure benefits. Legacy looks at long-term results in terms of what remains, or is considered a result of the successful implementation of the major sport event. Legacies can be intangible or tangible, planned or unplanned, and positive or negative, but often need 15–20 years after the event or more to be truly evaluated. This creates significant challenges when attempting to accurately measure legacies as it required the implementation of longitudinal studies to accurately evaluate the legacy of an event.

In contrast, impact is used more often as a result of its short-term orientation post-event. Most commonly used is a triple-bottom-line measurement and a reporting process that includes an evaluation of the economic, social, and environmental impacts that are relevant for sport facilities and events. The economic impact of sport facilities and events has been commonly assessed by estimating the spending stimulated (direct impact) and the flow-on effects of that spending (indirect and induced impact). Facilities and events can also render intangible benefits that are not typically accounted for in economic impact assessments. These include effects on the host destination's brand as well as effects on social capital.

The social impacts of sport facilities and events can affect the quality of life in the host community. Social impact assessment can identify the social effects of facilities and events, including which stakeholders benefit and which may be negatively affected. Social impact assessments can be used to identify policies and procedures to optimise positive social effects and to eliminate or minimise negative effects.

Sport facilities and events can also have a substantial impact on the environment. Facility managers can reduce their facility's detrimental impact on the environment by promoting efficient use of energy, using chemicals for cleaning and operations that are not environmentally toxic, using plants that are well adapted to the local ecology, being careful not to overload or erode the local environment, and minimise the impact of the facility on local breeding, nesting, and feeding habitats. Event managers can foster environmentally friendly operations by promoting, auditing, and rewarding staff and attendee behaviours that minimise stress on the environment. Environmental impact assessments are used to forecast, monitor, and manage environmental impacts.

But what does the future hold for measuring sport facility and event impact? There is a lot of work being done in the event impact analytics, with those results expected to also have a direct effect on facility impact. The following case study will look at one such structure.

CASE STUDY

The future of sport event analytics: the Global Sport Impact (GSI) project

The roster of quadrennial 'mega-events' including the FIFA World Cup, the Summer and Winter Olympic Games, and the Rugby World Cup dominate the global event calendar in terms of international audience reach. In addition to each sport's own international championships and the global F1 Grand Prix circuit, all compete for audience attention, sponsorship support, and host bids. However, the rising complexity of hosting mega-events and the bidding process itself now requires city and national governments to give increasing attention to the question of what is the actual value derived from hosting events.

Measuring event legacy

Understandably, as the costs of event bidding and hosting have continued to rise in the period since the debt-laden Montreal Olympics, prospective and past hosts have expanded definitions of the impact of events from direct, indirect, and induced economic benefits to include softer 'benefits' (e.g. social, health, cultural, community pride) – all together now commonly described under the catch-all term 'legacy'.

To improve the reliability of any pre-bid assessment as to the events' impact an historic assessment of past events and the scale of performance on each 'legacy' dimension should be foundational. Despite this, the predominant academic models of legacy proposed in the literature are conceptual only and fail to propose specific measures by which events could be assessed. A review of potential models noted that 'despite these prominent categorisations of legacies, only a few researchers have suggested actual indicators to measure legacies, and those who did, were restricted to a specific subcategory of their selected field of study' (Bob & Kassens-Noor, 2012).

The UK-based sports information service Sportcal developed an alternative approach to the issue of measuring event impact. Their approach was to create a single index score for events from mega-events to national championships, applying a 'point value' for events of differing scale and using the cumulative city and nation scores to produce their Global Sports Index (Sportcal, 2015). This model draws on Sportcal's 20 years of sports and events data to create benchmarks for events, based on standardised dimensions of event impact. This approach runs counter to the 'uncertainty' of legacy noted by academic authors.

As an approach to combining the direct measurement of events with establishing accountability for delivery for the taxpayer funds invested, a number of national authorities have developed localised event assessment models such as eventIMPACTS (UKSport, 2015) and NZ Major Events (MBIE, 2013) to assess an individual event's impact within a consistent framework. These are used to construct pre-bid assessments and post-event reviews. The assessment of events is by nature localised and hence output and findings from one model cannot be applied directly in another.

Measuring specific elements of event impact

While there are many models for event assessment, 'much of the growing body of literature on legacy focuses on either the economic effects or the infrastructural changes' (Preuss, 2015). Yet assessment of even the economic impact from direct visitor spending proves to be difficult as 'the methods used to research the economic impact of major events remain contested' (Davies, Coleman, & Ramchandani, 2013). This exemplifies the lack of consensus over the measurement and contribution seen in other impacts or legacies of events (Dickson, Benson, & Blackman, 2011) and that 'this lack of consensus has complicated the measurement of events' legacies' (Horne & Manzenreiter, 2006).

The default term for the outcomes from event hosting has in recent times focussed on 'legacy' rather than impact. The challenge that presents for events of scale below that of mega-event is that 'legacy' has unconscious associations with 'permanent improvements to the built environment' (Hiller, 2000).

The establishment of the 'legacy' narrative as the default viewpoint has a consequence in excluding smaller events that are unable to provide evidence of the required 'permanent improvement' to find their place in the legacy rhetoric. Indeed smaller events that do not require new infrastructure are potentially lower risk and offer higher economic returns but are potentially overlooked in favour of larger scale events promising a substantive 'legacy'.

An alternative terminology of 'impact' instead of 'legacy' has been used to connote a more direct time and event-bound constraint under which event benefits might be assessed and removes the 'permanent' and 'lasting' require-ment from the dominant definitions of 'legacy' that smaller events cannot expect to achieve.

Owner vs. host performance

Often unstated but embedded within the measurement frameworks are the benefits from a successful event that can also be accrued by the event owner. The IOC have, through the Olympic Games Impact (OGI) Study, established a 'prescribed set of indicators to measure impacts across three topic areas or spheres of sustainability – socio-cultural, economic, and environmental' (UBC, 2013). By being able to define the terms of reference for assessing the event's impact the event owner may seek not only to increase the perceived benefit the host but also to accrue incremental value to the owner (Barney, 2003) from successful edition to successful edition.

(Case study written by Michael Linley)

Questions

1   Given the foundational assumptions of event deliverables embedded in bid documents, how can a standardised model of event impact be used to refine and test pre-bid assessment? What modifications to the standardised scores might be needed to increase its applicability to a prospective host?
2   To what extent does localising the assessment of events obscure the value to other potential hosts? Is this a competitive strategy or simply a response to the lack of a standardised source and model existing that all prospective bidders might draw from?

3   To what extent might the growing usage of the term 'legacy' to describe the benefits of event hosting be about gaining political support for an event rather than a useful measure of its actual effect?

4   What dimensions of event performance might event owners consider critical? Are those at odds with the outcomes sought by the event host or just of a different priority in importance?

REFERENCES

Barney, R.K. (2003). The Olympic legacy of wealth: A double edged sword. In M. de Moragas Spà (Ed.) *The legacy of the Olympic Games, 1984–2000: International Symposium, Lausanne.* Lausanne: International Olympic Committee.

Bob, U., & Kassens-Noor, E. V. A. (2012). An indicator framework to assess the legacy impacts of the 2010 FIFA World Cup. *African Journal for Physical, Health Education, Recreation & Dance, 18*, 12–21.

Cashman, R. (2005). *The bitter-sweet awakening: The legacy of the Sydney 2000 Olympic Games.* Sydney: Walla Walla Press.

Chappelet, J.-L. (2012). Mega sporting event legacies: A multifaceted concept. *Papeles De Europa, 25*, 76–86.

Chappelet, J.-L. (2013). Managing the size of the Olympic Games. *Sport in Society, 16*(10), 581–592.

Chernushenko, D., van der Kamp, A., & Stubbs, D. (2001). *Sustainable sport management: Running an environmentally, socially, and economically responsible organization.* New York: Unipub.

Coates, D. & Humphreys, B.R. (2003). The effect of professional sports on earnings and employment in the services and retail sectors in US cities. *Regional Science and Urban Economics, 33*(2), 175–198.

Crompton, J.L. (1999). Economic impact analysis of sports facilities and events: Eleven sources of misapplication. *Journal of Sport Management, 9*(1), 14–35.

Crompton, J.L., Lee, S., & Shuster, T.J. (2001). A guide for undertaking economic impact studies: The Springfest example. *Journal of Travel Research, 40*(1), 79–87.

Davies, L., Coleman, R., & Ramchandani, G. (2013). Evaluating event economic impact: Rigour versus reality? *International Journal of Event and Festival Management, 4*(1), 31–42.

Deloitte (2010). *A lasting legacy. How major sporting events can drive positive change for host communities and economics.* Retrieved from http://www2.deloitte.com/content/dam/ Deloitte/global/Documents/Public-Sector/dttl-ps-alastinglegacy-08082013.pdf

Dickson, T.J., Benson, A.M., & Blackman, D.A. (2011). Developing a framework for evaluating Olympic and Paralympic legacies. *Journal of Sport & Tourism, 16*(4), 285–302.

Fredline, E. & Faulkner, B. (2002). Variations in residents' reactions to major motorsport events: Why residents perceive the impacts of events differently. *Event Management, 7*(2), 115–125.

Furrer, P. (2002). Sustainable Olympic Games: A dream or reality. *Bollettino della Società Geografica Italiana, Serie XII, 7, 4.*

Gratton, C., & Preuss, H. (2008). Maximizing Olympic impacts by building up legacies. *The International Journal of the History of Sport, 25*(14), 1,922–1,938.

Girginov, V. & Hills, L. (2008). The 2012 London Olympic Games and participation in sport: Understanding the link. *International Journal of the History of Sport, 25*(14), 2,091–2,116.

Hiller, H.H. (2000). Mega-events, urban boosterism and growth strategies: An analysis of the objectives and legitimations of the Cape Town 2004 Olympic Bid. *International Journal of Urban and Regional Research, 24*(2), 449–458.

Horne, J., & Manzenreiter, W. (2006). An introduction to the sociology of sports mega-events. *The Sociological Review, 54*(Suppl. 2), 1–24.

International Olympic Committee (IOC). (2012). Olympic *legacy.* Retrieved from http://www.olympic.org/Documents/Olympism_in_action/Legacy/Olympic_Legacy.pdf.pdf

Jago, L., Chalip, L., Brown, G., Mules, T., & Ali, S. (2003). Building events into destination branding: Insights from experts. *Event Management, 8*(1), 3–14.

Karadakis, K., & Kaplanidou, K. (2012). Legacy perceptions among host and non-host Olympic Games residents: A longitudinal study of the 2010 Vancouver Olympic Games, *European Sport Management Quarterly, 12*(3), 243–264.

Kidd, B. (2013). The culture wars of the Montreal Olympics. *Sport in Society, 16*(4), 472–481.

Liu, D., Broom, D., & Wilson, R. (2014). Legacy of the Beijing Olympic Games: A non-host city perspective. *European Sport Management Quarterly, 14*(5), 485–502.

MBIE (2013). Economic evaluation outcomes: Major events development fund. Retrieved from http://www.majorevents.govt.nz/pdf-library/news/MEDF-evaluation-report.pdf

Preuss, H. (2007). The conceptualization and measurement of mega sport event legacies. *Journal of Sport & Tourism, 12*(3–4), 207–227.

Preuss, H. (2015). A framework for identifying the legacies of a mega sport event. *Leisure Studies, 34*(6), 643–664.

Sportcal (2015). The global sports impact project. Retrieved from http://www.sportcal.com/Impact/GSI_projects.aspx

UBC (2013). Olympic Games Impact (OGI) study for the 2010 Olympic and Paralympic Winter Games: Post-games report. Retrieved from http://cfss.sites.olt.ubc.ca/files/2011/10/OGI-UBCPost-Games-Report-2013-10-23.pdf

UKSport (2015). eventIMPACTS. Retrieved from http://www.eventimpacts.com

INDEX